At last a book that offers the English-speaking world a window into a startling body of theory and practice on building democratic forms of economic organization. It offers challenging and stimulating material for anyone interested in practical and large-scale democratic economic alternatives. A critical contribution at a time when civil society offers great potential for catalysing progressive change, and yet is itself deeply vulnerable through its own susceptibility to inappropriate modes of organization. *Simon Zadek, New Economics Foundation, London*

This important book makes the work of de Morais accessible to an English-speaking audience for the first time. The Brazilian, de Morais, has developed the theory of 'large-scale capacitation' which provides the basis for an educational method that enables the poor to organize self-managed enterprises. This approach to employment generation makes possible the creation of secure livelihoods for all, which is the key to eliminating poverty in the Third World. The book introduces the theoretical conceptions of de Morais and focuses on examples of practice inspired by his ideas drawn from Latin America and Africa and also from the poorer countries of Europe. The success of these worker-owned enterprises make this book essential reading for anyone concerned with the issues of poverty and development. *Professor Frank Youngman, author of* The Political Economy of Adult Education and Development

The kind of book that comes only once in a while. With echoes of Paulo Freire's notion of conscientization, this book works around the notion of mass participation and mass training as a way to create a future for the excluded based on building forms of democratic control. An important book for progressive educators, community organizers, and all those concerned with non-formal education. *Carlos Alberto Torres, Professor and Director, Latin American Center, UCLA*

Carmen and Sobrado are to be commended for having made this book available to an English-speaking public with its innovative and exciting insight into organizational development. It is one of the few to cross the boundary between social and organizational change, and is a 'must' for all organization and social development practitioners. *Bill Cooke, Institute for Development Policy and Management, Manchester University*

Reviews of Raff Carmen's Previous Book

An incisive look at many of the new ideas around 'development'. Critical, original and accessible. *Ben Oakley, School for Policy Studies, University of Bristol*

A refreshing and welcome addition to the discourse on South World development. In an era where socio-economic disparities between South and North are increasing, and the mass media give consumers the world according to McCoke, voices like Carmen's are vitally important. A comprehensive analysis of both the barriers to and hopes for development in the South. Highly recommended for people interested in people-centred economics. *Professor Farah M. Shroff, University of Toronto*

Carmen's incisive arguments are thought-provoking and refreshing in their intellectual appeal and pragmatic 'development' prescriptions. His whole analysis is based on two pristine principles: people cannot 'be' 'put' first; development is people. People are not the problem, they are the solution. A readable book for the development policy and programme practitioners, social activists and Third World commentators alike. *P. Jegadish Gandhi, Vellore Institute of Development Studies, India*

A Future for the Excluded

**Job creation and income generation by the poor:
Clodomir Santos de Morais and the Organization
Workshop**

Edited by Raff Carmen and Miguel Sobrado

Zed Books

LONDON • NEW YORK

A Future for the Excluded: Job creation and income generation by the poor: Clodomir Santos de Morais and the Organization Workshop was first published by Zed Books Ltd, 7 Cynthia Street, London N1 9JF, UK, and Room 400, 175 Fifth Avenue, New York, NY 10010, USA, in 2000.

Editorial copyright © Raff Carmen and Miguel Sobrado, 2000

Individual chapters copyright © individual authors, 2000

Distributed in the USA exclusively by St Martin's Press, Inc., 175 Fifth Avenue, New York, NY 10010, USA

Cover designed by Andrew Corbett
Set in Monotype Ehrhardt and Franklin Gothic by Ewan Smith
Printed and bound in the United Kingdom by Biddles Ltd, Guildford and King's Lynn

A catalogue record for this book is available from the British Library.
Library of Congress Cataloging-in-Publication Data: available

ISBN 1 85649 702 X cased
ISBN 1 85649 703 8 limp

Contents

Preface

NIA

It is difficult to separate Clodomir Santos de Morais the person from his activities, or from de Morais the practitioner. As is often the case with seminal thinkers and activists of his ilk involved in social transformation, adult education, political action and autonomous development, they almost irresistibly form a following, a fact exemplified by Patrick van Rensburg (Education with Production), Manfred Max-Neef (CEPAUR), Helena Norberg-Hodge (Ladakh Eco Group) or Bernard Lédéa Ouédraogo (NAAM), all of whom, since the early 1980s, have been awarded the Right Livelihood Award (RLA). In the same way the Brazilian Movimento dos Trabalhadores sem Terra (MST) – the Landless Workers' Movement, which counts Clodomir among its founders – was awarded the RLA in 1991.[1] Ever since, the MST and IATTERMUND, founded by de Morais, have been at the forefront of 'doing enterprises' by means of the organization workshop (OW), so much so that mini 'MST republics' have sprung up in what used to be unemployment hotspots (see Chapter 17), and the PAE (Self-Employment Project), for example, has produced a ripple effect in the Brazil of the 1990s (see Chapter 18).

Although Clodomir is a prolific author of books, articles and conference papers, he is not, nor did he ever aspire to be, a producer of literature, even though, as a visiting professor at a number of universities, his academic credentials are beyond any doubt. Instead, he has been all his life, and still is, a prodigious generator of jobs and income, or rather, a source of inspiration, giving confidence to the most excluded in society that they, indeed, 'are able' and by showing them the 'how to'. As he says of himself and his extraordinary organization IATTERMUND in Brasília: 'We are not doers of work, we do enterprises instead.' As soon as new enterprises have been generated by the participants themselves in the course of those workshops, 'we start doing enterprises somewhere else' (see Chapter 10). Clodomir's unique OW method, indeed, represents not merely a pedagogy by which people learn 'for' some hypothetical workplace in the near or distant future (more often than not heavily subsidized by official or voluntary agencies), but a method that, itself, is 'generative of workplace', owned and managed by the new entrepreneurs themselves, where nothing existed previously.

Most of Clodomir's writing has been action-related or, as it were, produced in the thick of the action. Almost invariably, there was never sufficient time nor funds available for in-depth research or for extensive theory-building. This has resulted in a quarter of a century of vibrant practice on the ground, with critical examination, practitioners' and evaluators' feedback and steady theory-building consistently lagging behind. This undernourished theoretical prong of the OW-based 'capacitation' project can be attributed in no small part to the lack of knowledge about de Morais and his work in academic circles, some of the reasons for which are discussed, for example, by Miguel Sobrado in Chapter 2. Only a handful of Latin American universities – prominently, the Universities of Heredia in Costa Rica and Chapingo in Mexico, and, in more recent years, the Universities of Brasília and Rondônia – have taken an active interest in the de Morais approach at both the theoretical and practical levels. In Europe there is – apart, of course, from de Morais' own doctoral thesis, submitted in 1987 at the University of Rostock, in which he linked the core of his practice to the 'objective activity' concept of the Russian school[2] – the important theoretical work done by Cees van Dam in the early 1980s, at the Centre for the Study of Education in Developing Countries (CESO), The Hague, Netherlands (which, unfortunately, lacked follow-up afterwards), as well as the conferences and publications around de Morais organized by the University of Manchester in more recent years.

This book sees itself principally as an introduction to de Morais in which his ideas and his life's work are given a wider airing, especially in the important English-speaking development and academic communities, where he remains virtually an unknown entity. It is of course not possible to appreciate – let alone analyse and build the necessary broad body of informed comment, research and theory – about 'what one does not know'. The fact that the theoretical part of this book is relatively modest and that pride of place has been given to who de Morais is, and what his ideas have achieved on three continents over more than a quarter of a century, is therefore intentional: let the facts speak for themselves. The hope, however, is that, precisely because of this wider knowledge and deeper insight, a 'critical mass' of comments, criticisms and, above all, more generalized and intensive practice will be generated, prompting, in turn, more in-depth research, resulting in a necessary complement and sequel to this book that will be more reflective, critical and theoretical in intent and content. That the present English-language book saw the light of day is almost entirely due, in the best tradition of Zed books, to the commitment of Robert Molteno and his editorial team to give wider renown to that 'other Brazilian', the contemporary, compatriot and lifelong friend of Paulo Freire's.

It will forever remain difficult, though, to explain why de Morais' considerable achievements and revolutionary ideas in the fields of social psychology and adult education – to mention just two disciplines, and in sharp contrast to those of Paulo Freire, for example – achieved comparatively little recognition in either the former West or East, dominated by the monopolizing ideologies of right and left.

When everything is said and done, de Morais' OW allows people, specifically the unemployed who, literally, have nothing but themselves to rely or to fall back on, to gain autonomously ownership and control of the economic factor, or, in de Morais' words, the all-important *primo mangiare* for those who, without food, will simply die or become involved in crime and/or violent, destructive protests. Could it be that autonomy, genuine citizens' autonomy, was perceived as a threat by the West, obsessed for the last two decades by theories and practices around participatory development, as well as by the countries of the former Eastern Bloc, where de Morais' Organization Workshop – revealingly – never made any real inroads?

Clodomir's understanding goes far beyond the parameters of autonomous knowledge creation in the tradition of 'conscientization' and 'popular education'. He provides a genuine and workable answer to the all-important question: 'After conscientization: what?' and even more importantly: 'After conscientization: how, when and where?' The answer is the Organization Workshop, a point enthusiastically conceded by Freire himself.[3] 'Critical consciousness' (popular education) may, like the Duke of York, march its troops 'to the top of the hill', but, without 'organizational consciousness' to complement it and provide it with real autonomy and 'bite', they come all the way down again afterwards. This leaves them, as happened so often in the past, in a worse situation than the one they were in before: they will have tasted the fruit of 'freedom' but lack genuine means to sustain that freedom.

'Power', as we explain further in this book, is not just about 'feeling' (em)power(ed) and 'in control' (the political side of 'power'), or about 'allowing' people to 'participate' in power that is not theirs ('participulation'), nor does it come through 'small group dynamics', especially where the excluded and the dispossesed are concerned. 'Power' is also, and chronologically first and foremost, about constructing an economic base of genuine ownership. The organizational learning found in the OW exercise provides both 'ownership' and 'control' 'while-doing-it', inside the 'objective activity' (capacitation); where 'the need learns to know itself' (Leont'ev 1978), 'it becomes a motive'. Lacking this genuine claim to (common) ownership, political, social and educational activism will fizzle out into impotent idealism or verbalism, or be converted into the equally impotent (in terms of providing credible, genuine, sustainable livelihoods, that is) negative energy of Tupacamaru or Sendero Luminoso vintage, as illustrated in the tragic case of the failed reforms in Peru (see Chapter 8).

What Clodomir has to offer constitutes 'a genuine hope for the rapid transformation, on a massive scale and at a low cost to the public purse, of large groups of people' (Chapter 9) both in the so-called Third World and in the present and future 'World without Work' (Rifkin and Heilbronner 1996) in the post-industrialized countries. From 'excluded' (negative qualification) they become promoters of income and jobs, 'ambassadors of new work opportunities' (Chapter 18). When Clodomir was asked to sum up his position at the end of the one-day conference held in Manchester in March 1998, he could do no better than remind the audience of the wisdom of the Ancients, expressed in the Italian phrase: 'Primo mangiare, poi philosophare.'

Clodomir, who turned seventy in 1999, wrote to us in the spring of that year: 'As you keep pressing me for more, I just found some time to go back to some of the notes I made in my old work diaries, I managed to turn up some more data which could be used in the book.' These personal memories, which Clodomir, typically, never found the time to publish himself (he holds the view that 'memoirs are written by those who already have no memory left'), have been collated especially in Chapters 8 and 9 (Central and South America), Chapters 10 and 11 (Mozambique and West Africa), Chapter 15 (Portugal) and Chapter 17 (Brazil).

The foundations for this particular book can be found in the debates and efforts by the Latin American–European Research Group, which culminated in the Manchester conference of 23 March 1998 and in which most of the contributors to this book participated, either in Manchester itself, or over the subsequent 'Facilitate.Com' conferencing over the Internet. Others, such as Gavin Andersson, Walter Barelli, Benjamin Erazo, Leopoldo Sandoval and Paulo Roberto da Silva, joined us later, again thanks to the marvels of the Internet. To all of them goes our most sincere expression of thanks.

Raff Carmen and Miguel Sobrado
Manchester / Heredia

Notes

1. See Note 6, Chapter 17.

2. re: Vygotsky (1978), Luria (1976), Leont'ev (1978), an idea taken up and developed, much later, in the 1980s, by mainly North American researchers under the 'situated learning' aegis; (see e.g. Lave and Wegner (1991).

3. See p. 41.

References

Lave, Jean and Etienne Wegner (1991) *Situated Learning*, Cambridge: Cambridge University Press.

Leont'ev, Alexei, N. (1978) *Activity, Consciousness and Personality* (trans Marie Hall), Englewood Cliffs, NJ: Prentice-Hall.

— (1981) 'The problem of activity in psychology', in J. V. Wertsch (ed.) *The Concept of Activity in Soviet Psychology*, Armonk, NY: Sharpe.

Luria, A. R. (1976) *Cognitive Development: Its Cultural and Social Foundations*, Cambridge, MA: Harvard University Press.

Rifkin, Jeremy and Robert L. Heilbronner (1996) *The End of Work*, New York: Putnam Group.

Vygotsky, L. S. (1978) *Mind in Society*, Cambridge, MA: Harvard University Press

— (1986/1934) *Thought and Language* (trans Alex Kozulin), Cambridge, MA: MIT Press.

N I A

Preliminary Note on Translating 'Latino' Terms into English

Raff Carmen

The Concept and Practice of 'Capacitation' (and 'Discapacitation')

This book deals with the 'Latin' (South American, to be more precise) concept and practice of *capacitação/capacitación*, and, to a lesser extent, *formução/formación*, which reflect specifically different (adult) educational concepts and practices for which no equivalent term exists in current English dictionaries or academic literature. Imagine then the problem of devising an appropriate English book title that adequately expresses the idea while an adequate English term to express it is lacking. A similar quandary faced the (anonymous) translator of Paulo Freire's seminal work *¿Extensión o Communicación?* (Extension or Communication?) 25 years ago. The English translation of this seminal text can be found in the concluding part of *Education for Critical Consciousness* (Freire 1974). Jacinta Correia makes copious reference to it in Chapter 4. It would, indeed, have been wholly inconceivable to translate Freire's original idea of *capacitación técnica* – which he says is 'on the side' of the Learner, and not on that of the Teacher – by simply using the English blanket word 'training', which, precisely, as Freire stipulates, is 'not on the side' of the learner (and for which Latin languages have their own particular terminology, anyhow).

Thus, uniquely in an (adult) educational publication, we find the Spanish term *capacitación técnica* translated as 'technical proficiency capacitation', as, for example, in:

> Technical Proficiency Capacitation, which should not be confused with the training of animals, can never be dissociated from the existential conditions of the life of the peasants, from their cultural viewpoint, from their magic beliefs. It must begin at the level at which they are, and not at the level at which the agronomists think they ought to be. (Freire 1974: 163)

We decided, therefore, to translate, for the purposes of this book (and hoping that the idea and the term will 'catch on' in English) the Portuguese/ Spanish term *capacitação/capacitación*, which covers, among others, the generically different educational process of 'objective activity', i.e. in which it is 'the object' and not the trainer or educator, that 'teaches', simply as 'capacitation'. This term imposes itself, be it only from the mere practical viewpoint – for instance, Miguel Sobrado's 'mirror'-term *discapacitación* (see Chapter 18) can, in our view, be sensibly translated only as 'dis-capacitation'.

Another reason why we feel quite comfortable with the term '(dis)-capacitation' is that Freire came up against a similar problem with the translation of the concept and term of the 'Latin' term *conscientização/ conscientización*, which was, if not coined, then at least popularized by him in his 'psycho-social' approach to adult education (PSM). Some academics wanted to see it translated by, for example, 'awareness-raising'. Apart from the fact that 'awareness-raising' supposes a 'raiser' and a 'raisee', whereas 'conscientization' is now a term that has gained *droit de cité* in the English vocabulary:

> In Brazil we say 'esta estressado'(s/he is stressed). This does not mean that Brazilian Portuguese or other languages that have incorporated English terms, are inferior. These languages were forced to borrow those terms. When my work was first introduced in the United States, some people insisted that we put into an equivalent English phrase our concept of 'conscientização'. I refused. Why not accept this term? I do not have to accept 'stress', but I have. Why do you not accept 'conscientização'? (Freire 1974: 185)

The English/French verb 'to capacitate', as a matter of fact, does exist, and is used in legal documents and in the biological sciences, for example. Its educational potential, however, unlike in Spanish and Portuguese, has remained under-explored and it is woefully under-used or simply ignored in the anglophone world. There are some examples, though, of 'capacitation' being used in development literature: in the mid-1970s the Geneva-based United Nations Research Institute for Social Development (UNRISD), proposed the neologism 'capacitation' to 'emphasize[d] the building up of institutions for diagnosis and problem-solving, and of educational pro-grammes enabling societies to function better through the informed and cooperative action of their members' (Wolfe 1996: 39). For whatever reason, though, this meaning has now been completely subsumed in the quasi-universal 'capacity-building' parlance, about which more in chapters by other contributors.

'Capacitation' also propped up in an ILO World Employment Pro-gramme Research Report (ILO/WEP) called *Participatory Rural Develop-*

ment and the Role of the Animator (Tilakaratna 1987). Capacitation means, again, 'the availability of opportunities for people to build up their capacities to move from the status of objects (manipulated by external forces) to the status of subjects (guided by self-consciousness) and active agents of change [which] is central to the generation of Participatory Rural Development processes' (ibid.: 23). This meaning of 'capacitation' is more reminiscent of Freire's 'conscientization' but, as far as we know, it has not been picked up by other agencies or authors since then. In capacitation (objective activity), as used by de Morais, 'the need learns to know itself; it becomes a motive' (Leont'ev 1978: 116). This is what makes de Morais' capacitation into a generically different social psychological and adult educational concept and practice.

'Situated Learning' and 'Capacitation'

Unrelated to either the 'development' field or that of the Latin American experience with 'capacitation', 'situated cognition/learning' made its entry in North American and wider anglophone 'workplace' studies about ten years ago. 'Situated learning' (SL) field research was carried out mainly, if not exclusively, in formal school (including vocational training) contexts by, among others, Jean Lave and Etienne Wegner. Even though, strangely, SL at no stage concerned itself with learning from or interacting with the much older (by at least 20 years) Latin American scholarship or practice, the idea is of interest to us because, like de Morais' 'capacitation', SL draws inspiration from the same 'Russian school' of social psychology, in particular, the 1980s translations, by James Wertsch, of the works of the Russian social psychologists A. N. Leont'ev, Luria and Vygotsky (see e.g. Wertsch 1981).

Let us make it clear straight away, though, that de Morais' starting point and perspective differ widely from those of situated learning in that, rather than being concerned with how people learn 'in' the workplace and 'for' the (existing) workplace (school/vocational 'training'), 'capacitation' starts where SL does not tread, or leaves off: namely 'where there is no workplace', unless, as explained in this book, the excluded, the dropouts of capitalism, the unemployed and under-employed, create, through capacitation (OWs) a job, an income and a stable future for themselves. The common ground between the Capacitation and Situated Learning paradigms can be found in Marx and Engels' approach to the relationship between humans and reality. Soviet social psychology stresses the importance of active subjects whose knowledge of pre-existing material reality is founded on their interactions with it. No progress can be expected from a (behaviourist) psychology based on a framework in which the human passively receives input from the physical and social environment. Only interacting with the material world and with other humans can develop a knowledge of reality.

Formación/formação

English dictionaries use 'training' not only to translate *capacitación* but also to translate the educational term formación, commonly used not only in Latin languages, but also in French and a variety of Germanic/Scandinavian languages (in French *la formation*/Dutch *Vorming*) means: 'any kind of systematic teaching, learning or apprenticeship, whether geared to the acquisition of a technique or a trade, or whether it is aimed at the intellectual, social, moral or cultural development of a person' (translated from the French in UNESCO 1979: 140). *Formation/formación/Vorming* also refer to the way in which (even) adults continue to (be) 'form'(ed), to (be) 'shape(d)', or 'mould' themselves in order to fit any requirements of their role in life imposes, whatever this role may be. Training is part of that 'formation' can never express the full richess and specific meaning of *Formation/formación/Vorming*. That is why, throughout the book, the English term 'formation' is used where one 'normally' would expect 'training'; 'training' is used only if the text, context and term used in the original text indicate that this is what is specifically meant. De Morais' Organization workshops can be described as a form of 'formation' of and with adult individuals, cadres and groups. We see no objection, either, to using 'formation' in an educational sense in English, even if the term has already other (non-educational) uses. The same holds true in all the other languages that use 'formation' as an educational term too.

Assistencialismo/clientelismo/sociolismo

Assistencialismo comes from 'assistance' and conveys a concept closely associated with paternalism and 'compassion'. It covers policies of financial or social assistance that attack the symptoms, but not the causes, of social and other ills. *Assistencialism* is useful to and popular with politicians as it allows them to be seen to be doing something, assuring a good crop of votes in the short term. *Clientelism*, often going hand in hand with assistencialism, is a form of corruption of the common good: goods and services are channelled by political and other powerful patrons towards 'clients' who return the favour – for example, with a good crop of votes for the generous benefactor at election time. *Sociolism* is a popular sarcastic comment on the socialism of the *socios* (buddies) – the 'whom-you-know' favouritism and clientelism by those in power to do favours.

References

Freire, P. (1974) 'Extension or communication?', in *Education for Critical Consciousness*, London: Sheed and Ward.

Leont'ev, Alexei N. (1978) *Activity, Consciousness and Personality* (trans Marie Hall), Englewood Cliffs, N.J: Prentice-Hall.

Tilakaratna, S. (1987) *The Animator in Participatory Rural Development*, Geneva: ILO/WEP.

UNESCO/IBE (1979) *Thesaurus de l'Education Unesco* (with English and Spanish Equivalents), Paris: UNESCO.

Wertsch, J. V. (ed.) (1981) *The Concept of Activity in Soviet Psychology*, Armonk, NY: Sharpe.

— (1985) *Vygotsky and the Social Construction of Mind*, Cambridge, MA: Harvard University Press.

Wolf, M. (1996) *Exclusive Development*, London: Zed Books.

Notes on the Contributors

Gavin Andersson is executive director of the Development Resources Centre (DRC) in Johannesburg. Born in South Africa and raised in Botswana, he left university in 1974 to help rebuild the black trade union movement. Banned two years later and eventually detained in 1981, he returned to Botswana after his release. There he was hired as manager of a woodworking factory in a small village; he introduced worker self-management; and a ten-fold increase in production resulted. Among other activities, he helped launch *Mmegi*, a newspaper that now has the largest circulation in the country.

Walter Barelli is an economist. He is currently secretary for employment and labour relations for the state government of São Paulo and professor at the Institute for Economics, State University of Campinas-Unicamp. From 1992 to 1994, he was minister of labour. He has also served as technical director of the Brazilian trade unions' Centre for Statistics and Socio-Economic Studies.

Raff Carmen currently coordinates the masters and post-graduate research programmes in adult education, adult literacy and rural social/community development at the University of Manchester. Prior to that, he worked as a priest and a teacher in rural Zambia for fifteen years and then managed a UNDP/ICRISAT sorghum and millet research station in Burkina Faso for another five years. He is the author of *Autonomous Development: An Excursion in Radical Thinking and Practice* (Zed Books 1996).

Jacinta Castelo Branco Correia, Clodomir's wife, lectures at the Federal University of Rondonia, Brazil, where she has been closely involved in numerous rural and urban workshops in entrepreneurial capacitation. She has also directed the largescale OWs run by FAO and IATTERMUND in São Paulo under the PAE (Self-Employment Project).

Paulo Roberto da Silva is the current president of IATTERMUND, a Brazilian NGO he helped found in 1989. He is an Afro-Brazilian who has specialized in enterprise administration and agrarian economics. He has acted as principal adviser to the Federation of Wheat Producers' Co-operatives (FECOTRIGO) in Rio Grande del Sul. More recently he was appointed by the presidency as adviser on cooperatives to the federal government.

Benjamin ('Minchito') Erazo, a lawyer by profession, was in charge of the Honduran Social Capacitation programme from 1973 to 1977. He was also one of the founders of the Honduran Institute for Rural Development (IHDER). He has directed numerous workshops in Honduras, in Guatemala and Sandinista Nicaragua. More recently, he has acted as adviser to the Swiss Overseas Development Agency.

Isabel Labra and Ivàn Labra are social psychologists. In the early 1970s they worked in Chile on vocational training programmes and enabling workers to participate in the management of the nationalized industries. From 1988 to date, they have worked with the Organization Workshop method in southern Africa, where they have run some 60 large-scale workshops. They also provide consultancy services to major international NGOs including HIVOS, Catholic Relief Services (CRS), Redd Barna, Save the Children (USA), Terre des Hommes (Germany) and many others.

Clodomir Santos de Morais was born in Santa Maria de Vitoria, Bahia State, in 1928. At the age of 14 he emigrated from the northeast to São Paulo, where he worked for a time in a Ford assembly plant, an experience which undoubtedly had a strong influence on the theory and practice of organization that he developed later. He eventually became a lawyer and consultant to the Peasant Leagues in Recife and he was elected as a deputy for the state of Pernambuco. The seeds of the Organization Workshop were sown when he attended a clandestine study workshop for Peasant League activists in 1954. Arrested after the military coup in 1964, he at one stage shared the same prison cell as his friend Paulo Freire. He escaped to Chile and was able to return to Brazil only in the late 1980s when he set up the NGO IATTERMUND, in Brasília.

Juan José Rojas Herrera is a lecturer and researcher in the Department of Rural Sociology in Chapingo, Mexico as well as technical adviser to the Commission for the Promotion of Cooperatives at the Mexican Chamber of Deputies. He is author of *The Rise and Fall of the Agrarian Cooperative Movement in Mexico* (UACH, 1998) and of numerous articles on different aspects of the economics of solidarity.

Leopoldo Sandoval is an agronomist by profession. At one time he was minister of agriculture in Guatemala and President of the National Institute for Agrarian Transformation (INTA). For many years before that he worked for the Inter-American Institute for Cooperation in Agriculture and for the FAO as a specialist in agrarian reform. He has also been a consultant to the UNDP (United Nations Development Programme).

Miguel Sobrado is a Latin American social scientist. Among the many academic and research posts he has held, he was director of the School of Social Planning at the National University of Costa Rica from 1974 to 1982 and a member of the postgraduate University Council from 1992 to 1995. He has worked as a consultant in various Central American countries for the ILO, FAO and other organizations. He is the author of numerous publications (mainly in Spanish) and has long sought to apply Clodomir de Morais's thinking in concrete development situations. He is, in addition, a social commentator with a regular column in Costa Rica's leading daily newspaper. In 1998, he was requested by Costa Rica's newly elected President Miguel Angel Rodriguez to run the country's social development programme.

Abbreviations

ADERI	Association for Integrated Rural Development (Peru)
AGRITEX	Agricultural Extension Services (Zimbabwe)
ALEA	Latin American Association of Self-managing Enterprises
ANTEAG	National Association of Self-employed and Participatory Stakeholders (Brazil)
API	investment project assistant
BETGER	job and income-generating labour bank
CECODES	Centre for Ecology and Sustainable Development (Mexico)
CENCIRA	Centre for Agrarian Reform Capacitation and Research (Peru)
CEPAUR	Centre for Urban and Rural Development Alternatives
CIARA	Foundation for Applied Capacitation and Research for Agrarian Reform (Venezuela)
CNC	Campesino Central Office
CO	citizens' organization
CONAC	National Confederation of Campesino Land Settlements (Panama)
CONAN	National Federation of Human Settlement Associations (Brazil)
CONCRAB	Federation of the Agrarian Reform Cooperatives of Brazil
CONTAG	National Confederation of Agicultural Workers (Brazil)
COPERA	Capacitation Project for the Organization of Producers and Job Creation (Nicaragua)
CORDE	Cooperation for Research, Development and Education (Botswana)
CRS	Catholic Relief Services
CUT	Workers' Central Unit (Brazil)
DESMI	Economic and Social Development Institute for Indigenous Mexicans
DGTZ	Deutsche Gesellschaft für Technische Zusammenarbeit
DINADECO	National Directorate for Community Development (Costa Rica)

DRC	Development Resources Centre (Johannesburg)
EAP	economically active population
ECOMAL	Enterprise for the Provision of Construction Materials (Mozambique)
EMBRATER	Brazilian Enterprise for Technical Assistance and Rural Extension
ETC	Ecological Training Centre
EWTO	Experimental Workshop on Theory of Organization
FAO	Food and Agriculture Organization
FECOTRIGO	Federation of Wheat Producers' Cooperatives
FENAC	National Campesino Federation (Costa Rica)
FEWP	Foundation for Education with Production (Zimbabwe)
HIVOS	Netherlands Institute for Cooperation with Developing Countries
HRM	human relations movement
IAN	National Agrarian Institute of Venezuela
IATDE	Membership Institute of the Economic Development Experts
IATTERMUND	Institute for Technical Support to Third World Countries
IBAMA	Institute for Environmental Protection (Brazil)
ICIRA	Capacitation and Research Institute for Agrarian Reform
ICRISAT	International Crop Research Institute for the Semi-Arid Tropics
IDESE	Institute for Socio-Economic Development
IFAD	International Fund for Agricultural Development (Rome)
IHDER	Honduran Institute for Rural Development
IICA	International Institute for Cooperation in Agriculture
ILO	International Labour Organization
IMAS	Mixed Institute for Social Aid (Costa Rica)
INA	National Agrarian Institute (Honduras)
INAGRO	Institute for Agrarian Capacitation (Venezuela)
INCRA	Institute for Land Settlement and Agrarian Reform (Brazil)
INSCOOP	Institute of the Cooperative Sector
INTA	National Institute for Agrarian Transformation (Guatemala)
ITCO	Institute of Lands and Colonization (Costa Rica)
IWPR	Institute for Women's Policy Research
LETS	local exchange trading system
MST	Landless Workers' Movement (Brazil)
NAAM	('power' in Wolof) culturally embedded rural development movement pioneered by Bernard Ledea Ouedraogo (Burkina Faso)

NCPE	New Ejido Population Centre (Mexico)
NGO	non-governmental organization
NPA	Norwegian People's Aid
OCB	Organization of Brazilian Cooperatives
OD	Organization Development
OEA	Organization of American States
OTM	Mozambican Workers' Organization
OW	Organization Workshop
PAE	Self-employment Project, São Paulo, Brazil
PO	peoples' organization
PRA	participatory rural appraisal
PREALC	Regional Employment Programme for Latin America and the Caribbean
PROCCARA	Campesino Capacitation Programme for Land Reform (Honduras)
PRODERITH	Wet Tropics Integrated Rural Development Project
PROGEI	employment and income-generating project
PRONAGER	National Programme for Job and Income Generation in Poor Areas
RBM	Redd Barna Mozambique (Norwegian NGO)
RLA	Right Livelihood Award
SADET	Southern Africa Development Trust
SAHR	Agricultural and Water Resources Secretariat (Mexico)
SAP	structural adjustment programme
SEBRAE	Brazilian Service for Support to Micro-Enterprises
SINAMOS	National System of Social Mobilization (Peru)
SIPGEI	Social Participation System for the Identification of Job and Income Generation Projects
SUDENE	Supervisory Committee for the Development of the Nordeste (Brazil)
TDC	cooperative development expert
TDE	economic development expert
tdh	terre des hommes investment project
TOT	trainer of trainers
TPI	investment project specialist (Portugal)
UNDP	United Nations Development Programme

Part I

Context and History

1

Those Who Don't Eat and Those Who Don't Sleep

Raff Carmen and Miguel Sobrado

P16 015 017

F02 I30

The twentieth century was marked by conflict: apart from two world wars and countless local wars, there was the grand ideological divide between left and right, between socialism and capitalism, and more recently between governance by the public institutions of the state and the private institutions of the market. In the new century the only struggles that matter will be between the proportionally small group of the Included, whose success is based on ever greater concentrations of power and wealth, and the vast majority of the Excluded; between the global and the local; between individualism and solidarity; between the 'culture of power' vested in the institutions set up by global capital and the 'power of culture' vested in civil society. The millions of unemployed and the countless further millions teetering on the edge of survival in shanty-towns and urban slums all over the world, the losers, also known as 'marginals', in actual fact are as integral (or non-marginal) a part of the global win–lose economy as the winners. 'The margin' as a figure of speech trivializes and purposely marginalizes the vast majority of humanity who are, *de facto*, excluded. While poverty may always have been with us, its underlying causes have varied greatly according to the historical period. Capitalism, with its inbuilt unlimited competition drive, generates its own particular brand of poverty, generically different from the poverties experienced in any previous period, be it in feudal times or under slavery, for example, when the idea that the slave or serf should stay alive, be it only in the (self-)interest of the master, made good economic sense.

Globalization has changed all that. Globalization makes unprecedented concentrations of wealth ever more possible and feasible, with the new rich of the globalization era, a mere 225 of them, owning in excess of $1,000 billion, the equivalent of the annual income of 47 per cent of the entire world population (UNDP 1998). The extremes resulting from the disaggregation of well-being from development are at their most vivid in the 'gated city' phenomenon. These affluent ghettos, inside which the super-rich are cocooned in their sumptuous living spaces, are hermetically sealed from 'the rest of us'. There is little difference between the gated cities on the outskirts of Johannesburg and the phoney privacy of 'Alphaville', near São Paulo, Brazil, where mini-armies of paramilitaries, razor wire, dogs and closed-circuit television ward off the menacing ugliness beyond, which the inhabitants of the gated cities have in no small measure helped to create (Whitacker 1998; Martin and Schumann 1997).

Echoing Josué de Castro's 'geography of hunger' metaphor, de Morais speaks of a world divided *between* 'those who don't eat' and 'those who don't sleep', those 'not sleeping' not doing so because they are 'in permanent fear of those who do not eat'. The classical metaphor for 'prison', the steel-barred window, behind which not prisoners but citizens now cower, has become an almost 'normal' feature of end-of-century town architecture anywhere (de Morais 1997). With the gradual breakdown and subsequent disappearance of the 'economy of affection' (Hyden) – overtaken by the centripetal forces of the nuclear family, among many others – and the state's professed inability to continue to provide welfare, health and education for its citizens, just staying alive has become a never-ending act of almost superhuman resourcefulness on the part of the excluded. 'Families are becoming more nuclear. People, in the end, need more cash to survive,' declares a recent Oxfam report (Oxfam 1999).

Those living in tropical climes, to which foreign visitors travel great distances for holidays, would not normally think of emigrating to countries with colder, harsher climates, except, that is, in case of a severe dearth of local job opportunities. If things continue the way they are, the 'gated cities' of Jo'burg, São Paulo and elsewhere may soon prove to have been but a paltry foretaste of what is to happen on an international scale: namely the hungry, the unemployed and the excluded laying siege to a fortress Europe, USA or Australia, with 'millions upon millions of Africans, Asians and Latin Americans trying to slip between the mazes of the net or the loopholes in the legislation designed to keep them out' (de Morais, at the Manchester conference, March 1998).

Late twentieth-century neo-liberalism, the most recent stage of marketization, flooded into the space left by the now defunct social democratic consensus, while creating a huge social vacuum of its own. 'Social deficit' not only consists of in-country and inter-country inequities, but comes about also as the result of wholesale cuts in social provisions in health, education and social welfare, allowing for lower taxes which, in turn, must make the country concerned more attractive for foreign investment. Like Marxism, with which it has a lot in common, neo-liberalism generates an enormous leap of faith. Belief in the imperative of 'total market', or the doctrine of economic efficiency driven to its ultimate logical conclusion, demands that all barriers that are perceived to stand in the way of the pure individual(istic) pursuit of financial gain and the maximization of profit be removed (Bourdieu 1998: 3).

The Demise of the Welfare State

The world of globalized markets, globalized economies and global industries integrated by instant global communications is becoming so complex and so vast that there are very few people still able to keep track or see its outlines. 'Total market' has meant a systematic loss of autonomy for local and rural populations worldwide, bringing cultural, economic and social alienation in its wake. In small communities everywhere, people feel that power and culture are concentrated 'somewhere else' and that there is little they can do about it. Collective solidarity, expressed traditionally in the trade union movement, the family and the nation-state, in particular, has been in retreat for years. The modern welfare state, based on the principle of mutuality and reciprocality (rather than 'charity'), took root in the wake of the disasters of the great Depression and was urged on, in no small measure, by the example of the socialist regimes in the East.

Franklin D. Roosevelt's 'New Deal' (1933–36) in the United States stood firm for about thirty years, but started to crumble along the dualistic cracks that have always been present in North American society, i.e. the middle classes revolting against perceived 'state profligacy', with tax monies disbursed to the disadvantaged members of society, the majority of whom are black. The European version, along the lines of post-war Beveridgean full employment, social security and 'from-cradle-to-grave' social service provision, became standard policy in European countries (give or take a few variations). The institutionalization of the equal entitlement of every citizen to the goods and services of the welfare state ensured that wealth was redistributed before it was produced, rather than acting unidirectionally in favour of already existing capital. That was an important achievement by any standard.

The present crisis of the welfare state did not come about because of a crisis in the values which made it into one of the most noble mani-festations of democratic and civil progress an industrial society is capable of. Neither is it true that the welfare state is 'not affordable' any more, as conservative forces have been trying to argue all along: after all, the National Health Service in Britain, for example, now perceived to have become 'unaffordable', was established in the wake of an economy bled white by the war effort, with unprecedented scarcity of goods and wholesale rationing. Since then, national wealth in Britain has increased at least threefold. In other words, the wealth that is there is simply used somewhere else, and for different purposes. In real terms, welfare is more affordable now than it has ever been. When equity, however, is at odds with citizens' private liberty, the state, as primary agent of equitable distribution, is under attack. Hence the clamour, in the name of 'individual freedom', especially since the 1980s, for 'lower taxes', 'less state' and 'less big government'.

While, historically, the generation of new wealth brings with it a general improvement of living conditions (well-being), the late twentieth-century demise of the welfare state is both paradoxical (at the epistemological level) and perpendicular to the main direction of the flow of history. Or, in the words of Stefano Zamagni (1997), 'an extraordinary and worrying inversion of [this] relationship between the production of wealth and the reduction in uncertainty'. The breakdown of the social contract in post-industrial societies between the state and the citizens has, as already said, little to do with their lack of physical wealth, but rather concerns the gradual devaluation of social wealth, a social scarcity or a 'social deficit' engineered, fostered and maintained by a combination of mega vested interests on the one hand, and private citizens' greeds on the other, epitomized by Margaret Thatcher's 1980s declaration that 'There is no such thing as society.'

Hence, also, the steady deconstruction of the fiscal system and the adoption of the socially reactionary neo-liberal agenda, both on this and the other side of the Atlantic. It was Clinton-the-Democrat, after all, who, in 1996, signed the final death warrant of welfare-as-we-know-it. The way out of this one-way street, away from the abdication by the state of its social mission, cannot ever be 'less state' or 'less big government'. In many countries, this surrender has led to the usurpation of the institutions of the state by clientelist relations (as in Latin America) and Mafia interests (as in the former Soviet Union), as well as a drift to a devaluation of work, to more unemployment and more social exclusion all around. In both (former) Second and in the post-colonial Third Worlds in particular, it was the centralized, corporate, and in many countries, for all practical purposes, one-party state that, for many years, formed the backbone and guarantee of a fairer and more equitable distribution of wealth.

As described elsewhere in this book (e.g. Chapters 5, 10 and 11), unemployment, poverty and social exclusion were virtually a non-problem in, for example, Angola, Mozambique and Guinea Bissau immediately after those countries' independence.[1] As described by Miguel Sobrado in Chapter 14, in the former Eastern Bloc countries such as Poland and, of course, the former Soviet Union, every citizen was, constitutionally, treated as a state employee, assured of a job, and hence protected against poverty, destitution and exclusion. Considering the parlous state in which they find themselves at present, one would have thought that countries such as Angola or Mozambique would be the last countries on earth able to 'afford' and sustain a universal social security system. But a universal social security system did exist, was feasible, was possible and did operate satisfactorily until, of course, global politics, the rush towards privatization of public goods and services and, last but not least, the triumphalist 'capitalism-has-won' tsunami of globalization overtook them and swallowed them – a tsunami that reduced countries of truly gigantic economic potential such as Angola and a former superpower such as Russia to pathetic shadows of themselves, to the status of non-countries and of non-players on the world stage.

On top of those global trends, Latin American countries in particular had to cope with their inveterate, debilitating problems of assistencialism, clientelism and downright corruption. The very centralist nature of the corporate state, which is its greatest strength – the political will combined with the capacity to distribute wealth more equally and more fairly among its citizens, as it were 'by decree' – proved to be at the same time its greatest weakness and its ultimate undoing. A centralized bureaucracy detached from genuine democratic control, checks and balances soon becomes self-serving and irrational, inexorably leading to the common good being usurped by clientelist and Mafia interests. The phenomenon is known in Cuba as *sociolism* – the cosy 'buddy-ism' (*socio*) or the unspoken 'whom-you-know' inner network among civil servants who know how to 'get things done' and how to divert the state's goods and services to their own benefit and that of their 'clients' (clientelism), thereby making state services more expensive, less effective and a rich feeding-ground for corrupt practices, also known as 'bogus privatization' (*privatización espúrea* – Sobrado).

All this goes to show that when democracy and citizenship are merely nominal, when representative democracy is reduced and devalued to the casting of the occasional vote in local or national elections, without any genuine participation by civil society in the democratic process, the common good is bound to suffer, resulting in a radical weakening of the very foundations of the welfare state. Neo-liberal globalization processes were the final straw for the already exhausted and weakened corporatist state in Latin America as elsewhere. The universally proposed solution – 'less state' – invariably turned out to be the remedy that only makes the disease of unemployment and social exclusion worse. The obverse side of the social exclusion phenomenon are the 'rich ghettos' and 'gated cities' mentioned at the beginning of this chapter. In between those two equally obscene extremes, the quality of life of an entire society suffers and becomes moribund. Rich or poor resemble each other in that they are ghettos, far removed from a normal, dignified, humane way of life. The real solution has to go far beyond the sterile debate around more or less state. What is at stake is the kind of state and what type of social organization our society will need in the twenty-first century.

The neo-liberal agenda, trapped as it is in the blind alley of its own egotistic opportunism, can offer only attacks on the state, combined with uniform privatizations, in terms of 'solutions' to societal problems. Privatization, used as wholesale state reform policy, becomes a self-serving vehicle feeding the opportunism of the same political class that through its corrupt practices destroyed the welfare state in the first place. First they pillage the family silver, and then, when the state is down and out, they come riding to its rescue as 'privatizing knights', siphoning off public property for a few pathetic pennies. The consistently recurring feature of the massive privatizations in Russia, Latin America (and elsewhere, such as Great Britain in the 1980s) was the wholesale conversion of public monopolies such as electricity, water and gas into private ones. At the very least, in the case of public ownership (or part-ownership) a modicum of control (in favour of prioritization of the national interest, the ecological or social environment, for example) is possible, but this vanishes completely when private gain (of often distant shareholders) becomes the only criterion going.

A Sound Market Built on Sound Sociological Foundations

A sound market can be built only on the sound foundations of a society rich in human and social capital. By this we mean a society whose members are properly educated and formed in the knowledge and use of social and professional skills. This can happen only if they organize within their communities or when they are genuine owners of their own enterprises, in an 'economy of solidarity'. Without an organized society endowed with a high level of citizen culture, no market can be said to be 'free': it becomes a plaything and a tool for *participulation* and propaganda in the hands of the powers that be. Such a market built on social capital is much closer to Adam Smith's original idea and contrasts sharply with the blatant Thatcherite privatization frauds, which have resulted in the total destruction of Russia and inflicted the greatest income inequalities ever seen in Latin America where a mere 2 per cent of the wealth raked in by one-fifth of the highest-paid could solve all the problems of poverty of the entire continent.

Adam Smith, indeed, considered liberty (ensured by just laws) and security for all to be the ultimate objective of human endeavour (Rothschild 1995). A just and stable market can be established within a triangular relationship of a civil society empowered to control and hold the state to account and to enforce ecotaxes and taxes on market transactions (in the sense suggested, for example, by Riccardo Petrella and James Tobin – the so-called Tobin tax; see Tobin 1978). In other words, privatization in the absence of a genuine free market is an aberration and can only lead, as we now beginning to see, to social instability and ecological destruction.

Contributing to the crisis of welfare was also the ingrained, objective problem of the limitations inherent in the Cartesian tunnel vision, which inhibits the search for systemic solutions. The dependency-perpetuating assistentialist culture, which is the particular burden many a social worker is lumbered with, as well as the pedagogism of the educationist, which confuses neutral acts of 'transfer of knowledge' with capacitation (empowerment), or the self-righteous interventionism of the development worker, are all part and parcel of this almost genetic flaw. An effective social policy must be based on an operational epistemology and a consistent methodology, which hold the prospect of integral and permanent solutions. Central to this epistemology and methodology is the recognition, combined with a determination to act accordingly, of the organizational potential of the different social strata and citizens' ability to take initiatives towards the solution of their own problems.

The sorely needed cultural shift from the taken-for-granted 'people are not able' to a 'people are able' premise as a basis for any social policy is at long last in the making. The new debates, especially in development ethics circles, about people's entitlements, capabilities and functionings (see e.g. Nussbaum and Sen 1993) as well as assertions, in the Rawlsean tradition, that 'people ought to be capable to choose' – a language now increasingly being adopted by, for example, the UNDP as the new definition of development (as in the annual UNDP *Human Development Reports*) – are an enormous leap forward in terms of ethical principle and value-based strategy in public policy, which has remained for far too long technology-biased and, therefore, neutralistic. As long as this highly commendable new development discourse does not stop at the mere enunciation of statements of principle and assertions of what is morally right and what is possible in principle, leaving the excluded without any demonstrable, practical, new tools, and no wiser as to 'how?' the normative and the possible can be made feasible, in precise, concrete ways, preferably by themselves, in the end, the excluded have only themselves to rely on.

'Empowerment' is not to be taken for granted as if it were some transferable commodity. 'Power' is not just about 'feeling empowered', but about genuine ownership and control, starting with matters economic and politic. Genuine power cannot be transferred by dint of social assistance, by poverty alleviation measures, or by micro-enterprise strategies on their own. The latter tend to isolate problems into individual compartments that allow, at best, partial solutions with variable to doubtful degrees of sustainability. Nor can power be built, step by step, as implicitly suggested in the language and practice of 'capacity building', an idea and terminology that has become popular, not only with the World Bank but also with mainstream NGOs (see e.g. Eade 1997).

Capacitation is not produced by training – that is, knowledge and skills transfer – or by critical awareness-raising, on their own, but by autonomous agents who, in the productive activity in which they are engaged, learn to discover ('become conscious') in a real(istic) way, of 'needs' that 'become a motive'. This discovery can and will also lead to the need for training suited to the activity/-ies they are already engaged in, as exemplified in the type of capacitation that is at the heart of the de Morais organization workshops (OWs) (the subject of this book).

People's organizations (PO) or citizens' organizations (CO) tend to have no hierarchy or headquarters in capital cities, no general secretary, central director of operations or central funds, nor do they see themselves as agents with a 'mission to intervene'. Indeed, strictly speaking, one 'intervenes' not in one's own affairs but only in those of people who are perceived as 'the other' ('beneficiaries' or 'target' populations). Intervention and interventionism, translated into all forms of social, political and economic projects ('projectile projects' – Carmen 1996), have increased phenomenally over the development decades, at the expense of genuine concerns for the primacy of autonomous human agency and capacitation.

'Agency', by contrast, primarily means autonomous action, or operation by subjects, as distinct from persons being acted upon as objects, or being used, in a roundabout way, as 'part-icipants' in interventionist initiatives, projects and programmes which, ultimately, are not theirs ('participulation' – ibid.). Robert Putnam, in his book *Making Democracy Work* (1993), advances the examples of credit unions in Peru, football clubs in Italy and peasants' cooperatives in Costa Rica as all equally representative of what he understands by social capital. Because it is generative of confidence and relies on horizontal networks that facilitate coordinated action, a high correlation was found to exist between civil action and good governance. Wherever civil action traditions are found to be strong, people are much more likely to cooperate for each other's mutual benefit and to look for collective solutions to problems. Citizens organized around civil action are also much less likely to put higher demands on their government, and because they contribute more, they are also likely to receive more. Putnam even goes so far as saying that social capital is not just one of the many elements that make up a sound democracy but is a vital ingredient of sound, sustainable economic development, too.

The Italian sociologist Riccardo Petrella estimates at half a million the number of interest groups, voluntary and not-for-profit associations and networks around the world, united on the basis of the principle of solidarity, equality and partnership (social capital). They represent an impressive 600 to 800 million members and supporters, with five to six million leaders (Petrella 1995a). In Britain where, after almost twenty years of Thatcherism, one would have thought any vestige of mutuality and co-operativism to have been extinguished for good, 30 million people are still members of mutuals, with an annual turnover of £25 billion; there are still five million Friendly Society members with £11.5 billion in assets; much of Britain's food comes from 550 agricultural cooperatives (which, for example, produce 95 per cent of all apples and up to 75 per cent of common vegetables); and new mutuals, such as Linux, one of the fastest-growing software providers, are springing up all the time. Older cooperative ventures such as the Co-op and the John Lewis Partnership continue to survive and thrive. As explained in Chapter 15, LETS and new economics find fertile ground, particularly in the UK. The Workers' Educational Association (WEA), which relies on member-run branches, is one of the largest adult education providers in the country (Leadbeater and Christie 1999). In the United States, too, there are hundreds of examples of successful cooperatives in a whole range of enterprises that employ one to ten people, all the way to larger industrial enterprises that employ over a hundred (Mumm 1999: 11).

'Where There is no Workplace', and Hence no Future

The traditional small producer (artisan) has been in retreat ever since the Industrial Revolution: 'surplus labour' (a chillingly dehumanizing term if ever there was one, but quite accepted/-able in mainstream economics) was artificially created and converted into capital on behalf of a proportionally small minority of the 'included'. With allowances for the different forms and shapes in which it presents itself, it is a story that is still unfolding. Even in the USA, home of the proud, independent 'homestead', 4.2 million small agricultural enterprises disappeared between 1940 and 1960 alone. With the disappearance of the commons (as in Europe and more recently in India), exponential population growth and the further encroachment of modern production methods, especially the mechanization of agriculture, it has become increasingly difficult for the small family business to continue living off the land anywhere in the world, hence the universal phenomenon of massive rural exodus to the towns. Structural adjustment programmes (SAPs) have wreaked havoc with health, education, subsidized food and public services, with women and children disproportionally represented in the poverty statistics. Even in the USA 15 per cent of the population live below the poverty level, while in France two million have to rely on food aid. According to the UNDP *Human Development Report 1998*, over one hundred million people in the industrialized countries suffer from deprivation and exclusion.

Welfare-as-we-know-it, for the unemployed, is, as pointed out above, on the way out, to be replaced by 'workfare' and 'welfare-to-work'. The idea of 'positive' welfare, meaning that support will continue and even be increased for welfare recipients such as the elderly, the disabled and the young, but that those physically capable to work will have to find themselves work, is gaining ground (see Chapter 16). 'Poverty alleviation', championed by organizations as diverse as IFAD (Rome), the ILO (Geneva) and the World Bank (Washington), has traditionally been concerned with 'correcting' the adverse effects on the poor of SAPs and compensating for the deficiencies in the market, by means of macro policy interventions, such as stabilization programmes, the creation of social funds and the promotion of poverty research institutions and an array of micro-interventions.

'Capacity building', a neologism of uncertain parentage (but, as already mentioned, one now fully embraced by the development community) is, as a transitive, interventionist and development-inducing concept, well within the parameters of mainstream development practice. Capacity building or development of capacity is the language and strategy now increasingly being adopted at all levels. This notwithstanding, it is, as Southern critics like to point out, a 'concept used by Northerners towards Southerners, with reference to others rather than themselves, and within a context which sees Southern development organizations as local implementing agents for Northern policies. In this sense, "capacity" refers largely to the "absorption capacity" of Southern organizations' (Kaplan 1999).

'Enterprise' and 'enterprise training', too, have seen a gain in prestige, especially over the last decade and a half. Entrepreneurs have come to be recognized almost universally as the true torch-bearers of the free market society and of development efforts. In the early 1990s the 'creation of a climate of enterprise' and the 'need for a worldwide propagation and expansion of enterprise' has gained centre stage, not only of the World Bank's unambiguously market-friendly approach to development (World Bank 1991), but also in most of the governmental and NGOs' development agendas. The German DGTZ overseas development agency's CEFE Programme (Competency-based Economics through Formation for Enterprise), for example, is illustrative of the great leap forwards 'small' or 'micro' enterprise has taken in 1990s development parlance and initiatives. CEFE's D. Kolshorn hails micro-enterprise as 'one of the most significant and dramatic developments of the last decade' (DGTZ 1996). The need for the propagation and expansion of small enterprise has now become widely accepted as a promising way out of the development impasse.

Conclusion

Micro-enterprise no doubt occupies an important place in poverty alleviation and the search for a solution to the massive unemployment problem. But as Walter Barelli, for example, demonstrates (see Chapter 18), while some of the enterprises generated under the PAE (self-employment programme, São Paulo, Brazil), were of the micro-enterprise type, the great majority are membership and cooperative enterprises, based on the economy of solidarity (social capital). Even in the case of micro-enterprises, the emphasis, in the PAE context, is on the pooling of resources, which not only alleviates the cost factor – thereby increasing competitiveness – but, above all, cultivates, maintains and strengthens 'social capital', which was the driving force behind their common effort and the decision to go ahead with the OW capacitation workshops in the first place. This proves that, using the right philosophy and capacitating methodology which equips large groups of people with 'entrepreneural literacy' (massive capacitation), civil society can, indeed, be a powerful source of self-induced energy for genuine and sustainable poverty alleviation and capacity building. Micro-enterprises, provided they are supported by an economy of solidarity, rather than leading down the logical path of internecine competition, can play a powerful role in the regeneration of economies in crisis and become part of often sorely needed wholesale state reform (see Chapter 20).

Historical inertias and allergies, mostly the product of a blinkered, partial vision that continues to insist on knowledge transmission, dis-embedded training and individualist(ic) entrepreneurship, can be overcome if the willingness exists to 'learn from Brazil' (Carmen et al. 1999). There is a lot of mileage, not only in Brazil, but wherever the de Morais method has been applied, in the discovery of the power of capacitation and the joys of discovering a 'win–win' society built on solidarity in action. This is what this book will try to demonstrate.

Note

1. In Angola the exchange rate is now 2 million kwanzas to the dollar and 'greed has overtaken ideology' (*Guardian*, 1 July 1999).

References

Bourdieu, Pierre (1998) 'L'Essence du Néoliberalisme', *Le Monde Diplomatique*, March.

Carmen, R. E. (1996) *Autonomous Development*, London: Zed Books.

Carmen, R. E., I. and I. Labra and M. Davis (1999) 'Learning from Brazil'/'Aprendiendo de Brasil', Manchester Monographs no. 38 and 39.

DGTZ (Deutsche Gesellschaft für Technische Zusammenarbeit) (1996) *Competency-based Ecomics through Formation for Enterprise*, CFE WWW Cybertext.

Eade, D. (1997) *Capacity Building: An Approach to People-Centred Development*, Oxford: Oxfam.

Hyden, Goeran (1980) *Beyond Ujamaa*, London: Heinemann.

Kaplan, A. (1999) 'The development of capacity', NGLS Development Dossier, Palais des Nations, Switzerland.

Korten, D. (1995) *When Corporations Rule the World*, Boulder, CO: Westview.

Leadbeater, C. and I. Christie (1999) *To Our Mutual Advantage*, London: Demos.

Martin, H. P. and N. Schumann (1997) *The Global Trap*, London: Zed Books.

de Morais, Clodomir Santos (1997) 'Efficient labour markets: a challenge for Latin America', keynote speech at international CIEDIA/ICEP Conference, San José, Costa Rica.

Mumm, J. (1999) 'Victory in sight: community organizations and popular governance', Online paper <http://uac.rdp.utoledo.edu/comm-org/papers.htm>

Nussbaum, M. and A. Sen (1993) 'Capability and well-being' in *The Quality of Life*, Oxford: Clarendon Press.

Oxfam (1999) 'Oxfam Report', Oxford: Oxfam.

Petrella, R. (1995a) 'Interview with Petrella', *The Courier* (Brussels).

— (1995b) *Limits to Competition*, Massachusetts: MIT.

— (1997) 'For the Common Good: In Praise of Solidarity', Brussels: Vrije Universiteit.

Putnam, R. (1993) *Making Democracy Work: Civic Traditions in Modern Italy*, Princeton, NJ: Princeton University Press.

Rothschild, E. (1995) 'The debate on economic and social security in the late eighteenth century: lessons of a road not taken', WWW Hypertext.

Tobin, J. (1978) 'A proposal for international monetary reform', *Eastern Economic Journal*, nos 3–4, July–October.

UNDP (1998) *Human Development Report 1998*, WWW Hypertext.

Whitacker, R. (1998) *Independent* (London), 2 July.

World Bank (1991) *The Challenge of Development*, Oxford: Oxford University Press.

Zamagni, S. (1997) 'The crisis of the welfare state', *Etruria Oggi* (Italy) no. 46.

2

Clodomir Santos de Morais: The Origins of the Large-scale Capacitation Theory and Method

Miguel Sobrado

Introduction

Clodomir Santos de Morais was born on 30 September 1928 in Santa Maria da Vitoria, a small rural town in the state of Bahía, in Brazil's Nordeste Province. He attended a state school and afterwards a private one in his town of birth. Because of his restless character he was expelled from both, which meant that technically he failed to finish his primary schooling. His father sent him to go and live with a friend in the hope that he would learn the trade of a tailor. He stuck it out for a year and a half in this occupation, but what he had really set his mind on was to emigrate to the 'big town', as most Nordeste youngsters had to do in the harsh years of the Great Depression. So it was not long before he was off to São Paulo, where he completed his primary schooling while living with a member of his family there. Later he joined the Salesian College, where he paid for his studies by working. The Salesian had 603 students, most of whom were children of Italian and German immigrants. He stood out there for being the only black student, which earned him the nickname 'the Flathead Nigger'. Expelled once more, this time because of his student activism (he was president of the governing board of the Student Union), he was accepted at an Adventist college. To finance his studies he enrolled at the Ford Motor Company where, after two years, he made it to line supervisor. It was while working at Ford in São Paulo that he got involved with the trade union. He also got involved in work stoppages and strikes at a couple of other factories where he worked. Later, while he was finishing his secondary studies, he worked part time as a journalist at a newspaper in São Paulo.

All these experiences served him well in his later life: he worked as a journalist at a number of important newspapers in São Paulo and Pernambuco. He was eventually able to set up his own news agency in Recife, which allowed him to graduate as a lawyer in the same city. Journalism drew him almost inevitably towards politics. He was elected deputy for the state of Pernambuco, in which capacity he got closely involved with the Brazilian 'Peasant Leagues', then led by Francisco Julião. These and other activities led to his imprisonment for two years when the military took over in the coup of 1964. He was in several Brazilian prisons, one of them in Olinda, near Recife, where he shared the same (tiny) cell with his lifelong friend and compatriot Paulo Freire.[1] His civil rights were taken from him for a period of ten years, but he managed to escape from prison and found asylum in the Chilean Embassy in Rio de Janeiro, from where he moved to Chile.

The rich tapestry of experiences early in his life – he was a tailor, a musician in a jazz band and an orchestra, a journalist, when he came in daily contact with hundreds of ordinary workers, and a worker on the Ford Motor Company conveyor-belt – in no small way contributed to the forging of his unique insights into the inadequacies of the peasant mode of production, his involvement in the peasant struggle for the reclamation of land, and his intimate knowledge of what makes the industrial 'worker' culture and associated mode of organizing so efficient and competitive. He came to the conclusion that it is the particular production culture of the peasantry – those 'artisans of the field' – that, by dint of reproducing itself indefinitely, puts them at a severe disadvantage when confronted with repressive mechanisms of all kinds.

In the 1950s he became a clandestine member of the communist movement.[2] It was in those early days that he underwent an experience that put an indelible stamp on the subsequent development of his method. This consisted of a seminar on political economy in which he took part with 60 political activists in a small residential house in Recife. The cramped conditions of the house, combined with the need for secrecy so as not to arouse the suspicions of the police – which would have cost them dearly in the political climate of those days – imposed on the group a strict organizational discipline in terms of the division and synchronization of all the tasks needed for such an event, run in such a small space with so many participants, to run smoothly. In approximately his own words: 'I learned nothing new about the theory, as it was a pretty elementary course for militants from different cultural backgrounds, but I learned an enormous lot in matters of organization; above all, how the existence of a commonly owned resource pool becomes a capacitating factor in the organization for popular movements.'

Years of Exile and of Further Development of the Method

After Chile he spent time in Panama, Costa Rica, Honduras, Mexico, Portugal and Nicaragua. In all these places he set up production and

communal projects, especially in Honduras and Portugal. The latter are
described more in detail in Chapters 6 and 15. In 1987 he moved to the
former German Democratic Republic, where he was awarded his doctorate
at the University of Rostock. From Rostock he made several visits to
Angola and Mozambique, where he mounted and evaluated a number of
massive capacitation projects, until his eventual return to Brazil in 1989,
completing a total of 24 years in exile.

In the late 1960s and in the 1970s he worked as United Nations consultant in Central America, in a number of agrarian reform development
projects, tirelessly promoting the cause of autonomous organization among
the peasantry. It was through his active involvement in all these projects
that both his theory and method, then still known as the Experimental
Workshop on Theory of Organization (EWTO), became progressively more
focused. De Morais' Theory of Organization (Teorìa de la Organización)
is a unique interpretation of historical materialism, which embodies, again
in a uniquely original fashion, a typology of social layering (referred to in
his work as 'artisan', 'worker', 'semi-worker' and 'social mifits' ['lumpen']).
The social behaviour and organizational capacities of each of these groups
are determined by the nature of the work they are (or, in the case of the
lumpen, are not) engaged in. It is the work culture (work experience) of
each of them that will dictate the need for establishing a close relationship
between the composition of a group, on the one hand, and the particular
way a development project ought to be organized with them, on the other.
The same logic also underpins the way in which capacitation processes are
formulated: as perfect as possible a 'fit' needs to be achieved between
people's mental organizational models and the need for a social division of
labour (which is an integral part of de Morais' capacitation pedagogy).

The Theory[3]

In de Morais' theoretical conceptualization, 'artisans' (or small producers) are those producers who are engaged in the entire, seamless
production effort from beginning to end. Salaried 'workers', on the other
hand, typically 'earn their crust' by means of some form of work that,
unlike the artisan mode, involves a social division of labour; the same is
true for 'semi-workers', although they get part of their income from working
as artisans, too. The 'lumpen' or social outcast neither works nor seeks to
work, regardless of the social stratum he or she originally hails from. To
each of those strata corresponds a specific 'mental organizational structure'
or a corresponding organizational capacity that is a reflection of their daily
activities and of their varying life experiences. Artisans and small producers,
of whom the peasantry form the numerically largest and most important

category, have been the social stratum most negatively affected in the way industrial and technological development has massively displaced them all over the world. At the root of the peasantry's problems is the very nature of their artisan/small producer activities in which work is organized in the 'simple' (non-complex), self-sufficient fashion of isolated workers operating on their own or on a family basis. The 'ideological structures of organization' that are typical of the small producer — however excellent in their own right and in a non-conflictual environment — become, in the words of de Morais, 'bad habits', 'deviations' or 'vices' when transferred to the totally different – that is, complex – social organization, with social division of labour and the specialization of the production process.

The Organization Workshop Method

As the small producer (artisan) mode, according to de Morais, is destined to disappear (not counting a few niche areas) as a significant way in which work and society are organized, the only way forward is for artisans and small producers, who have been displaced by encroaching modernization and by 'development' in general, to become 'entrepreneurially literate' ('capacitated') in 'the other' mode of production and organization, which will allow them to develop self-managing organizations based on the division of labour. These will allow them to survive as members of associative organizations, provided that they go through a capacitation (learning) process that, alone, will allow them to overcome the 'deviations' particular to the artisan mode and acquire a new 'organizational consciousness'. Neither of these can be learned through conventional ways of knowledge and skills transmission ('training'). Such a capacitation and such a new consciousness requires that they become involved in a real-life practice.

This practice can be generated in a process in which no fewer than 40 people (with no upper limit set in numbers) participate. One of the distinguishing features of the large group – as compared to the small group – workshop is that it imposes the need for a set of commonly pooled resources, which imposes on the group the need to unite and organize. This practice, to be genuinely capacitating, requires full autonomy of the group and lasts between four and six weeks. The process is moderated by a director[4] who arranges the input, as local circumstances require, that will facilitate the capacitation process and the development of the participants' organizational consciousness. As mentioned above, this method of capacitating and consciousness-altering learning was referred to by de Morais in the early years (1960s and 1970s) as the Experimental Workshop on Theory of Organization while its effectiveness was still being tested and when progressive adjustments to the proceedings were still being made. It was only later that his approach came to be generally known under the present name of Organization Workshop (OW) (LO – laboratorio organizacional, in Spanish).

The OW is a practice in organizational capacitation that unleashes a prodigious amount of social synergy. Inside this practice 'the worker' will emerge as a new positive social value and force. Being a 'worker' means to have learned to cooperate with others; to be modest (to know one's place in the whole), but, at the same time, to be disciplined and systematic in the planning and execution of the set tasks of the enterprise. Setbacks and failures are usually attributable to the 'simple' (non-complex) and self-sufficient 'artisan' ways, which are dysfunctional in the context of a complex organization, as well as to the 'opportunist' artisan character and behavioural traits that will tend to subordinate the needs for proper planning and organization by the group to immediate, short-sighted individual(istic) needs. Thus, in the context of the workshop as envisioned by de Morais, the 'artisan way' will soon acquire negative connotations because of the pettiness and self-centredness of the individualistic spirit that is typical here. 'Organizational vigilance' is therefore required to counteract and continue to overcome those artisan 'deviations'. The need for group vigilance is an important topic during the seminars on theory of organization that are run throughout the length of the workshop.

No texts expounding this method were known to exist until the Bataán OW in Costa Rica, where a first systematization of the method, albeit limited, was carried out. This initial characterization and subdivision of the workshop process into different stages or phases was further complemented and nourished by actual practice by de Morais himself, especially during the important years he spent as programme leader of the agrarian reforms in Honduras from 1973 to 1976. Here also the first foundation stones were laid for what, in later years, would become the Job and Income Generation Programmes (PROGEIs) and Systems (SIPGEIs). De Morais' involvement with the agrarian reform in Honduras, under the PROCCARA-INA-FAO programme (1973–76), resulted in the eventual establishment of over a thousand membership organizations there, all based on the application of the OW methodology in their initial stages, and while Honduras, where the first cadres for the Costa Rican team were also trained, can count a strong work team among its achievements, there were nevertheless no major advances of a theoretical or methodological nature during that period. The successes were due to a large extent to the remarkable intuition, experience and skill demonstrated by de Morais and his work team in the management of situations. In other words, the 'technology' (OW method) demonstrated, in actual practice, a degree of efficiency far in excess of the advances made at the theoretical level or in terms of methodological formulation.

The drawback of this lack of theoretical exploration of practice is, of course, that success depends to a large extent on knowledge, personal skills and charisma, which are difficult to verbalize and therefore difficult to reproduce. In his doctoral thesis, de Morais explores in more depth the epistemological foundations and other aspects of his method, which find resonances in Lenin and Marx, but also in the theories of social psychology of the Russian school (Vygotsky, Luria and Leont'ev), which were buried under Stalin.[5]

In his thesis de Morais advances the epistemological foundations of his theory, while at the same time throwing light on the methodological process. The most significant theoretical advance consisted in the incorporation in his theoretical framework of A. N. Leont'ev's concept of objective activity, which came to replace the rather imprecise and *ad hoc* conceptualizations he had soldiered on with until then. This allowed him to explain, in operational terms, what is actually happening in the relationship of the subject in the process of becoming capacitated with the aid of the object, i.e. the very object the subject wants to become adept (capacitated) in managing. This newly acquired attribute allows the subject to make a key distinction between what it is to educate, on the one hand, and the process of capacitation, on the other. The epistemological foundations of the OW were thus further enriched with an operational base.

It was while working for UNDP/ILO in the INSCOOP programme in Portugal (Institute of the Cooperative Sector) in 1978–79 that the first national PROGEI (Job and Income Generation Programme) was set up. This new approach was later perfected when, in the late 1980s, he was allowed to return to his home country, Brazil, where he founded the Institute for Technical Support to Third World Countries (IATTER-MUND) with the support of the University of Brasília. This became the launching pad for his work with the Landless Workers' Movement (Movimiento do Trabalhadores sem Terra, MST) who applied the workshop with the support of the Workers' Party (PT). Still later, following the successes obtained with the method in establishing concrete enterprises and organization with the landless movement, other governmental and non-governmental organizations and institutions became interested. The PROGEIS were reproduced under different names all over Brazil, sometimes promoted by federal government, as in the case of the National Programme for Job and Income Generation in Poor Areas (PRONAGER), in other cases by federal state goverments, as in the case of the Self-employment Project (PAE) run with the assistance of the FAO in São Paulo and surroundings(see Chapter 18).

In each case de Morais took great care to ensure that the PROGEIs did not – apart from a short initial stage – have to depend on institutional support, but that they would become as soon as possible self-sustaining (autonomous) by turning themselves into a 'system', i.e. a (nationwide) System for the Identification of Job and Income Generation Projects (SIPGEI). For all practical purposes this meant that the creation of a popular institutional base belonging to civil society and independent of the political powers, rooted in autonomous people's enterprises, was always uppermost in his mind. With some exceptions, this has not always been possible to achieve in the case of the PROGEI. In reality, the task is far from easy as the evolution from (local) PROGEI to (national) SIPGEI requires the root and branch reform of a nation's institutionalized services and the usual channels for the provision of credit which, from now on, need to take account of the entrepreneurial initiatives and needs of those who are least favoured in society. This either implies that they be excluded or, at the other extreme, favours them with one-off special concessions with clientelist overtones whenever an electoral campaign appears on the horizon.

This also means that the investments made in them should be related to those similar investments in the market and that the advances in organizational development (entrepreneurial literacy) of their enterprises be appreciated on their own merit, even if the totality of the benefits achieved may not be clear as yet. A sea change is required in official attitudes and appreciation: their future economic potential should be evaluated at its genuine market value and the advances in organizational development (or burgeoning entrepreneurial literacy) held as a genuine security set against the monies loaned out. The construction of PROGEIs has therefore been an important step forward in the application of the theory and method of organization as proposed by de Morais. This has made evident the great need for a new type of specialist, capable of integrating knowledge into the development of the organization rather than developing knowledge inside their own particular disciplines and specialisms. What we are talking about here are 'alley cat' experts, capable of operating in the most adverse circumstances, daring to put their faith in the organizational potential of the people themselves, rather than 'house cat' experts, comfortably settled in their easygoing inertia and the ways of the traditional, institutionalized bureaucrat.

What we are in the presence of here is a revolutionary theory and method of capacitation that fundamentally challenges received ideas about training and has shown, in its practical applications, the severe limitations under which traditional professional training disciplines labour in attempts to come to grips with the problems of modern development. All of this poses a serious challenge to the academic community, but above all to the powers that be in their pursuit of effective designs by which to reform the state along more self-sustaining lines.

Why a Method That Has Shown Such Excellent Results Has Not Spread More Widely

'Capacity building' or 'organizing and training for the promotion of people's initiatives and capacities' are mottos readily subscribed to by agencies over the world, and with access to multi-million-dollar resources, all with disappointingly meagre results. This has been the case not only in the so-called 'developing' countries, but also with the poor and the excluded in the 'developed' world. Clodomir de Morais has achieved unrivalled results and successes in this very field, and in three continents, wherever his vision and interpretation of reality, his method of capacitation and his programmes for job creation and income generation have been applied over the last quarter-century. It is a real mystery, then, as to why his achievements have passed almost unnoticed, especially by the afore-mentioned agencies, and why his method has not become standard practice all over the world.

The first reason lies, we think, in the fact that a method that offers a sure-fire way of developing the autonomous capacities of the poor annoys those organizations and institutions that appear to operate according to a more or less cleverly disguised clientelist hidden agenda. This autonomous capacity goes against the grain, not only of the vested interests of the powers that be, but also of the culture of dependency and slavish con-formity that is typical of a mutually reinforcing clientelist culture, typical of experts who put the organizations they are working for at their own service rather than serving them.

A second inhibiting factor and one that, we think, has weighed extremely heavily is the conceptual mode and language, a throwback to the 1950s, in which the Theory of Organization is couched. Even though Clodomir's discourse, from a purist Marxist-Leninist perspective, is ideologically un-orthodox in that he bases his theory and practice on the organizational capabilities of people and not on the principles of class struggle, this mere association was enough to brand him and his ideas as instruments of 'the Evil Empire', which was then only too easy for politicians and development experts who, for whatever reason, felt that his ideas needed rejecting. Paradoxically, as readers of Chapter 6 (on the Honduran experience) can see for themselves, it was precisely in those places where de Morais' ideas were applied on the most massive scale that people's energies were channelled positively, towards the transformation of the agrarian landscape, rather than being wasted on guerrilla warfare, as happened in many neighbouring countries.

Third, de Morais' vision and method – unlike those of Freire, which were published and written about quite extensively worldwide – were starved, for too long, of the proper research, systematization, conceptual-ization, theory-building and dissemination that might have made him more accessible to social scientists coming from a variety of epistemological frameworks and academic traditions. Linked to this is the need to explain the nature of the process and to highlight the potential it holds, far beyond that of basic organizational training, going into the process in which management skills develop in people in the course of the different stages of the Organization Workshop.

This gap in concept formation and in-depth research has equally grave consequences when it comes to reproducing the experience in different contexts and determining how workteams need to be formed. In practice, the pedagogical need for forming *esprit de corps* during the OW so as to produce a vigilant counterforce against the ever lurking danger of back-sliding into 'bad habits' (see above) is only too easily interpreted as a form of demonification and condemnation of the artisan way (which it definitely is not). Thus the very conditions that need to be fostered for the facilitation of a climate of healthy creative and vigilant tension, which helps the group to be on its guard against organizational culs-de-sac and to create an organizational identity inside the group, may also, under certain conditions with less well-motivated groups, lead to a form of ideological McCarthyism.

This is important in view of the fact that, although taking theoretical short-cuts may be found to be effective in the short term, the potential for better understanding and human enrichment of a theory that so exception-ally explains the historical character of the artisanal modes of organization, and the ways in which they can be overcome, can be lost, especially when working with less sophisticated groups. The latter is a particularly important point and represents one of the strongest aspects and in-built richness of a method that has been neither adequately developed nor sufficiently exploited. The theory of the organization applied in the context of the OWs generates those specific conditions that allow the participants and groups to recognize the origin of their organizational deficiencies and of their own past work experience. It is precisely these handicaps and limita-tions that have put them at a disadvantage in the past, as compared to other, better-placed social groups and sectors, and have misled them in believing that it is all because of some genetic inferiority that they simply have to put up with. The OW not only creates the ideal conditions in which the origin of those limitations can be traced but also, even more importantly, creates the means by which to overcome them: organizational capacitation.

This 'aha!' experience has a deep impact on the way the participants subsequently organize their lives, and this impact goes far beyond the acquisition of mere organizational skills. It forms the very basis of a renewed sense of self-esteem. In the very process of becoming masters of their own destiny, gradually acquiring skills of self-organization and self-management, the participants experience conditions that require strict principles of self-discipline.

Moreover, the method is centred on the cross-cultural transition from the artisanal (small producer) to the industrial (complex 'worker') mode. Even though the post-industrial sector has just started to make inroads in the developing world, its presence is none the less important: these new forms necessitate new mental models that are a far cry from the era of the chimney-stacks of the Industrial Revolution. In the absence of a true recognition of the implications of the onset of a new age, the theory and method of organization may appear, to some, as a mere throwback to the industrial era that idealized 'the worker' who, in actual fact, is now already disappearing from many areas of production. This is one of the factors that may help to explain why the method has been judged to be less useful in post-industrial societies – or in Eastern Europe, for that matter – even though the principles on which the method is built are flexible and adaptable enough to allow for organizational capacitation learning whatever the nature of the transition processes may be.

Is It Possible to Overcome the Allergy?

In order to ensure people's participation and make it real, the prevailing discourse and the technology used must, as the logic of the method requires, be in tune with the attitudes of those involved. It is no use talking about participation and autonomy if, at the same time, and behind the scenes, people are being manipulated into doing what the development agents have decided should happen anyway: as, in the words of Carmen, 'participipulation' leads not to autonomy but only to increased dependency.

In the teeth of the contradictory opinions of bureaucrats, politicians and experts who, weaned on disaggregated disciplines, are always in favour of interrupting organizational processes 'so as to reduce stress', de Morais developed 'defence mechanisms' that support the favourable development of his workshop experience. That is why he always steered the discussion clear of pure theorizing in favour of concrete action; by creating space for experiences that have the power to offer solutions to real problems in people's lives, he almost by coincidence also proves the theoretical validity and value of his theory. De Morais has been able to safeguard the purity of his proposals. One cannot escape the impression, though, that this has had the negative effect of a certain allergy to other forms of organizational development and technology. This aloofness from other approaches has limited his sphere of influence, has inhibited the growth of his teams of collaborators and, looking from the outside in, has raised the hackles of some leading quarters leading to his method being dismissed as mere 'ravings of a guru'.

I want to conclude this chapter with two questions:

* What are the risks, in terms of the efficacy of the method, of introducing changes that strengthen it in theoretical terms and enrich it from a human resource development perspective, but may not necessarily add value in methodological terms?
* How far can the PROGEI–SIPGEI be advanced as a solution to the important changes taking place in contemporary society in terms of a shift towards the active involvement of civil society and of the excluded?

Notes

1. Just a few weeks before his death (2 May 1997) Freire, on a visit to Clodomir's *alma mater*, Rondônia Federal University, gave a resounding testimony to his 'velho de guerra, amigo-irmão'; see also Paulo Freire (1987) *Aprendendo com a propria historia*, Rio de Janeiro: Paz, p. 135; also Chapter 3.

2. Movement, not party. The party was outlawed in Brazil until as late as 1989.

3. Take away the 'commonly pooled resources' element, and the group will disperse, with individuals working in isolation, relapsing into the small/micro entrepreneurial mode, which has been already identified as the problem, not the solution.

4. For more details on 'The tasks of the OW director', see Carmen, Labra and Davis, 'Learning from Brazil', Manchester Monographs 1999.

5. But which were recently (re)discovered in the West, thanks to, among others, the work of James Wertsch and Jean Lave on 'situated cognition' (in a formal school context) and 'situated learning'. See Nick Boreham (ed.), 'Situated learning and the workplace' (forthcoming) by the *ad hoc* Manchester research working group.

Part II

Theoretical Perspectives

3

The Large Group Capacitation Method and Social Participation: Theoretical Considerations

Clodomir Santos de Morais

Large Group Capacitation

The organization field workshop can take place with forty, a hundred, a thousand or more participants. The only limitations are those imposed by physical space, local conditions and the amount of 'common pool resources' that can be put at the disposal of the participants.[1] Created with the specific intention of nurturing the process of social and organizational conscientization, it displays, in its rich detail, the entire spectrum of the capacitation process. The weekly work plan is drawn up by the organizations dealing with the management and the execution of all the activities, which take place in a large group context, and are structured, as from day one, with the building of a large-scale enterprise in mind, allowing the participants operational control of the means and the very instruments that facilitate the capacitation process. These means may include office stationery, computers, typewriters, photocopiers, vehicles, kitchen installations, audio–visual instruments and installations of all kinds. Over these, the community exercises a true right of ownership or of temporary tenancy (usufruct). What we have here is a true case of real social ownership of all the means that facilitate the capacitation process.

The fact that the Capacitation Enterprise – embodied in the collective ownership of all those who participate in, for example, the organization field workshop – is set up on the basis of the ownership (or virtual ownership) of all the means of production guarantees that all the work performed within this enterprise has a 'directly social' dimension, in contrast with 'private work' in which producers operate in isolation from each other. All those involved in the organization field workshop produce for the benefit of the collectivity of persons, so that the individual work of each individual person, in a very direct way – and not merely indirectly, as happens in the market economy – becomes an integral part of the totality of the work produced. As Engels put it, when society becomes the owner of the means of production and begins to use them in a directly social way, the work of each member of society, however dissimilar it may be – more specifically its utility factor – becomes work with a 'directly social' dimension. This is to say that when, as happens here, both ownership and production are collective, or belong to a community (a 'common unity' of people), the work of each individual producer in terms of goods and services produced is an integral part of the totality of the socialized work.

In addition, and in the context of the OW, each person is responsible for the completion of a well-defined part of the weekly workplan on which the collective economy is structured. This means that, in this instance, it is not the market that, unrelated to the needs of the producers, regulates the output of the collective enterprise, but, on the contrary, the producers themselves who spread continuously, and as the needs arise, the means of production and those of the common resource pool to the different areas of the OW production process. We already know that the degree of maturity of 'directly social' forms of work depends on the nature of the ownership of the means of production. These may vary, ranging from community cooperative and from structures of common ownership linking a number of independent producers together, all the way to forms of associative self-managing enterprises such as Hondupalma, Coapalma (large enterprises in Honduras) or the Silencio and Vaquita cooperatives in Costa Rica, or the big agro-industrial enterprises of the Landless Workers' Movement (MST), and the industrial enterprises affiliated to the National Association of Workers' Self-employed and Participatory Stakeholders (ANTEAG) in Brazil.

Guiding Principles for the Analysis of the Concept of Organizational Consciousness

From whatever angle one may want to look at it, the model of social participation must always take into account the organizational structure of the production process, for the simple reason that the latter forms the material basis of the different manifestations and styles of management – self-management or co-management – that will guarantee that the enterprises are genuinely socially participatory. That is because the organizational structure of work – from its earliest embryonic stage, as in the case of the natural economy, up to the most complex forms, which make full use of the social division of labour – is always an expression of how humans act when faced with nature, be it in the pursuit of their most immediate needs to sustain their livelihoods, or through vital social networks, or through to the spiritual representations that arise from these.

The objective factors that govern the agricultural economy gradually led to the first steps on the road to the social division of labour and of human labour processes, always in tune with the surrounding geography or with the types of hydrography, vegetation, soil, climates and natural products prevailing in a particular area and a particular unit of time. On the basis, then, of factors that directly dictate their needs, humans start out on a journey of discovery in search of the organizational structures best able to mediate their newly found capacities and *modus operandi*. As so frequently happens in the small peasant economy, dedicated as it is, almost exclusively, to the production of use value (commodities owned by individuals who support themselves in the natural economy) the interaction between humankind and nature, because it is direct, determines the former's overwhelming dependence on it.

The initial break – on the surface tentative and weak – in the bond between humankind and nature finds its origin in the impact of the changes introduced by the division of labour, bolstered by the private ownership of the article produced. Work (humankind), from this moment, acquires and subsequently develops a new organizational structure, less dependent on nature. This structure is aimed at guaranteeing the maintenance of the subjectivity threatened by the reduction in the dominion the producers previously held over their own destiny, as, from now on, the commodities, which are the result of work executed in common, escape the workers' control, given the fact that this control has now been withdrawn from the area of production and is left to the capricious sphere of the circulation of goods mediated by trade and commerce. It is for this reason that the expansion of the relationships governing market interchange (the mercantile economy) was in many instances the first and immediate goal of social participation in the sphere of agriculture. That is why the consumer cooperative and the needs of commerce can be seen as the primary mould in which models of social, local or regional participation, which correspond to the level the productive forces in a particular area or region have reached, can be tried out, developed and nurtured. The organizational 'mechanisms' of the market interchange must therefore be structured in accordance with the level of consciousness that the members, or participating beneficiaries invited to share in the control and management of the enterprise, have reached. Thus we see the 'ontogenesis' of the social mechanism of management, starting with simple commercial transactions, which give rise to other agro-industrial activities and services. What should not be forgotten is that the social organisms (principally the richly endowed entrepreneurial structures around production and services) can be compared, *mutatis mutandis*, to those superior forms of organization that can be found in organic matter and function, sometimes, in a way similar to biological organisms. From this can be deduced that social organisms cannot survive or thrive unless they are continuously nurtured by the inputs of the other members of the group.

When setting up an enterprise with social participation in a rural development context, it is obvious that the way this enterprise is managed will be social in nature, too. By this we mean that the primary as well as the secondary organizational structures that underpin the enterprise, and will allow the rural economy to develop, will have to be generated from the inside out, from inside the lived reality of the producers, and not from the outside in, as commonly happens with 'blueprint' or 'desktop' planning. In the light of this, it has been observed, again and again, that the absence of proper, organic organizational structures in peasant groups is always a serious obstacle to the proper running of agricultural development programmes. What is equally obvious is that, in the face of persistent failure, and notwithstanding the over-abundant research and evaluation data available on those programmes, no one seems to have been able to devise modules of social participation that deal effectively with criteria set by the government's political project as regards place, costs and the need to duplicate those programmes on a wider and larger scale.

This is due to the preference given to a purely 'technicist' alternative, which is characterized by the conception and design of modules that fly in the face of the otherwise easily observable rural reality on the ground. This, however, will not happen, if, from the very beginning, the social participation mode is favoured (as indeed occurs in the OWs), all the way to the level of socio–economic research. Indeed, it is not the specialists and experts, equipped with cultural toolboxes dominated by urban values and criteria, however vast their powers of abstraction and of deductive reasoning otherwise might be, who are best placed to set priorities and decide the scales of deprivation and need as they apply in various rural cultures. Rural development happens with people, not with blueprints, not with plans, not with maps, with surveys or even with projects: these all have their use, provided they are put and kept in their place, i.e. the actual reality on the ground with which people try to cope, let alone try to transform.

Plans and blueprints only combine theoretical references. These can be ascertained to be correct only if they emanate from actual practice in the field. The practice of co-management and self-management in the production of goods and services comes not from plans, but from the lived experience of the social group in the actual exercise of social participation. Plans are good and proper in organizing around theoretical frameworks but these, too, can be correct only if they emanate from practice on the ground. So, for example, the practice of co-management or self-management in the production of goods and services derives from the actual experience of the social group in social participation. Indeed, from the moment industrial machinery comes into the picture as an integral part of the enterprise or project and so determines the technological level that, in turn, reflects the development of the 'common resource pool' (above all as regards fixed capital), a new management profile reflecting the new organizational structure of the production process will inevitably and inescapably ensue. In effect, on the basis that the new industrial machinery, on its own, already represents a new form of working in common, the need to organize labour in a cooperative manner will have become already a necessity, inherent in the medium itself, which is put at the disposal of the cooperative members. The reason for this is simple: we are dealing here with an impersonal, objective factor of production that, in the case of salaried labour, is already part of a ready-made work environment.[2] There is more: the intervention of industrial machinery always cancels out manual labour as principal regulator of the production process, so much so that in many sectors of the industry – for example the machinery needed for the production of sugar or cooking oil – most of the indispensable operations to be carried out in the process of producing them require hardly anything more than routine vigilance and attention on the part of the operator, who is reduced to the status of mere instrument.

In a rural environment increasingly taken over by agricultural industrialization every day the production process reflects more and more the stark law of value of economic rationality that governs it. Under those historical circumstances the above process incorporates, in geometric proportions, scientific criteria of knowledge that have made the value of individual achievement ever more obsolete. It is for this reason that the artisan and small producer (rural or urban), however great their manual and mental virtuosity, have to give way to science, in this case massive forms of socialized production embedded in a system that heavily relies on all sorts of industrial equipment. From this we can deduce that humans and their work, in their natural training environment, necessarily tend to depend on the social network of which they are an integral part, i.e. their historical 'habitat'.

To the extent that human agents manage to free themselves from the laws of causation that apply in nature, they will seek refuge in the objective laws of social causality that accompany the new levels of development achieved in the production of goods and services. As social beings (which sets them apart from other beings) humans and their work tend to spread out into social relationships, an environment in which they are as at home as fish in water. Starting from small-scale production the tendency will always be towards the large(r) scale. Likewise, the unicellular structure of the peasant economy (subsequently replaced by other, intermediate forms) will culminate in the complex organizational structures that govern the highest forms of cooperation.

The social division of labour, be it at the level of manufacture or on the factory floor, creates, or at the very least determines, the level of complexity of the organizational structures that human actors use as an interface with their social practice. In effect, they will want to find the same degree of secure knowledge about how to act as the one encountered in the division of labour of the production process of which they are part, be it in 'manu'-facture or in industry. Hence the tendency to form cooperatives, membership associations, trade unions, political parties, etc. They will therefore try to find the same social objective logic that is part and parcel of the productive organizational structures needed by cooperating agents. They will try to find in the social organizational structure the objectivity inherent in the productive organizational structure of the cooperative. They will try to find that structure in their work environment, be it a manufacturing workshop or in a factory. This objective logic is part and parcel of the analytical nature of the socially divided production process; in the inescapable discipline that subordinates the parts to the whole; as well as in the synthesis expressed in the sole centre of control of labour collectives.

The Need to Realign Workers' Ideological Behaviour

It stands to reason, therefore, that individuals who are being integrated in the production processes of a large-scale enterprise will adapt their behaviour patterns with difficulty to the needs of a complex, analytical and objective structure, if they have not first been initiated in behaving differently by means of mass capacitation courses in which they learn how to analyse as well as how to link practice with theory so as to realign the ideological behaviour typical of that 'rural artisan': the peasant. This is because, just as happens when components of a basic organism (such as the membership association or the cooperative) become integrated into one of a higher order such as the membership enterprise) so the membership (the individuals) of those organizations, too, pass through a transition process consisting of three stages: *syncresis*, *analysis* and, finally, *synthesis*.

The first stage is characterized by the *syncretism* of different ideological manifestations, how accumulated experiences, particular interests and expectations, all fight for supremacy in their attempt to comply with a particular organizational structure. However, the stage of syncretism also denotes a certain 'disorder' and heterogeneity of the forms and content of different capacities to reflect reality. In other words, as the activity of integration progresses, the path is clear for the next stage, namely analysis.

The stage of anomy, so characteristic of the stage of syncresis, can be overcome only by the *démarrage* of the process of integration itself. That is to say that the activity of integration opens the way for the following stage, i.e. the analysis stage. No social organism, no individual, as pointed out by Hegel, 'can determine the object of its action while it is not acting'.[3]

We are in the presence here of that self-same phenomenon called 'objective activity';[4] in the case we are describing here, the integrating activity rigorously takes place in an analytical fashion, in that the leading role belongs to the object that imposes its particular organizational and management characteristics on the subject. In the case of the object, upon which it falls to guide the integrating activity (be it the group of individuals or the group of organisms that compose them), the objective 'channels of conveyance' reflect the same contradictions and heterogeneities as those found in the syncresis stage. The activity of the subject then follows, guided by the object, which, in turn, will indicate which 'tools', or tactical instruments, are needed in each operation required by each activity in which the subject engages.

The character of the *synthesis* stage will also depend on the nature of the confrontation of the subject of the activity with the object, i.e. on the subject's ability to perceive and assimilate the 'conveyance' imposed by the 'objective' channels during the entire analysis stage. This is because the character of the synthesis results from two concurring factors: on the one hand there is the the subject (the learner of the organization and management skills) who acts consciously, compelled by concrete need(s) and, on the other hand, there are the specificities (the 'objective' channels) of the object, in other words, the integrating activity itself. The activity, in as far as it is a process that integrates individuals or entire membership organizations, can be interpreted as a circular structure: an initial confrontation with the new reality (syncresis phase); followed by the processes and the effects that are the direct result of the contact with the 'objective' channels (analysis phase); and, finally, the synthesis phase, when corrections as well as improvements are made to the original activity with the help of relationships that provide an inverse image to the one that originally prevailed.[5] Indeed, as the object of the (integrating) activity, in the case of complex cooperative organizations, will *de facto* and principally occur with poor peasantry, the 'objective' channels that emerge will flow from the immediacy of their needs; from the subjectivism of their expectations; from the voluntarist nature of their actions and from the social–psychological traits of their social consciousness, all of which impinge on the way in which the 'conveyance' to the subject occurs.

Associative membership enterprises such as Hondupalma and Coapalma in Honduras and the Silencio and Vaquita cooperatives in Costa Rica, for example, resulted from just such an integrating activity. This means that the conveying factor, the factor that guides the processes of the integrating activity, happens to be the object itself. For this reason the transition, from process to product, will occur not only on the part of the subject, but also, and much more obviously so, on the part of the object that is in the process of being transformed by human activity. What we see happening, then, is that it is the *object* that conscientizes the *subject* in the integration process. By 'object' we mean no other than the activity of social participation itself and the management forms – self-management and co-management – that flow from it.

Indeed, economic rationality, in the ambit of capitalism, is geared to the acquisition of 'plus-value' and therefore, as the technical division of labour spreads out horizontally in the direction of the production of goods and services, the more intense will become the vertical social division of labour of the administrative forms shoring up the large-scale enterprise. In this manner, as the volume of the means of production increases (which implies an expansion in the horizontal social division of labour) so will the overall supervision (expansion of the vertical social division of labour), so as to avoid profligacy: 'To the extent that the dimensions of an organism expand, the means by which to control it become correspondingly elaborate. These are determined both by the structure of the social labour process itself, as well as by outside ownership which allows authoritarian forms of administration to gain sociological relevance.'[6]

The fact that in agro–industrial complexes of major socio–economic and technological impact on national development most activities are conducted factory-fashion, i.e. in a pronounced mechanical way, means that the organizational set-up will reach high levels of rationality due to the strict analysis and synthesis of the labour processes. From this it follows that the social character of work in the mechanized sectors of transformation will inevitably impose a rigid observation of rhythms and norms of behaviour, as well as an abiding dependency of its workers on the irreversible nature of the social or collective production process. Evidently, the situation will be different in the bureaucratic sector and in the repair and agricultural machinery maintenance workshops, where the technical laws of the division of labour leave a wide margin for individuality (because, even though part of the cooperative, the predominantly artisan technology is still the general rule in these types of activities). Indeed, it is impossible systematically to transfer the scientific method of analysis and synthesis to the types of cooperation prevalent in production processes of the 'manu'-facturing (artisan) kind, given the preponderance of subjectivist elements present in manual operations and given that the workforce consists of artisans (small-scale producers). By contrast, the large-scale enterprise (whether co-managed or self-managing) typical of the major agro-industrial socio-economic and technological development projects does allow for the transition from traditional, customary activity to the lucrative, rationalized way of profit-making operations. But such an objective imposes a special structuring of the means of production at the service of just one objective: revenue.

It is clear, then, that this concentration of the mind on one single goal will naturally lead to the rational use of all the means available to reach that goal. It then becomes easy to distinguish between fundamentals and what is of mere secondary importance, leading to the gradual hier-archization of the activities.[7] At this level, the degree of organizational consciousness will lead it to a methodological rationality and, consequently, to the management of the economic category of 'profit', which, in the end, will be proportionate to the efficiency of the actions.

Social Engineering

In order to facilitate this change in consciousness in the subject who is becoming an integral part of an enterprise, it is necessary to call on the help of the modern sociology of organization's concept of 'social engineering', more in particular as it is applied in the method of mass capacitation: the OW. The key to and basis of the method, leading participants to understand the nature of the psychological reflex that triggers changes in social consciousness (a product of the particular society and subject to its own social norms and relations) – and we include here the intentional introduction of 'organizational consciousness' into groups, can be found in the analysis of organized activity – i.e. cooperation understood as activity. Only thus can the analysis of structured activity (the proper attribute of social groups), as well as that of the specific activities by individuals forming part of this group, reveal – given proper sociological and organizational research – how the transition from the material world to the world of ideas occurs. Only in this way can concepts such as 'peasant psychology', the category of 'petite-bourgeoisie', the 'psychology of the worker' and the 'bureaucratic mentality' or 'technical expert', all of which reflect the organizational structures of different social groups, be properly understood as merely reflecting phenomena encountered in the objective world. Whatever the modalities of the transition achieved by social units (structured groups) or by a combination of all of these, it is always the structure that acts as causative mediator.

Nobody can, therefore, remain in any doubt as to the fact that the capabilities of the individual not only manifest themselves, but are also formed (shaped) in the course of being engaged in the activity. This is because capabilities are never fully 'finished' before they start manifesting themselves. Therefore, 'in each stage of the activity shared in common [meaning: socially useful activity] ... and as long as socially significant results ensue ... humans progress qualitatively in their psychological development, i.e. in the development of their capacities'.[8] It is at this point that the change in consciousness, i.e. the transition from the 'psychology of the "Artisan"' to the 'psychology of the "Worker"' (in other words: the final coming to terms with the prior ideological behaviour typical of 'the artisan') comes to fruition, thanks to the very fact of being involved in the activity, and based on the pedagogical attributes of that activity. Here, then, is the profound reason as to why it is possible intentionally to modify, by means of real, collective cooperative practices, the consciousness of the peasant/small producer and to reduce all inclinations towards individualism, spontaneity, voluntarism, self-sufficiency and other similar behavioural forms. These, drawing on artisan/small producer ways, can be rightly dubbed deviations or 'vices', because they are inimical to efficiency and optimization.

The Methodological Phases

In order to ensure experimental and intentional replicability of the capacitating power inherent in the objective activity, it is absolutely necessary to adapt rigorously the methodological phases to the comprehensiveness with which the division of labour is being implemented and to the character of the means of production that are in place. Indeed, and not least in the sphere of cooperative work, 'organization always starts with a division of labour and with the centralization of command, be it in the economic sphere or in all the manifestations of social life'.[9] This intensity (which can extend to the level of the socially divided production process) stands in intimate relationship to the 'use value' of the 'individual resource pool', expressed mainly as 'fixed capital' (installations, machinery and work teams). The indivisible nature of this resource pool translates into the equally indivisible nature of the operation, in which many hands act together and thereby configure one, single cooperative reality. When a social group acquires means of production such as machinery and installations, whether by way of outright ownership, or under collective ownership, or under conditions of simple, collective usufruct (temporary ownership), the need for the socialization of the management of the said common resource pool will become more than persuasive. That is because important elements, such as machinery, form the fundamental underlying 'assumption', the 'objective' factor from which the capitalist mode of production arose, i.e. social production mounted on collective activity.

This collective activity at no stage reveals itself as the means of labour the individual worker is accustomed to. Its specific difference lies not, as in the case of labour, in the transmission to the object of the activity of the worker, but in the fact that the worker's activity is calibrated in such a way that the individual is left with little else to do than simply transfer the labourer's work to the raw materials or to the machinery, which requires only 'watching for breakdowns'.[10] It so happens that in the technologies that preceded capitalism, or indeed in those economies where capital does not exercise an overbearing influence – as is still the case in so many Third World countries – the tool has the function of interface between work and nature. Work is therefore the tool's initial and active term of reference, while nature is its final and passive term of reference: in other words, the tool is mere intermediary.

With the introduction of automated industrial machinery, however, this relationship is turned on its head because the tool has ceased to be the intermediate term of reference. The producer, who, before machinery came into play, occupied the position of active initiator, is now reduced to an intermediary role, to mere instrument. The introduction of automated industrial machinery, even more so when dominated by capital, has thus resulted in a process that escapes the sphere of influence of human subjectivity or of human needs. The process pursues its own ends and its purpose is exhausted inside the process itself. And this purpose is, simply put: adding value to existing value.[11]

The appearance of automated factory machinery will inevitably result in the withering away of any influence of the subjective human psychology of the small isolated producer, until then always associated with artisanal forms of labour. The machinery supplants any form of subjectivity from the moment work stops being the initiating factor of the relationship with nature (or the object of work), which was previously mediated by (hand)-tools. Work, thereby, becomes the mere instrument of the machinery; it becomes 'reified' because it is now subordinated to that other 'thing': the machinery. At this point, the production process also loses all its former 'natural' characteristics and becomes purely 'technical' in nature, 'taken out of realm of the direct skill of the worker and turned into mere "appliance of science"'.[12] And because the knowledge of the logic of this technology does not reside any more in the worker, but has acquired an independent existence outside the worker, i.e. in the machinery itself, the machinery takes over: it controls and 'educates' the worker in its own ways, imposes 'its' consciousness, imposes another psychology, because the worker and the worker's activity is being forced into adopting 'another' existence.

Consequently, self-sufficiency and all the other characteristics of subjectivity atrophy and die. The former master and initiator of the relationship of technique with nature is now being taught to be a humble servant. The former active agent is reduced to an instrument, turned into a mere 'thing', subjected to master 'machinery' and its immediate corollaries: new parameters, new values, new collective conduct imposed by the new subjective conditions (organizational above all) are imposed on the evolution of the activities. So, for the artisan or small producer to acquire the consciousness or psychology of the 'worker', it suffices to transfer them, in the technology process, from their original position (where they had a direct influence on the object, nature) to the intermediate one.

In a similar fashion, from the moment that the management of the productive process becomes collectivized – be it by the mere physical presence of industrial machinery, or by the common organization it induces – the producer loses the centre-stage in the production process. The productive process becomes totally detached from the subjective influences of the producer, and from any accompanying individualistic traits (which we have already referred to as the 'vices' belonging to the artisanal way of working), i.e. from the trademarks of the small producer, be it in a rural or urban environment. What happens, in reality, is the transfer away from the control of the technical knowledge vested in the 'artisan' using (hand)-tools, to the machine and the organizational framework it demands.

A large group or mass capacitation method, therefore, which aims to establish the primacy of the psychology prevailing in the culture of the worker inside those social groups that have very little acquaintance with this (worker) psychology (or ideological behaviour) must be constructed on the firm basis of a common resource pool – which means, in practice: machinery first and foremost. Here, then, in a nutshell, is the basis for the intentional and premeditated practice, adaptable to each particular case, of the method of the organization workshop for capacitation with large groups of people, or mass capacitation. Outside this method, there are those training and education practices that confuse 'education' with 'capacitation'.

A case in point are the learning practices promoted by the idealists of 'popular education'. Practices such as these reduce what are the real causes to their external symptoms, invert the link between cause and effect and inevitably hold a superficial and simplified view on what is involved in the transition from the culture of the artisan to the culture of the worker. This transition, this 'other literacy', is necessary, vital and inevitable from the perspective of the high level of organization that rural and urban development requires.

Notes

1. The 'common pool resource' concept comes from what Karl Kautsky calls 'means of production shared in common'. This is especially the case when machinery is involved, which 'requires that production processes be regulated (coordinated), independent from the whims of various collaborators'. See: Kautsky, K. (1972) *Comentarias al Capital*, Mexico: Edicianes Cultural Popular; (1973) *El Marxismo*, Mexico: ROCA; and (1978) *Origen y fundamentos del Cristianismo*,

2. Marx, K. (1973) *El Capital*, Vol. I, Buenos Aires, p. 373 (English version *Capital*, Moscow, 1954).

3. Hegel, G. (1959) *Obras Completas*, Vol. 4, Moscow, pp. 212–13 (English version *Works*, Moscow, 1959).

4. A social psychology concept introduced by A. N. Leont'ev. According to Leont'ev, 'the organic meeting of need with its object allows the object to orient and regulate the activity' – Leont'ev, A. N. (1989) *La Actividad*, Mexico.

5. Ibid., pp. 68 and 74.

6. Marx 1973, p. 407.

7. Lange, O. (1974) *Political Economy*, Mexico, pp. 143–5.

8. Traspenikov, S. (1979) *Leninism and the Agrarian Problem*, Moscow: Progress, p. 284.

9. Fedosseiev, P. (1978) 'The social problem', *Journal of Social Sciences*, no. 1, Academy of USSR Sciences, Moscow, p. 50.

10. Marx, K. (1972) *Fundamental Elements for a Critique of the Political Economy (Draft) 1857–58*, Mexico: Siglo XXI Editores, p. 218.

11. Basmanov, M. and B. Leibson (1979) *The Revolutionary Vanguard*, Lisbon: Avante, p. 136.

12. Marx 1972.

4

(Brazil)

From Paulo Freire to Clodomir Santos de Morais: from Critical to Organizational Consciousness

Jacinta Castelo Branco Correia

A Final Treasured Moment with Paulo Freire, March 1997

The starting point of this chapter is the very last conversation we were privileged to have with Paulo Freire, merely a month and a half before his death, when he was the guest in our house at the occasion of the inaugural speech he was to make on 16 March 1997 in the new lecture hall at the university in Rondônia, Brazil.[1] At that occasion we spoke at length about the complementarity between his work and that of Clodomir Santos de Morais, his great friend, former cellmate and co-exile, especially in matters related to rural development. We watched videos about our field experiences in Rondônia and Mato Grosso, the two Brazilian states which have played a particularly important pioneering role in the application of Clodomir's method. We also talked about how this method opens up avenues for a genuine and strongly dialogical practice, because, in its essence, the OW method, from the very beginning, starts from the dialogical engagement of the participants and communities involved in the workshop process.

We also discussed how the lack of a method for community participation based in the objective reality, and using democratic, dialogical principles as proposed by Paulo Freire, had remained the abiding and fundamental problem with mainstream government and university-based extension practice and was a great obstacle to getting projects off the ground. It is now almost thirty years since Freire wrote *Extension or Communication?*, the first version of which was published in Chile. In this seminal text, Paulo critically questioned the prevalent use of the very word 'extension', a term that, until then, was being used unproblematically by agronomists working for the government extension services in the field.

Extension and Extensionism

For Paulo Freire the problem was not merely a question of hollow terminology unrelated to actual practice, but, on the contrary, to put it in his own words, one of capturing the 'operational force of concepts' and what the underlying ideological associations were of the term 'extension' – 'transmission, delivery, provision, messianism, mechanism, cultural invasion' – which he referred to as actions that 'reduce humans with the capacity to transform the world to the status of mere objects', 'denying them their proper role in transforming the world'. '[Such] assistencialist notions of "education" anaesthetize adults and reduce them to "uncritical simpletons, when faced with the world"'; 'education which recognizes itself (and has the courage to live by this insight) as a gnosological situation, challenges them to think, and not to memorize' (Freire 1974). While the former is rigid, dogmatic and authoritarian, the latter is mobile and critical: that is why authority should not be confused with authoritarianism, nor liberty with libertarianism. In spite of those warnings, which have been with us for almost thirty years, the term 'extension', bar a few rare exceptions, not only continues to be used, as was the case, for example, in the recent University-Based Extension Congress held in Costa Rica in September 1998, but continues to underpin the very diffusionist and authoritarian practices that were so roundly condemned by Paulo Freire.

Such practices navigate, purely and simply, between assistencialist and diffusionist interpretations of academic theoretical notions, thereby generating immobilism and the subsequent accommodation with the discapacitating tendencies, in organizational terms, for the great masses of the excluded – who are increasing in numbers and becoming more alienated by the day – in their search for organizational solutions to the problems they face.[2] This regrettable state of affairs is only made worse by the actions, imbued with paternalism, of bodies with social responsibilities, such as academia, which, when everything is said and done, reveal themselves incapable, apart from a few rare exceptions, to generate programmes and projects capable of transforming the reality on the ground. Specifically turning now to the task of academia, the contradictions or the backtracking are all the more serious if we remember that one of the main demands of the student revolution at the University of Córdoba, Argentina, 80 years ago, for example, was that the university should get actively involved in the search for solutions to the ever-changing challenges posed by society. This was one of the earliest examples of a extension-type engagement of academia with the real world outside.[3]

Paradoxically, extension, over time, has come to be identified with practices promoted by the political right, which, in turn, has helped to keep in check the student revolutionaries who came in the wake of the the pioneers in Córdoba. Interrelationships between society and academia have, until now, remained as much on the agenda as before, as the problem of poverty, already so widespread, is progressively getting worse. The fear is that this will lead to social exclusion on a global scale, with the vast numbers of the excluded not so much (any more) fighting for their rights, but instead banding together in armed struggle and/or turning to criminal activities. This fear is justified: wherever the dominated class falls short in its liberatory task, and when popular movements are not properly organized so that they can cope with the challenges at hand, a backsliding into violence has almost always been the result. In the end, dreams turn into nightmares, or we see a flight forward into right-wing reactionism on the part of the very movements that originally were of leftist persuasion.

It is 30 years now since Paulo Freire traced the outlines of what genuine extension ought to be: a process of mutual learning rooted in communication and dialogical learning, in which all involved become critically aware. The fact that virtually nothing has changed in this long intervening period has to be attributed to the fact that critical consciousness, based on dialogue, on its own, is fundamentally incapable of transcending the dialogical stage and generating those very changes that are most required by society and by the poor and the excluded 'here and now'. What one has to be clearly aware of here is that Paulo Freire's methodology, in the end, did not provide an objective methodology (i.e. a methodology actively engaged with objective reality), but that, based on dialogue, it largely remained within the ambit of the socialization of academic knowledge, mediated by a liberatory education process. It is for this reason that, with Freire, the 'what-to-do' and the 'how-to-do-it' always either remained unarticulated or were explained by each extensionist differently, as their own limitations and personal experiential backgrounds dictated.

Paulo Freire himself readily conceded that the 'how-to-do-it' was still to be discovered by those taking up the teacher–learner challenge within a dialogical posture. However, the fundamental problem lies in the fact that the peasantry, accustomed as they are to paternalistic interventions, and to assistentialist relationships, for reasons of a long history of relationships of domination, remain rooted in their conviction that they will be forever inferior and 'incapable': they therefore refuse, if not in words, then in deed, to participate in actions based on precisely the type of dialogical analysis proposed by Paulo Freire. On this very subject, Freire comments in his early work *Extension or Communication* that 'it only is natural that they [the oppressed] should show an extreme reluctance to dialogue. Nor is it surprising that they tell the educator after a mere fifteen to twenty minutes of active participation: "Excuse us, sir, we-who-don't-know should keep our peace and listen to you who know"" (Freire 1974: 121).

An identical situation presented itself as we watched the videotape about the Organization Workshop in Urupá (Rondônia, Brazil), on the occasion of the above-mentioned visit of Paulo to our house. In this film, local people's resistance to calls, by the personnel of the State Rural Extension Service, for them to come and participate in the various training sessions organized by EMBRATER, the state rural extension enterprise, was only too obvious, as compared to the very positive response given by the very same people to the invitations to attend job-generating OWs. The great difference lay in the fact that the OW courses were proposed at the behest of the peasants themselves, and were negotiated beforehand between them and the director. As soon as this fact was established, participation and community support were assured. On this very topic, namely the enormous difficulties encountered when calling for community 'participation', Paulo Freire was categorical: 'No doubt: that [the organization workshop] is the way to go about it!'

Freire has the following message for those who continue to argue that dialogue is all a waste of time: 'Those who declare dialogue is impossible will probably say that these observations only serve to confirm their hypotheses. This is not true. What those considerations clearly reveal is that the difficulty of dialogue with peasants does not come about because of their peasant status, but because of the social structure, perceived by them as "permanent", oppressive and keeping them hostage' (Freire 1974: 121). These are, then, some of the difficulties and the reasons why we propose here to analyse the very problems which cause agronomists – and not just them – to brand all attempts to dialogue as 'time wasting' (ibid.: 122).

Starting in the 1980s, the state extension service in Brazil made its first attempts, coordinated by EMBRATER, to use Paulo Freire's ideas in extension work.[4] As a result, a group of male and female specialists was formed under the aegis of the 'New Extension Proposal'. One of the problems that emerged was that the extension workers were very clear about the 'what-to-do' but extremely reticent when it came to the 'how-to'. Their great fear was to be overheard talking technical jargon and thus being accused of being of the 'diffusionist' tendency, a term that, by then, had acquired a number of pejorative connotations.[5] The upshot of these developments was that other extensionists, who had far more first-hand field experience, started seriously to question the technical competence of the New Extension Proposal recruits: a lot of wind but little wool. A great number of experiments were run in those days that tried to adapt field communication and extension methods – all broadly diffusionist – to new approaches that would live up as closely as possible to the ideals propounded by Paulo Freire.

All of this coincided, in Brazil, with the final stages of military dictatorship, with new winds of democratization blowing, favouring the ideals of those who had been exiled for what they believed in. In educational matters, the ground was definitely shifting in the direction of more equality, social justice, freedom and a search for the re-establishment of human rights that had, for decades, been trampled on by successive dictatorships. That is why the state extension service saw itself now obliged to move away from its authoritarian ways and to democratize its relations with the public, starting with the peasantry. Towards the end of the 1980s, the first experiments in Brazil with the new OW method took off with the support of EMBRATER, in the hope that a way could be found to change fundamentally the ingrained extensionist protocols in tune with the democratic transition taking place in Brazil at that time.[6]

These experiments were based on the aforementioned method of mass capacitation called the Organization Workshops systematized by Clodomir Santos de Morais. The OW method in very real terms allows for the very type of dialogue recommended by Paulo Freire, in that it starts from the organizational knowledge already embodied in the community. Thanks to the 'objective activity' of the workshop, new information and new organizational skills of a type far more complex than the pre-existing ones are acquired.[7] These skills allowing the participants to cope with complex forms of organization, and on a large scale, are generically different, it needs to be pointed out, from those prevailing among traditional small-scale producers in the small 'family'-type economy. The different methodological phases, therefore, establish a relationship completely at odds with those usually established by mainstream extensionists, given the fact that what is at work here is the immediate delivery of the means of production to the participants involved.

The OW usually starts with a grand assembly of those who have volunteered to participate, where all, men and women, make clear their wishes about the type of courses they want, where they want them, the time they want to spend on them and who are willing to subscribe to them. Everything that subsequently happens in the workshop is patterned on the type of courses requested by the participants, including at least ten teachers or specialists versed in the subjects chosen by the collective, whose numbers are often in the hundreds, with no numerical upper limit, except the physical facilities. It should be plain from all this that the driving force of the workshop originates not in the extensionist project but in what the group themselves have decided they are interested in learning and under what conditions. It is then the proper function of the specialists engaged by the workshop to respond instantly to any request coming from the workshop participants: this includes content, time and place, in the way the participants have requested.

In practice, this means that the ultimate responsibility for organizing the proceedings of the subsequent 30 or 40 days that the workshop lasts rests with the locals, be they peasants or urban unemployed, and their families. There are no restrictions as regards age or sex. Once the participants have set up the structures necessary for the smooth running of the workshop and of the courses requested, a series of texts are made available on the Theory of Organization, as laid out in the several publications of a pamphlet of the same name written by Clodomir Santos de Morais.[8]

Those involved in the holistic capacitation process of the workshop gradually learn to appreciate the importance of organization in a socially divided work context, indispensable in bringing the proceedings of the capacitating event to a successful conclusion. This complex structure, namely, the membership enterprise, is indeed the 'object' that capacitates, in matters of entrepreneurial organization, the collective 'subject' (the community of learners) involved in the process. The inevitable problems (referred to by Clodomir as 'anomy' in Chapter 3 of this book) that always arise in the course of getting organized for a complex production process will themselves become the very 'needs' and objectives that will guide the 'collective subject' in the 'how-to?' use of a number of instruments in the collective problem-solving effort. In this sense, the very problems that turn up in the process of getting organized become the very needs and objectives that orient the 'subject-collective' in the use of the various organizational instruments and in the ways to arrive at a successful conclusion. In that sense, the problems that pop up in the course of the capacitation process take on the form of authentic pedagogical instruments of organizational experimentation.

This lived experience, taking place under new conditions of existence the participants have never experienced before, becomes, little by little, the key factor underpinning a new social consciousness, referred to as 'organizational consciousness' by de Morais (see Chapter 3). It is this new organizational experience, and this experience alone, that makes it possible for the participants to make the transition from individual to collective consciousness. At the moment of becoming involved in the OW experience, the consciousness of those 'artisans of the field', as well as the consciousness of the 'urban artisans', can be called, at best, informed or critical, according to the classification provided by Santos de Morais.[9] This informed consciousness is determined by their conditions of life.

By 'artisan' de Morais understands those small producers involved in a seamless production process over which they have complete control from beginning to end. The peasant, for example, is alone, in charge of the sowing, the harvesting and the eventual marketing of the crop. In this process there is no need for a social division of labour and even less for a socially divided production process (technical division of labour) because production is organized parallel to other, similar, productive groups. That is precisely the reason artisans are so averse to associative processes in search of solutions. The large group capacitation method is rooted in the practice that establishes a reversal in the relationships of power. This is in stark contrast with virtually all other educational processes, in which the centre of power (educator/communicator) dictates the means and methodologics to be used. Under those conditions the situation prevailing in capitalist production, where the workers are neither in possession nor in control of the means of production and remain alienated from the goods themselves they produce, is being reproduced indefinitely.

The organizational regime prevailing in the OW, on the other hand, creates the opportunity for the participants, for the month or so that the experience lasts, to achieve a change in the living conditions they have been used to, due to a radical change in the position of power, which is now entirely in their hands. The fact that they have ownership and control over not only the means of production, but also over the manner in which the process is conducted, fosters confidence in the values of unity that flow from actually working together and being in charge of their own destiny. Being in firm control of the instruments of the capacitation process in which they are the principal actors, they successfully achieve an analysis of their own life conditions, the origins of which they have now learned to understand in a critical manner. This experience will restore their self-confidence at the same time as they develop new and vital capabilities that permit them to succeed in the capitalist market economy in which, hitherto, they found it so difficult even to survive.

Thus, the principal objective of the organization workshop is that the group as a whole takes part in what is, at the same time, a real enterprise, and learns to stand on its own feet, efficiently, competently and speedily. The soundness of the principles that apply in the OW methodology is confirmed by the fact that those already working in industrial or factory environments where the technical division of labour, or the social division of the production process, prevail, find it easier to engage in associative forms of cooperation. The nub of the problem is how to generate opportunities conducive to operate the necessary change from 'artisan' to 'worker' consciousness. Without this all-important change, artisans will never be able to ensure their own survival in the complex market economy. They will continue to be exploited by the so-called 'coyotes' (profiteering middlemen) in the first stage of the commercialization of the economy, while, in the productive stage, they find themselves not up to the task of installing the technology necessary for the efficiencies and speed needed in the increasingly competitive production environment. What the capacitation process above all aims at, therefore, is the total and unconditional exposure of the 'enterprise-object' to the 'subject-collective'. To use a metaphor, only in the total surrender of the bicycle to the learner can the capacitation in bicycle-riding be fully achieved. In the case of capacitation in organization for enterprise, it is only in the surrender of the entire enterprise, with its entire complement of the means of production, the so-called 'common resource pool', that full entrepreneurial capacitation can be achieved.[10]

Extension, Popular Education and Capacitation

For far too long mainstream extensionism has confused fundamental issues, including matters at the heart of its natural vocation of diffusing technology. Extensionism is agnostic about the distinction between 'education' and 'capacitation'. Education is a process that takes place between a teacher and a learner, aimed at transforming (the knowledge world of) learners. This is done by means of the transmission of an already existing store of knowledge, via channels, to the learner. In the case of capacitation, the opposite is true: here it is the object that capacitates the subject. The role of the educator consists in transmitting and socializing academic knowledge with the aim of teaching the learner. The transmission of knowledge to the learners (who thus become objects, recipients and beneficiaries) can be deemed successful only if the knowledge of the teacher has been properly introduced into the heads of the learners – to use another metaphor: the way one does when 'installing' software on a computer. Without that 'software' it is impossible to interpret the discourse or the lecture.

The role of the facilitator in capacitation, on the other hand, is to assist and encourage the relationship between the subject (in this case group of workshop participants) and the object (the real enterprise) so that the material facts pertaining to the object become comprehensible to the subject. In other words, it is only when the subject has been challenged by the object that the need to change will become obvious to the subject. The facilitator is not a transmitter of knowledge, only someone who makes the capacitation process possible in actual practice (in the process of being engaged with the object). The specialist or trainer in the capacitation process is a facilitator and an adviser whose principal task it is to avoid all the forms of gratuitous, overbearing authoritarianism that normally come with the possession of superior knowledge (knowledge is power). The facilitator acts only when and if requested to do so. These actions have to be free of all assistentialist or paternalist overtones, allowing the problems that come up to act themselves, as pedagogical tools. It is precisely this capacity to solve problems in actual practice that allows the collective of learner/workers to move in the direction that leads to the proper solutions. If, however, the facilitator becomes a problem-solver, it will only result in a gradual set-back in genuine capacitation, because those who ought to be subjects of their own learning fall into the old trap of being mere passive objects and relapse into the state referred to by Freire as 'absolute ignorance', which in the past has held such a stranglehold on 'artisans of the field', due to centuries of domination and oppression.

Objective Activity

On the subject of objective activity, Paulo Freire, in the third part of the work we have already extensively quoted, even while not referring to it by name, makes some extremely important comments that coincide with de Morais' theoretical-methodological position:

> I should once again emphasize that problematization is not an intellectual diversion, both alienated and alienating. Nor is it an escape from action, a way of disguising the fact that what is real has been denied. (Freire 1974: 153)

> Problematization is not only inseparable from the act of knowing, but also inseparable from concrete situations ... problematization implies a critical return to action. *It starts from action and returns to it.* The process of problematization implies a critical turn to action. (ibid.: 154; emphasis added)

> There can be no problematization without reality. Discussion about 'transcendence' must take its point of departure from discussion on the 'here', which for many humans is also the 'now', too. (ibid.)

Continuing to take our cue from the same work by Paulo Freire, we summarize here what he has to say about genuine capacitation:

> *Technical Proficiency Capacitation* is something more than mere instruction, because it is a search for knowledge, using the appropriate procedures. (ibid.: 160)[11]

> *Technical Proficiency Capacitation* can never be reduced to the level of mere 'training' (e.g. in the way animals are trained), since capacitation only takes place in a human setting. (ibid.)

> Unlike animals, whose activity is themselves, human beings are capable of reflecting not only on themselves but also on their activity, which is something separate from them, just as the product of their activity is separate from them. (ibid.)

Technical Aid, of which Technical Proficiency Capacitation is a part, can only exist through praxis, if it is to be genuine. It exists in action and reflection and in the critical comprehension of the implications of the method. (ibid.)

Technical Proficiency Capacitation, which should not be confused with the training of animals, can never be dissociated from the existential conditions of the life of the peasants, from their cultural viewpoint, from their magic beliefs. It must begin *at the level at which they are*, and not at the level at which the agronomists think they ought to be. (ibid.: 163; emphasis added)

Theory-building, Research and Evaluation

A great number of enterprises, cooperatives and associations have resulted, in three continents. The work of simply putting on record, classifying and writing up of reports has, so far, lagged behind, partly because lack of personnel and funding, partly because the primary objective of the OW is not research, but people learning how not only to survive, but also to lead a dignified life. What is certain is that the workshop is not an employment or enterprise 'factory', but it is a space for a practice, of vast dimensions and potentialities, in which people make this vital transition in consciousness, the outcomes and long-term consequences of which cannot be plotted in advance. This notwithstanding, there is an urgent need for more researchers to get involved and to recognize the value of the OW on its own terms, the more so as it is the proper role of universities and academics to respond to the challenges constantly being thrown up by society at large. When those problems are inherent, structurally embedded in an economic system that now encompasses the world, the importance of this research cannot be overstated.

Notes

1. Freire gave a rousing testimony to his 'velho de guerra, amigo-irmão', Clodomir (see also Paulo Freire *Aprendendo com a propria historia*, Paz: 135). On that occasion, reminiscing about the time they spent together in prison, he said: 'But even so, when I saw [that] food, I could not restrain myself from jumping on it. All this while Clodomir would not touch any food at all until he had brought food to his fellow prisoners, the peasants. It was the kind of thing one would have expected Christ to do – in that sense Clodomir was far more of a Christian than I ever was. All I was interested in was jumping on that food' (translated from Portuguese)

2. On the concept of 'discapacitation' see Sobrado in Chapter 20 of this book. In Jacinta Correia's book, *IATTERMUND*, Brasília, 1994, the term is used in a way which complements the ideas of Sobrado.

3. On the influence of the student revolution in Córdoba, consult Jorge Fernández

Varela et al. (1981), in *Notes on the Conceptualization of University Extension*, UNAM 1981.

4. EMBRATER (Empresa Brasileña de Asistencia Técnica e Extensión Rural–Brazilian Enterprise for Technical Assistance and Rural Extension) acted as coordinator for SIBRATER, the federal system that groups all the enterprises in existence all over the country.

5. Diffusionism is the model used in governmental extension work. It is a model that originated in the USA and was most intensively applied in the diffusion of agricultural innovations for accelerated development. Extension saw it as its proper vocation to diffuse those technological innovations regardless of the attitudes, the cultural embedding or the needs of the target populations. For more about this model and other extension models, see Bordenave, Juan E. Díaz (1977) *Communication and Rural Development*, Paris: UNESCO.

6. About the changes in the extension model, see in Jacinta Correia (1995) *Comunicaçao y Capacitaçao*, IATTERMUND, Brasília, 2nd edn.

7. 'Objective activity' (or objectivized activeness/*dyatel'nost* in the original Russian – see Labra 1992) is one of the foundation stones of the OW approach. For more around the theme of social psychology and objective activity see Labra, I (1993) *Psicología Social – Responsabilidad y Necesidad*, Santiago, Chile: LOM Ediciones.

8. *Theory of Organization* by de Morais is the base text for and during the proceedings of the organization workshops of mass capacitation (entrepreneurial literacy). It is during this workshop that the collective of learners become 'literate' in complex forms of organization through the division of labour as the main instruments by which both the internal and external 'enemies' of the budding organization are overcome. The external enemies are the external pressures on the self-managing organization, such as the capitalist system of organizing labour and its promoting agents of individualism and exploitation. Among the internal enemies we count the 'vices', those habits that are inconsistent with the new mode of production and inherent in the small producer or artisanal forms of production. Together those 'enemies' wage war against the two pillars on which the complex organization rests: unity and discipline. Without those two, the enterprise will fail. The main 'bad habit' characteristic of the artisanal or small-scale production culture is opportunism, which finds its origin in the private ownership of the means of production, such as: individualism, subjectivism and self-sufficiency (which differs from the spirit of reliance on self) (see also Chapter 2).

9. On the different types of consciousness, see de Morais, *Theory of Organization*, where the bad habits of the artisanal or small family mode of production are described. In those forms of production the peasant or small family unit producer typically execute all the production activities themselves, on their own. Naïve or simple consciousness is characteristic of small subsistence producers, be they rural or urban, who produce mainly for the immediate needs of the family (with or without a small surplus). Their work produces hardly the equivalent of 'use value' – this consciousness will be called 'critical' when they have understood the difference of what it is to produce 'exchange' or 'market' value.

10. See in de Morais, *Theory of Organization*, about the commonly pooled resource base. This is another category that plays a role of great importance in the organization workshops. The OWs indeed start from the principle that a group of people who come together also share a certain number of resources together, or a 'common pool'. The latter consists of those things that cannot easily be broken up and divided among each member of the group (e.g. a 45-ton lorry for the marketing of the produce or perhaps

a tractor). For example when they need to fill the Maracana stadium when there is a football match in Rio de Janeiro, the match is not shown on TV. Should this happen, the 'commonly held resource' is divided up, with the result that people will stay at home (to watch the match there). When the need to organize is an essential requirement, and when people are motivated to get organized, the commonly held pool will become the binding factor.

11. Translator's note: the translator of Freire's original *Extensión o Comunicación* uses the term 'technical proficiency capacitation', which, in Freire's mind, is clearly distinct from training in that it is 'on the side of' the learner, but does not contain the full meaning of 'objective activity' that we find in de Morais (see also Preliminary Note on translating terms).

References

Carmen, R., I. Labra, I. Labra and M. Davis (1999) *Learning from Brazil*, Manchester Monographs.

Correia, J. C. B. (1994) *Comunicaçao e Capacitacao* (Communication and Capacitation), Brasília: IATTERMUND.

Corzo, F. and J. Ramon (1984) *Practica, Conocimiento y Valoracion* (Practice, Knowledge and Appraisal), Havana: Fundacion de Cuba.

EMBRATER (1987) *Comunicaçao e Diretrizes Operacionales* (Directives and Communications), Brasília.

Freire, P. (1974) 'Extension or Communication', in P. Freire, *Education for Critical Consciousness*, London: Sheed and Ward.

Labra, I. (1992) *Psicologia Social, Responsabilidad y Necesidad* (Social Psychology, Responsibility and Need), Santiago, Chile: LOM Editoriales (English translation forthcoming).

Leont'ev, I. T. (1964) *Papel de las Condiciones Objetivas y de los Factores Subjetivos en la Educación de los Trabajadores*, Havana, Cuba: Editoria Política.

— (1981) *Activity, Consciousness and Personality* (trans. M. J. Hall), London: Prentice Hall.

de Morais, C. S. (1986) *Notes on a Theory of Organization* (trans. I. Cherrett), Newcastle: ETC UK.

— (1987) 'Condiciones objetivas factores subjetivos da la incorporación de las masas rurales en el proceso de desarrollo progresista de la agricultura en Centroamerica', doctoral thesis (Spanish only), Rostock, Germany: Rostock University.

— (1989a) *A Capacitaçao Massiva: Uma Proposta para o Desenvolvimento Rural* (Mass Capacitation: A Proposal for Rural Development), Porto Velho, Brazil: EMATER.

— (1989b) *El Reencontrado e lo Perdido de las Reformas Agrarias* (Agrarian Reforms Lost and Found), Brasília: IATTERMUND.

Monteiro, S. T. (1993) *A Capacitaçao para Formaçao de Empresas Associativas* (Capacitation for the Formation of Membership Enterprises), São Paulo, Brazil: IATTERMUND.

Part III

The Organization Workshop in Practice

The OW in Central and South America

5

From Navvies to Entrepreneurs: The OW in Costa Rica

Miguel Sobrado

The elaboration of the theory and the practical application of the OW methodology in Costa Rica took place principally during the 1970s. It all started with Clodomir Santos de Morais, who, as ILO adviser for Costa Rica (1970 to 1973), organized a series of conferences at the University of Costa Rica and at other public institutions. These conferences attracted a keen interest because of the originality and freshness of their theoretical outlook. Although as yet no examples of what the method was capable of existed in the country, a great expectation had been raised in academic and institutional circles about the theory and its practical possibilities. In 1972, spurred on by the increasing clashes around land reclamation, the Mixed Institute for Social Aid (IMAS) and the Institute of Lands and Colonization (ITCO), in collaboration with the National Directorate for Community Development (DINADECO), developed a plan for intra-institutional co-operation called the National Plan for Land Settlements. This plan, of distinct Moraisean inspiration, provided for the formation of 'peasant community enterprises'. It had particularly in mind the campesinos and unskilled labourers who at the time were involved in land invasions. Behind the plan, originally inspired by the IMAS, there was a silent agreement with an organization of communist inspiration, the FENAC (National Campesino Federation), which campaigned on behalf of the disinherited against expulsions from the lands they had occupied. This made the need for community enterprises all the more urgent, and whenever groups expressed such an interest the community enterprises initiative was ready to comply.

The FENAC had become aware, by then, that once the land had been seized, the backsliding into land concentration usually took less time than when the land had first been claimed. The organizational power that had been generated at such great cost dissipated rapidly, thereby impeding the grouping of forces in the campesino movement. The requirements of the

National Plan prompted the then director of ITCO, don Teodoro Quirós, to put in a request with the ILO for an Organization Workshop to be held in Bataán, a campesino settlement established under the aegis of the institute, in the Atlantic region of the country. The OW took place from 13 to 28 February 1973. These dates coincided with the last two working weeks of Clodomir Santos de Morais in the country as ILO consultant. Participating in the event were IMAS and ITCO officials, students from the University of Costa Rica and members of six cooperative and pre-cooperative groups. Out of this original workshop came several leaders who later organized cadres of enterprises, as well as a number of officials and students willing and able to act as workshop directors in the future. They were responsible for the emergence, in 1973 alone, of 80 pre-cooperative groups and 15 membership enterprises, some of these among former banana plantation workers who had become displaced because of rapid technical innovations on the plantations themselves, combined with their diminished market value as manual labour due to their age. Nevertheless, the intra-institutional cooperation arrangements and the agreement for cooperation struck with FENAC was maintained until 1974, when a new government team took over in Costa Rica.

This team belonged to the same Social Democratic party which won the elections that year (the National Liberation party), but it replaced the officials who had directed both institutions until then. The new ITCO executive did not believe in cooperatives and believed even less in community enterprises, which were branded 'communist' because of their links with the FENAC. The new ITCO director was of the opinion that the Costa Rican is inherently individualist, and he started zealously to implement the repartition of the land into smallholdings as ITCO's new official policy. The active promotion of the breaking up of the emerging community enterprises formed part of this same policy package. These changes in institutional policy stopped the process of further promotion of cooperatives, which had gathered strength in the new land settlements, in its tracks, and provoked, further along the line, the parcelling up of less cohesive cooperatives or those whose membership was made up predominantly of former traditional farmers, accustomed to individual land exploitation. It is important to highlight here the fact that the break-up into individual plots happened especially in those cooperatives where the membership was accustomed to traditional work on an individual basis, whereas in those cooperatives where the majority of the membership were agricultural (day) labourers, in particular former banana plantation labourers, cohesion was generally maintained in the face of external pressures. In the end, only six cooperatives, which enjoyed the support of the extension programme of the Universidad Nacional (in Heredia) for community enterprises in the rural areas, remained. This university extension programme, financed by the Interamerican Foundation, remained all along in close touch with Santos de Morais who, by that time, was in charge of the agricultural reform programme in Honduras (see Chapter 6).

Those cooperatives, as well as standing firm against the parcelling up of land, set up a cooperative federation called FECOOPA R.L. The cooperatives and their federation went through very difficult years due to the fact that the land was not registered in their name, which, in turn, meant that, in order to secure credit, they had to apply for guarantees from the institute, as there were no other convenient alternative sources of credit. No wonder then that those difficulties, long drawn-out over several years, led to desertions, especially among the younger members, and inhibited the hopes and prospects of the other members, leading to a considerable reduction in the capacities and the drive with which the rural enterprises had started out. With the change of government in 1978, the Christian Socialist Unity Party (USC) having won the elections that year, and the subsequent formation of a new goverment of Christian Democratic inspiration, the politics pursued by the agrarian institute became more flexible and made it possible to bring in a specialist in mass capacitation from Honduras, who had been one of Clodomir's pupils there.

The upshot was the creation of three new self-managing cooperatives in the former cattle ranches. The new cooperatives affiliated themselves in the FEDERAGRO, the federation sponsored by the institute. Former seasonal labourers of the cattle farms and some local campesinos joined in this experience. These cooperatives lasted for many years, until, yet again, the institute came under the jurisdiction of the same partisan leadership favouring the parcelling up of land. For its part, the Ministry for Planning of the 1978–82 administration presented the president of the republic with the demands emanating from FECOOPA that the land titles be transferred to the cooperatives. This objective was finally achieved by FECOOPA in 1982. The same year also saw the introduction of important modifications in cooperative law in self-managing cooperatives and a new, differentiated sector inside the national cooperative movement gained a new juridical status. This gave them right of representation in the National Council for Cooperatives as well as new negotiating powers. There is not the slightest doubt that those changes were vital for their survival, but the relations inside the National Council and inside the cooperative movement in general kept them vulnerable to the pervasive clientelist culture, which sets a greater store on loyalty than on efficiency.

From the moment of its recognition as a sector within the cooperative movement, its premises in San José, containing a small supermarket-cum-capacitation centre, made possible thanks to a grant from the Dutch NGO

CEBEMO, could be inaugurated. These premises were also to act as a guarantee for the operational autonomy of the federation and the co-operatives that were part of it. Thus an era of recuperation set in. They suffered a slight setback due to a case of embezzlement involving the supermarket, which affected the financial stability of the federation. The 1980s and 1990s saw a number of ups and downs. First, there was the then prevailing climate of mistrust towards the federation because of its leftist ties as well as the war atmosphere then prevalent in the entire Central American region. Second, there was the exodus of the youngest cooperative recruits, sons and daughters of the founding members. Several cooperatives in succession entered the federation while others, again, left it, which meant a slow rate of growth for the federation, although its entrepreneurial focus became keener as time progressed.

At the moment of writing 13 cooperatives belong to the Costa Rican FECOOPA (see Table 5.1, overleaf).

It is important to add COOPESA to the list in Table 5.1. COOPESA is a large co-managed cooperative, with more than 800 workers, which deals in aeroplane repairs, with an annual yield in export sales of $30 million. It became self-managed at the time of the law reforms initiated by FECOOPA, and it maintains strong links with the latter. The reason for its non-incorporation in the main federation is that FECOOPA is limited by law to agricultural and cattle-producing sector cooperatives. It is equally important to note that those Costa Rican cooperatives that survived tended to enjoy a majority membership of ex-banana plantation workers and had usually been able to secure good pieces of land. Those with a majority of campesinos and cattle ranch day-labourers with less familiarity with socially divided forms of labour were less successful in their endeavours, although it must be said that they usually found themselves with the worst types of land.

The land invasions by former banana-workers in the 1960s ran parallel with those in other countries, such as Honduras, during the same period. These were set in motion partly by the modernization of agriculture then gearing up, which meant a considerable loss of workplaces and subsequent displacement of workers, especially the older ones. Costa Rica has been lucky in that it has not to cope with serious problems of unemployment, except for a short period following the 1982 crisis, which lasted for five years. At the moment of writing (beginning 1999) and notwithstanding a strong immigratory influx from Nicaragua, estimated at at least 10 per cent of the economically active population (EAP), Costa Rica's unemployment rate now stands at 5.4 per cent.

A combination of factors – a more democratic approach to internal politics, ample social policy measures, the long and hard road to final

TABLE 5.1 Cooperative enterprises associated with FECOOPA

Name	Area (ha)	Members	Product(s)	Location	Years
Coopevaquita	407	18	Oil palm/ cereals/ecology	Puntarenas	2
Procercoop	34.2	12	Pigs	Laurel Corred	1
CoopeGuaycara	148	12	Oil palm	Rio Claro Golfito	14
Cooprosur	1,000	37	Oil palm/banana/ ecol. protect.	Rio Claro Golfito	15
CoopeAndelante	225	16	Banana	Palmar Sur Puntarenas	12
CoopeSierra Cantillo	600	22	Banana/palm/ pawpaw	Puntarenas	22
CoopeMangle	12	13	Carbon extracts/ ecotourism	Ciudad Cortes	13
Coopesilencio	980	49	Oil palm/refores- tation/cereals/ ecotourism	Savegre, Quepos	26
CoopeSanRafael	3.5	13	Broilers	S. Rafael de Alajuela	12
CoopeSan Juan	460	20	Tubers/cereals/ dairy products/ reforestation/ eco/agrotourism	Zarcas San Carlos	14
CoopeOrtega	170	14	Sugarcane/organic products	Guanacaste	14
CoopeUnioro	8	15	Ecotourism/med. plants/reforestation	Rincon de Osa	13
Ecopavones	600	60	Fish/cereals	Golfito	5

recognition of FECOOPA cooperatives – meant that in the case of Costa Rica the cooperative movement did not reach the size and importance it achieved, for example, in Honduras, but the experience in Costa Rica is nevertheless full of lessons for other countries applying the workshop method:

• Individualism is not an inborn Costa Rican characteristic. This may have been the case to a certain extent in the past, when a greater part of the population was still settled in the rural areas. Today the majority are in paid jobs and economically active. Also, the very practice of working in situations with a high level of social division of labour generates organizational mental models that transform those whose lived reality it becomes, into disciplined persons capable of working in an organized manner and as a team.

• The more specialized former salaried workers are, the better aptitudes they show for teamwork. Their capacity to organize is their strong point and for that reason can and ought to be used to bolster social policies. In the case of Costa Rica, we have two distinct types of enterprise: the commercial and the survival. Even though, initially, all enterprises have many characteristics in common, due to the fact that the range of their operations is as yet limited, they gradually start to differentiate. Those enterprises that have better organizational skills and better land succeed in transforming themselves better, in due course, into medium-sized enterprises capable of competing in the open market. Others, such as Coopetulga, which had to make do with mediocre land, never went beyond the subsistence stage. But it has to be recognized that, by dint of their cooperative efforts, they were able to fend off at least the spectre of hunger and to provide for themselves and their children without having to rely on social assistance handouts.

• This means that concrete options do exist, as proved in the Costa Rican case, for development and poverty alleviation that go far beyond the traditional parameters of the micro-enterprise; options that also draw on people's work experience and on their organizational mental models. All of this is of great practical significance for employment and income-generation policies that are far more efficient than the traditional ones pursued at present.

• The experience with the ex-salaried workers organizing themselves into cooperatives lifts one particular corner of the veil covering the problem of unemployment and poverty that no one seems to have taken the trouble to analyse in the past. What I am referring to here is the – so far – hidden problem of manual labourers' under-employment, which is caused by their diminishing ability to work, due to their progressing age, the disappearance of their specialized skills, to technological innova-tion, and competition from younger workers with superior manual prowess and educational credentials to themselves. These factors boost the problem of under-employment, drastically cut financial income potential, and thus contribute directly to increased poverty and social exclusion. Under-employment has tended to be perceived as something of a lesser evil, as those who fall victim to it at least continue to draw some form of income, which may allow them to survive without too much trouble, a luxury not given to the fully unemployed. Policies in the past have, therefore, tended to concentrate almost exclusively on male and female full unemployment, which affects especially young men and women, who tend to be targeted by the usual micro-enterprise and training programmes. This omission is all the more serious as the problem of under-employment continues to increase at a rapid pace, resulting in the progressive loss of more and more income opportunities. The end result of all this is, as we have already mentioned, increased levels of exclusion and chronic poverty among men and women alike, who then go on transmitting it to their children, allowing the problem to fester and to reproduce itself.

• It is interesting to note that this process of gradual exclusion is becoming more intense as technological change progresses, not least in the Costa Rican banana plantations, which use leading-edge technology packages with peak forms of socially divided of labour. These are the companies that are using First World technology in Third World countries. This does not prevent them from generating exactly the same exclusion processes that can be observed in the more technologically developed world.

Conclusion

The Costa Rican experience with the application of the OW method to agrarian production processes in the 1970s and the 1980s did not have the same repercussions as it may have had, for example, in the case of Honduras, but it fostered, nevertheless, a movement towards self-management that promises to play an important part in the future. On the other hand, the Costa Rican case has thrown into sharp relief the theoretical-practical importance of the sociological theory and of the capacitation method expounded by de Morais, especially in his identification of social strata and the potential of the workshop in organizational terms, as well as the avenues it opens up for capacitating entire populations in organizational and entrepreneurial skills. The results of the experience allow us to devise new ways of understanding the genesis of poverty and to open up new options in the elaboration of new social policies and programmes that go far beyond the traditional solutions, which limit themselves to youth employment and the setting up of micro-enterprises.[1]

Note

1. Costa Rica played a leading role in the setting up of a 'disaster relief'/'social participation' project in the wake of Hurricane Mitch. The $4 million proposal was submitted by the SP-CSUCA (Permanent Secretariat of the Supreme Council of Central

American Universities) with headquarters in San José de Costa Rica, and is planned to run until December 2000 for the zones devastated by the hurricane. It is proposed that, with the cooperation of 17 Central American universities, 40 TDEs (Experts in Economic Development), per country, will be appointed, as well as 200 APIs (investment project assistants), with 40 communities to be capacitated per country as an ultimate objective. The Moraisean field OW is proposed as the main engine of those developments in each of the intended geographical zones. De Morais, based at the time of writing in Mexico, is actively involved in the project. Additionally, a nationwide Costa Rican 'Job and Income Generation System' (on the pattern of the original SIPGEI in Portugal of the 1970s and 1980s) and the present nationwide SIPGEI in Brazil has been proposed, in the spring of 1999, by the National University of Costa Rica in conjunction with the Costa Rican National Institute for Training (INA), the Ministry of Labour (FODESAF), the Ministry of Agriculture and the Mixed Institute for Social Aid (IMAX).

6

Sacked Agricultural Workers Take on the Multinationals in Honduras

Benjamin Erazo

F23 J43 017
Q13 013
015

Short Overview of Development in Honduras in the 1970s

Honduras is known as one of the lesser developed countries of Central America. The agricultural sector has always accounted for the bulk of the country's social and economic make-up. Seventy-two per cent of a total population of 2,755,608 people in 1972 were agrarian-based. Agriculture also accounted for 36.3 per cent of the Honduran GNP and 62.4 per cent of total exports. Those exports consist mainly of bananas, a monoculture that makes for an extremely fragile economy.[1] Between 1960 and 1962 per capita income was $192, and it rose to $242 in 1970–72. Average incomes of the rural population stood at $156. During the 1960s Honduras went through a period of social strife, which had its root cause in the prevailing socially divisive land tenure structures. As many as one-third of the 350,000 rural families had no access to land in 1972, and 67.50 per cent of all smallholdings had to make do with only 12.3 per cent of the total cultivable land, whereas a mere 0.2 per cent of the large landowners owned 19.6 per cent of the cultivated land area. The focal point of these struggles for land was the area where the most developed sector of agriculture was concentrated. It was in this same area that most of the rural migrants from the most impoverished and backward areas of the country were also concentrating. During this decade there were incisive readjustments in the agricultural export sector, especially in terms of labour-saving technologies, which drastically cut job opportunities in that sector and resulted in countless numbers of people being pushed off the land.[2]

Campesino Organizations and Context of the Reforms

It was during this same period that the campesino movement in Honduras took off. Its field of action geographically coincided with the areas of export agriculture or rapid industrialization, which meant that the vast majority of the membership consisted of landless peasants or former agricultural labourers. The struggle concentrated around the reclamation of the land, especially land left idle by the large agro-industrial and export companies, and in the areas peripheral to those sectors. The smallholders in the agricultural subsistence sector – the majority of the rural population – were poorly represented in this movement. The Alliance for Progress, which saw the light of day at the end of the 1950s, was significant in that it coincided with the only civilian government able to vote in a land reform legislation, a process cut short by the intervention of the military in the political process in 1963. The persistence of social conflicts encouraged the state, until the end of the 1960s, to engage in a number of peasant collective land settlement pilot projects situated mainly on lands abandoned by the agricultural export companies. Finally, the 1969 war between Honduras and El Salvador left behind a legacy of fervent reformist nationalism favourable to revisionary policies, of which the Land Reform Act became the strategic centrepiece. These developments coincided with an international climate that favoured the type of populist reforms taking place all over Latin America in that period.

The Workshop

The most salient features of the agrarian struggle were the land invasions by groups of peasants, from a couple of dozen individuals to much larger groups. The peasants tried to give legitimacy to their actions by engaging in land cultivation as soon as lands were seized, thus giving a new legitimacy and destination to lands that had been left fallow for considerable periods of time. This practice raised a number of questions: was the work on the land to be done on a collective or on an individual basis? If the former, then the question as to how the group ought to organize so that the problems threatening its survival as a group could be tackled arose immediately from there. How best to use the available time of all the members in the group? And how to administer goods held in common? What structures were to be created for a smooth flow of information and the build-up of confidence among the members? How to organize, also, so as to obtain and consolidate outside help?

The contribution of the Campesino Capacitation Programme for Land Reform (PROCCARA), and in particular its proposal that experimental workshops might contain the right answer to those questions, was very important, for the good reason that the workshop dealt with precisely the type of real-life questions posed by the majority of the new land settlers and also because it provided an institutional framework capable of rapidly converting an idea into an action and a force.[3] Subsequent agrarian legislation gave preference to collective endowments and retrospectively legitimized the *de facto* land seizures that had taken place.[4] The problem of how to administer land held in common then became a matter for the agricultural extension services. The experimental workshop approach was taken on board in Honduras by the public sector. In practice, the capacitation of the land settlers and peasant leaders took place by means of 'course'-type workshops, which provided for the formation the technical personnel needed in the first instance. In the rural areas the method was multiplied and became the backbone in the formation of cadres or enterprise leaders who would typically attend 15–20-day workshops in *ad hoc* capacitation centres.[5] Of the 210 workshops held in that period, 126 (60 per cent) took place in capacitation centres, while the remainder were field workshops organized especially in the land settlements.[6] The heaviest level of workshop activity was in the agricultural export sector, in the northern zone of the country. In total, 17,400 campesinos attended those workshops, representing 39 per cent of all the members or the heads of household in the new land settlements in operation by 1976 (44,700 families in total). This demonstrates that it is entirely feasible to apply the method on a massive scale. On the other hand, such a massive cover by the method was possible only because participation in the OW learning events does not require preparatory schooling or a minimum level of literacy.[7] After all, to organize oneself for survival does not require much more than the need to do so, and having an idea on how to put to the best advantage scarce resources.[8] An intense level of national as well as international (Latin American) interest and participation in the workshops was noted on the part of employees, students and public sector officials, involving, in all, more than 450 persons. But the principal emphasis of this form of formation of adults was on the capacitation of the capacitators in the method. This formation goes to the very roots of the workshop and demands that one experiences it in practice; this, alone, will allow a proper, experiential knowledge of how it works. In this way 300 persons were trained on behalf of the National Agrarian Institute (INA) of whom one-quarter came to occupy positions of direct responsibility in the capacitation of the campesinos. Eventually 500 persons in total were appointed.

The OW and the Private Sector

By 1976 there was a marked slowing down in the agrarian reform process. But, at the same time, there was also a decline in the rate of occupancy of new land; land settlement nevertheless remained the main arm of INA strategy until the beginning of the 1980s, which meant that the methodology remained in constant use, albeit not on as massive a scale as before. This also meant that the method was able amply to demonstrate what it was capable of. As from 1977 a start was made with transferring the method to the private sector. There it was used principally as a working model in the development and strengthening of enterprises, cooperatives and peasant groups. This happened principally in two ways: through the new practices the personnel trained on behalf of INA brought to other institutions, and by the method being adopted as an institutional practice. A leading private institution in the application of the method was the Honduran Institute for Rural Development (IHDER), which first concentrated its technical training methods on the enterprises, groups and cooperatives of the Atlantic region, the export crop-producing zone of Honduras. This lasted from 1978 to 1982.

Strengthening of Group Management

Both public and private sector capacitation initiatives in Honduras were concentrated in the Atlantic region, where the communal settlements consisted of an average of 25 peasants per enterprise, with a person-to-land ratio of 6 hectares, concentrated in relatively compact zones (15 or more settlements each) with a high agricultural potential, which allowed them to become bases for second-degree organizations, such as Choloma, Guanchias, San Manuel, Guaymas, Lean, Música, Jutiapa, Isletas and Bajo Aguan.[9] These enterprises specialized in export or agro-industrial produce and came to represent a sizeable section of total land under cultivation in the country. This provided the objective conditions for enriching the organizational expertise of simple agricultural hand labour in coping with production processes of far higher complexity than they were typically accustomed to in their former peasant environment. Another important dimension was the ownership in common of a number of indivisible resources held in common (common resource pool), which implied the need to organize along the type of democratic principles prevailing in businesses held in common. This in turn gave rise to an important inversion in the way people learn management methods. The workshop became wellspring and basis of the process; it also led to a more selective training of administrative cadres and of technicians competent in rural development promotion matters. The about turns in the way productive capital is structured that were realized in those zones represent the most salient features brought about in the course of the agrarian reform and possibly represent the most important achievements, on a national level, in the 1970s. Of these three zones, three managed to develop themeselves: Guanchias, Guaymas and Bajo Aguan. Of those three, Guaymas was without doubt the most successful and noted for its innovations in terms of capacitation for conditions of collective ownership. We will come back to this later.

The 'Centre' Workshops

As we have seen, 'centre' workshops played an important role in Honduras. They were responsible for the formation of cadres for the implementation of collectively managed enterprises. Most of those taking part in the centre workshops were ordinary peasants, and they were joined by experts and functionaries of the national public sector, the international development organizations and representatives from other countries in Latin America. The results of those centre workshops were less well documented, mainly because doing so was a massive enterprise. But we can venture the following hypotheses concerning the graduates of the workshops:

- Where participating peasants came from an enterprise that enjoyed some form of field assistance, this enterprise was intended to become a support base for others, which, in most of the cases, was what actually happened.
- Where campesinos came from enterprises or settlements that did not benefit from any form of support, their principal objective was to improve the organizational management skills of their own enterprise. However, some factors did not seem to correspond with the hypothesis. In the case of technical personnel, they made use of the workshops in a variety of ways:
- Where technicians were already involved in capacitation work, the experience helped them to deepen their knowledge of the method in a practical manner so that they were able to better reproduce it for the benefit of others later. At a later stage they would add to this a better knowledge about the role of the workshop director and the different phases through which the director had to accompany the group.
- In the case of experts not attached to national institutions or belonging to national institutions not involved in development projects, the main benefit for them consisted in gaining inside knowledge of the method and in finding ways and means of applying it. In Central America the method was thus applied in many instances, based on the Honduran experience, for example in a number of cooperative contexts or in land settlement initiatives.

An Example: The Agro-industrial Complex of Guaymas

As mentioned before, the most successful enterprise to come out of the workshops, and one that, moreover, has survived for more than twenty years and continues to develop, is the agro-industrial 15,000-hectare complex of Guaymas. Guaymas is situated in a zone on the Atlantic west coast. Agriculturally, it belongs to the wet tropics area. In that area there are 66 settlements boasting campesino enterprises representing, at the last count in 1995, 1,800 families, who, in turn, represent 10,000 people. Thirty-two of those enterprises cultivate African oil palm (5,200 ha). In 1995 this complex represented 23.5 per cent of the total land area in Honduras planted with oil palm. It also represented 23 per cent of the total national production of fresh palm products, which means a yield of 22.5 tons per ha, better than the 17.92 per cent national average. The primary producers sell their produce to Hondupalma, an agro-industrial complex they themselves have set up. It comprises a processing plant capable of yielding 25 tons of oil per hour. They sell their produce at a price slightly lower than that of similar processing plants in the area. The enterprise itself refines the different types of oils: crude, almond oil, almond flour, refined oils, oil fats and margarine. More than 60 per cent of the production is exported, thus generating foreign exchange for the country. By 1995 the agro-industrial enterprise was the largest in the country, generating, in 1994, American $1.9 million, while its assets cover 2.68 times its liabilities.

The group was able to acquire the factory plant thanks to a loan obtained from the Dutch government, guaranteed by the Honduran government. The sum involved amounted to $12.5 million, with a remaining balance of $3 million. The enterprise that runs the processing plant is a joint venture by the 32 primary enterprises and is juridically an entity separate from them. Each primary enterprise boasts its own organizational set-up, normally based on the structures created with the help of IHDER and the capacitation acquired in the course of the OWs. The agro-industrial enterprise is structured along the lines of a general assembly, with three representatives from each field base (primary) enterprise. Together, they elect the administrative board. The president of this board is in charge of the overall running of the enterprise. The board is elected for two years so as allow the administration the necessary continuity. There can be only one election in those two years. Ten operational departments, all operating on the basis of the division of work in the plantations, the processing and marketing of the product, report back to the management. Specialized technical tasks are performed by contracted-in personnel, but there is a general policy of continuing formation of cadres drawn from the primary enterprises so as to relieve dependence on non-member expertise. Also, as a general policy, the enterprise provides secondary and higher studies scholarships to one son or one daughter per member per year. Investment in education stands at $70,000.00 per year. The membership draws an annual income equivalent to $2,700 per year, which is almost four times the average Honduran annual income. The enterprises represent an astonishing 19 per cent of the total rural population considered to be affluent. With these kinds of above-average incomes (for Honduras) the families can provide for their basic needs as well as launch into small family enterprises, as many do. Not counting the membership, another 600 permanent jobs have been generated with an annual pay of $1,250.00, almost double the local average income.

As regards social provision, there are a total of five centres with 700 houses that have running water and electricity. The enterprise also provides health services in a health centre erected in the area, serviced by medical personnel from the surrounding urban centres. Primary schooling also receives subsidies from the enterprise. The enterprise is the biggest fiscal contributor to the three municipalities over which it is spread out; it contributes to the diversification of exports and is a substantial contributor to the national finances though direct and indirect taxes.

Limitations and Problems

Needless to say, the *in situ* capacitation by means of the OW has yielded the highest returns in economic, social, educational and other terms. This result is almost always assured in all capacitation that seeks to be an exercise in transformation of practices and habits and aims at equipping people with better options for tackling economic and productive challenges in life. But this is possible only if the exercise takes place in conditions that confront the genuine daily problems of the person at whom the exercise is directed. The workshop was successful mainly in those campesino enterprises that grasped the opportunity of capital injections allowing the creation of a common resource pool and the associated economies of scale these allowed. Once the principle of a common resource pool has been accepted, organization on the basis of a more or less complex division of labour and an – of necessity – collective form of management will naturally follow. This means that producing on an associative membership basis brings with it comparative advantages as well as being a necessary condition for an adequate profitable return on capital outlay. This does not take away from the fact that particular circumstances have contributed to the failure of certain enterprises that otherwise may have looked promising, the agro-industrial complex of Bajo Aguan being just such an example. The differentiating factor is that, while Guaymas works on a basis that is far more independent from the state, occasionally even opposed to the state, Bajo Aguan has been constructed almost solely on the basis of state support involving a costly land colonization process. Nor was there any private input in the technical and social infrastructure of Bajo Aguan. In either case, the level of participation by the primary enterprises marks the main difference in the way they are managed. While the level of participation in the administration of the agro-industrial enterprise of Guaymas is very high, participation at Bajo Aguan never got off the ground. The result was that in the latter high-level corruption and misuse of resources became the rule.

Lessons to be Drawn

Since 1985 the laboratory method along the lines indicated by the IHDER came to be used less, above all because of problems related to an increasingly difficult political conjuncture in the country. Instances of casuistry and insistence on punctuality, for example, became more prominent. This notwithstanding, the continued learning and relearning of the principles of capacitation continued at a steady pace, not only among those directly participating in the experience, but also on the part of institutions and persons involved in development work. Among the lessons learned we can highlight the following:

- Only lived practice capacitates.
- Capacitation must start from the experiences and needs of the *capacitandi* (the learners).
- The necessary conditions must be created opening the necessary space for experiences to be applied in the intended field.
- Only when the learners have adjusted their behaviour and conceptual models to the theme is it possible, little by little, to introduce new alternatives to tackle the same theme.
- A move towards a new practice that allows the adoption by the group of new tools will allow it to live up to its new tasks.
- The new tools and the new, lived practice need to be fed back to the conceptual domain.
- A spirit of constant innovation and of adaptability to constantly changing circumstances needs to be fostered to allow for a harmonious evolution of the method.

These principles are visible in many of the capacitation proposals by public or private sector development organizations. In the period between 1980 and 1998 many other development projects with new training proposals presented themselves to the country. Some have made important contributions in several fields, such as the investigation of the rural sector together with the campesinos and in their actual working conditions, the transfer of knowledge and skills from campesino to campesino, etc. Wherever those methods have met with success, we can recognize the same principles that underlies the success of the workshops.

In matters of campesino organization for agricultural production many proposals have been put forward over the years, especially in terms of participation in, for examle, integrated rural development projects. Many, possibly hundreds, have failed, or have simply been abandoned after the expiry date of those projects. The only experiences that survive and continue to grow are those where a *common resource pool* forms the basis of a collective activity that none of the associates could accomplish on their own; that is to say, wherever there is a comparative advantage in associating with others to produce and grow, people are always well-disposed to make a contribution to that growth, as a group, and not on a mere individual basis. This was the very learning curve the workshops of Guaymas went through: individuals are ready to associate with others and make an enterprise grow in the same measure as the growth of the enterprise also allows the growth of the common good and thereby the good of each member, i.e. in the measure that the members can see the future for themselves and their families. As Fausto Martinez, ex-president of Hondupalma, put it, 'The workshop teaches us to organize and the organization is a seedbed of human values which need to be nurtured and allowed to grow.'

Notes

1. In 1978 coffee overtook bananas as the first export item on the list, with the additional advantage that this crop, unlike bananas, was owned and controlled by local farmers and enterprises.

2. Improved production methods and new banana varieties led to a higher productivity per hectare cultivated. Banana cultivation became much more intensive, with a concomitant reduction in cultivated areas and labour needed. It is estimated that by the end of the 1950s 15,000 land labourers had been thrown out of work.

3. According to a description by PROCCARA at that time, the experimental workshop consists of 'a practical exercise, as well as a theoretical one which allowed a group of participants to internalize the participatory mechanisms of organization at the highest level which the status of the workshop participants would allow. In each case this level will be determined by the praxis which emerges from the role which each individual plays in the productive process with social division of labour. The self-managing enterprise created in each Experimental Workshop will itself provide for the most urgent needs for production-related technical training. More intensive and permanent training emerges from the way itself, the multiple production and service provision activities

organized during the 15 to 20 consecutive days the Workshop lasts' (PROCCARA/INA, 1976) *46 Meses* (46 Months), Honduras, p. 4.

4. Law Decree of Compulsory Lease of 1972 and the Agrarian Reform Law of 1975.

5. Established as from 1976 onwards

6. In the field workshops the level of participation was determined by the number of members of the enterprise plus a number of participants invited from outside.

7. As recently as 1972, 75 per cent of the population could not read or write.

8. It is obvious from case studies of persons who had taken up positions of responsibility in the workshops that these persons had on average a higher level of education than the other participants. This is merely a reflection of what actually takes place in the field. (See IICA, 1978, *Evaluation of the Experimental Workshops*, Costa Rica.)

9. By second-degree enterprises we mean that they were capable of fulfilling, and continue to fulfil, the role of bases for service delivery to grassroots production activities or to the process of rural transformation in general.

70 - 80

7

The Mexican Experience

Juan José Rojas Herrera

The First Field Workshops in the Lacandona Forest (Chiapas)

Mexico came to know about de Morais and the OWs almost by accident, when their originator, Clodomir Santos de Morais', contract with the UN, at the end of 1976, could not be renewed, and because he was unable to go back to Brazil, because of his exile status. He therefore came to Mexico at the invitation of CECODES (Centre for Ecology and Sustainable Development). The first experimental workshop for the formation of organizational cadres took place in the New Ejido Population Centre (NCPE) of Velasco Suárez, municipality of Ocosingo, Selva Lacandona, Chiapas, from 18 February to 18 March 1977.[1] The formal closure took place in the presence of Clodomir Santos de Morais on 11 June of the same year. The new settlement was created in a desperate attempt on the part of the state government to relieve the strong pressure being exerted on the land by the new peasant movement in the high Chiapas. The majority of the new settlers were of Tzeltal extraction, known for their long history of struggle for land. At the time of the workshop, there were 800 Ejido settlers. Together with their families this made for a population of approximately 5,000. Four hundred hectares of the settlement were set aside for collective exploitation. The workshop in Velasco Suárez followed the usual pattern of the 'field'-type workshop (FOW). The commissions that emerged from the introductory processes of the workshop concentrated on health, production, communication and education activities. The courses requested were in automechanics, typing, first aid, woodwork, forestry, accountancy, lime production, rural journalism, baking and cooking. One of the important outcomes of the workshop was the construction of a 'people's house', large enough to hold all the heads of household of the NCPE and entirely constructed by the community itself. Other achievements were: a Spanish–Tzeltal newspaper, printed with appropriate technology; the renovation and repair of the Tumbo–Velasco–Suárez road and the acquisition of two pick-up trucks for collective use by the community.

The 28,000 peso grant ($4,000) from the Economic and Social Development Insititute for Indigenous Mexicans (DESMI) was used to finance the launching of different projects, such as the bakery project and the construction of a 5-ton lime oven, which was later sold cheaply to the settlers of NCPE. During the capacitating event a goods and services production enterprise called Benito Juárez was founded, with Nicolas Bolom as its first president. Perhaps the most important aspect of this mass capacitation experience, and one that more fully casts into relief the full extent of its original objectives, is that a number of persons who passed through the Velasco Suárez capacitation event at a later stage became the coordinators of three other field workshops that took place both in Velasco and in Nueva Palestina, in the Lacandona forest area proper and on the basis of which the membership organizations Emiliano Zapata, Lazaro Cárdenas and Francisco Villa were set up.

The Field OW of Tampaón San Luís Potosí

Tampaón is in the Gulf region of Potosí, a region dominated by shrubland vegetation and with a rainy tropical climate. One of the most salient features of this coastal region area of the Gulf of Mexico is its enormous hydrological potential, as thousands of millions of cubic metres of turquoise water pass through the plain where the rivers Pujal, Coy and Tampaón join with the Moctezuma to form the Pánuco river, which, unfortunately, carries this enormous hydrological resource straight to the Gulf of Mexico, without bringing any significant benefit to the agricultural and cattle-ranging industries of the region, for lack of hydrological infrastructure. Until the end of the 1980s beef cattle formed the predominant industry, which, as a widespread practice, was predatory and was never actually profitable, either, because it was inherently incapable of harmoniously integrating the region. Unprecedented rural and urban unemployment and under-employment were the hallmarks of this region. Most affected by the unchecked growth of the industry were the Tenek, Nahuatl and Pamé ethnic groups, who, since the time of colonization, were forced to seek refuge in the wooded hill areas of the Potosí watershed. It was the marginalized and socially excluded status of this sector that made it into the trigger region that was to play a leading role in the most important agrarian struggles in this region. This struggle for land culminated in the formation of the so-called Land and Freedom Camp of 1974. It was a movement that was subjected to strong repressive measures on the part of the paramilitaries operating on behalf of the large estate owners of the region. July 1975 marked its terminal decline with the murder of its leader, Eusebio García 'Chevo'. No sooner had the independent peasant organization been beheaded than the government, both state and federal, embarked on a strategy aimed at the creation of different semi-official organizations willing to collaborate, from a 'no-contest', institutional position, in the execution of a number of agrarian reform and development plans. It was in this context also that the organizations Populations in Needing Land in the Potosí Bay Valley, at the beginning of the 1980s, and the Alliance of Peasant Producers of the Potosí Bay, in 1991, were set up. Both institutions formed part of the national Campesino Central Office (CNC).

Traditional large-scale cattle farmers of the Bay of Mexico, such as Gonzalo N. Santos, had, by the 1970s, become a huge obstacle to the economic and political modernization of the region. The federal government, through its Secretariat for Agrarian Reform, therefore embarked, in 1976, on a series of massive land expropriations. Not only were the farmers indemnified but they were also allowed to hang on to important pieces of land provided they complied with the 'small cattle range' provisions of the law. Around the same time, as part of the National Hydrological Plan, the Agricultural and Water Resources Secretariat (SAHR) put its weight behind the Wet Tropics Integrated Rural Development Project (PRODERITH) set up by Clodomir Santos de Morais, who, by then, had been appointed national director of the FAO–UNDP Mex74/006. It was the intention, to launch, with the financial support of the World Bank, the most ambitious irrigation project seen in recent times, with the damming off of the rivers Pujal, Coy and Tampaón, so as to form an enormous water catchment. The project also included the refurbishment of old canals, roads and other hydrological works, which would convert the bay area of Potosí into an agro-industrial region of international significance.

The new *ejido* (Common Land) Population Centres (NCPEs), such as Tampaón, was part of an overall effort to push public landownership from 18.3 per cent to 78.2 per cent, leaving 21.8 per cent of the remainder to small landholding occupation. The *ejido* settlement population was made up to a great extent of racially mixed (*mestizo*) people from the different urban centres. They therefore only partly integrated with the indigenous Tenek and Nahuatl peasants of the region. In fact, two indigenous groups in the region refused point blank to join, because they could not abandon the land of their ancestors. They entertained the hope, however, that some of the settlement area would be established as near as possible to their communities, as they had always advocated.

In Stage I of the project the federal government put hydrological infrastructure, rural credit, modern machinery and equipment at the disposal of the new *ejido* inhabitants. The intention was to create the material conditions for the emergence of a new type of *ejido* farmer, free from the inhibitions of mini-fundism (small leaseholding). Three such *ejido* settlements were established on 31 March 1976 in the new *ejido* settlement of Tampaón. Tampaón itself was at one time a small cattle, agricultural and pasture holding, which was expropriated, against idemnification, from its previous owners. By the end of 1978, the year the OW was first experimented with in Tampaón, a total of seven *ejido* common landholdings covering a total of 3,386 hectares – 3,196 under irrigation and 190 of all-weather fields – had been established. As these lands had been recovered from the rough scrubland surfaces without preparatory land-levelling works, they were interspersed with important stretches of existing woodland. The initial group was 306 strong, each receiving an allocation of 10 hectares of irrigated land. The 326 remaining hectares were set aside for collective use. Tampaón, at the time of the introduction of the OW, held 230 palm and wooden houses anarchically scattered all over the area. Even though the new settlers, by force of circumstances, were confined to the same space, they were in reality segregated from each other and did certainly not form what one could call a 'community'.

The original motivation to take part in the OW appears to have been a general feeling that it would help them in devising ways and means to manage the public services needed in a burgeoning human settlement as well as in getting to grips with the management of the irrigation district. There was also a feeling that by setting up an autonomous organization, they might prevent the district from falling again into the hands of the landowner class and being managed as a pure business venture, as had happened so often before. Here was a unique opportunity for laying the foundations for the emergence of an authentic integrated community, notwithstanding its original heterogeneous make-up. From this perspective the capacitation of the new settlers appeared as an ideal instrument with which to reach the set goals. It was even more attractive because it differed from the traditional training provided by the government-sponsored 'INCA Rural', which all miserably failed because of their distinct clientelist and paternalist style. The challenges were enormous: what was at stake was not just getting the settlement going in a functional and profitable manner, but also establishing an entirely new, properly equipped and socially integrated urban centre. A final decision made by PRODERITH, in conjunction with the federal government, was to call in the services of CECODES and to request the services of Clodomir Santos de Morais, then head of operations of 'Project 74/006'.

The Tampaón OW

The Tampaón 'Field Workshop for the Formation of Organizers of Peasant Enterprises' was run in the *ejido* centre Nueva Tampaón, Tamuin municipality, from 23 January to 26 February 1978. In the beginning it stuck to a 18–21-hour timetable but at a later stage, it ran for as long as and whenever the groups felt needs arose. Participating institutions were the former Secretariat for Agriculture and Hydrological Resources (at present known as the Commission for Hydrological Planning, the National Hydrological Plan – CPNH) and the Multiservice Educational Enterprise, which integrated seven *ejidos* of the region. This enterprise was created at the time the OW itself was being set up. The workshop was part of a number of promotional and organizational activities realized in Mexico under the wings of PRODERITH (Wet Tropics Integrated Rural Development Project), which, as already mentioned, was set up in the 1970s with the help of the World Bank to initiate large irrigation schemes that would boost agricultural output considerably, thereby improving the living conditions of the peasants. The workshop was inaugurated on 24 January 1978 with a total attendance of 485 peasant farmers who came from seven common land *ejido* settlement inside Tampaón, although, in the end, only 277 men and women were accepted.

Overall coordination of the workshop was in the hands of the agronomist Frederico Porras, of Nicaraguan nationality, whose services as organizer of peasant enterprises were used to good effect by CECODES. He was assisted by the agronomists Gerardo Valencia and Msc. Ofelia Casamadrid, both in the employ of PRODERITH. Participating in the proceedings, as evaluator, was Clodomir Santos de Morais, representing the UN organization FAO and fulfilling the functions incumbent on the leadership of the FAO–UNDP project Mex74/006. There were 23 instructors involved in the theoretical lectures provided during the workshop: ten PRODERITH representatives; eight from the representative body of the the Panuco lower river plain, the SARH; a representative of the Bank of Mexico; one from the Commission for the Study of the Guayas River Plain (Guayaquil, Ecuador); two from the enterprise 'TV and Sports', and one from the Ecological Development Centre. These persons, because of their competence in theoretical matters, also acted as evaluators of the work commissions that got together the participants of the capacitation event.

As a first organizational measure, the participants decided to set up a joint commission of seven directors, one from each *ejido*, which they called the Educational Entreprise New Tampaón. They also immediately elected a person in charge of stores, where the 'common-pool resources' of the enterprise were held, consisting of typewriters, cooking implements, electrical tools, duplicators, calculators, soil drills for collecting soil samples, medicinal stores, as well as educational materials. An editor for the new journal, *The Voice of Tampaón*, was also elected. The first issue of the journal was published on 25 January. In total five issues of this journal would have appeared by the end of the workshop. On 25 January the first of the very important 'Theory of Organization' lecture series was given, arranged by the OW course director Nemesio Porras Miedieta. On the 27th the Education Committee announced the 23 courses in which the participants had expressed interest. Here are the different kinds of courses requested with the learner numbers in parentheses: health nursing (35), plumbing (4), sewing (31), accountancy (5), carpentry (12), radio and television (18), general mechanics (80), adult literacy (17), veterinary sciences (10), entymology (10), needlework (31), apiculture (10), electricity (18), cattle raising (10), brickwork (4), mechanics (14), baking (19), agriculture (10), cooking (6), soldering (18), confectionery (16), tractor mechanics (80), driving skills (80). The courses started officially on 30 January.

On 28 January the board of the education entreprise determined that it would be necessary to group the peasant participants into work committees. Twenty committees were created: Finance, Irrigation, Education, Security, Administration, Consumption, Agriculture, Cattle Raising, Forestry, Journalism, Storage, Water, Electricity, Health, Sports, Social Work, Marketing, Transport, Industry and Construction. These were formally integrated on 1 February. Each one was assigned an evaluator. The basic tasks of those commissions consisted of: a) realizing practical tasks related to mastering the art of self-management; and b) elaborating simple projects for the coordination of immediate activities to facilitate participation of the members of the enterprise. On 3 February, the General Assembly met for the first time, with 260 farmers present. The general coordination of this assembly was done by the capacitation team.

Twenty Years on: Some Preliminary Evaluations

Twenty years after the Tampaón workshop drew to a close, a workteam, composed of personnel of the Department of Rural Sociology of the University of Chapingo, returned there in July 1998 and carried out an evaluation from which we relate the most important points, both good and bad.

Positive points On the positive side there are some striking features: first, the transformation of the former backwater of Tampaón into a real, full-sized city of 4,000 inhabitants covering eleven *ejidos*. It is an adequately planned town, moreover, with all the usual urban services and infrastructure, except for a drainage system and proper street hardening. Some features of the town have a definite modern touch – there is a wide central four-lane avenue with a central divider, as well as a generously big central square with its typical kiosk constructed on the model of the kiosk in the central square of the town of Tamuín. The urban allotments are 40 by 25 metres and the majority of the housing is built with brick walls and concrete roofs. There are also plenty of green and recreational spaces, piped water, street lighting, electricity and two public phone-booths. Transport to the Tamuín–Tampico trunkroad and to Tamuín is frequent and cheap, serviced by a flotilla of microbuses owned by Tampaón locals. There are virtually no public safety problems because security is a community affair in which the whole community takes part; also because alcohol consumption is out of bounds for the under-20s. There is, moreover, a clinic staffed by the Ministry of Health and Welfare, and there are two educational centres leading from primary all the way to the baccalaureate.

Second there are the advances in 'human development': the emergence of a culture of conviviality, i.e. knowing 'how to' live together in a plural society imbued with tolerance for racial, religious and political differences among the inhabitants of the settlement. Therefore, all the participants in the OW, to a lesser or greater degree, achieved a noticeable increase in personal self-esteem. The realization of the enormous internal potential allowed them to reproduce inside the family circle less 'macho' relationships than are common in the wider rural environment in the country. As a collective, they learned to rely on their own resources and to resolve the problems that affect them as an urban centre through democratic consent in the General Assembly. For the management and representation of issues that affect them in relation to the different government instances, they use the method of the social division of labour by appointing rotating task commissions with the more responsible persons in the community in charge.

Negative points On the minus side, we have to signal, first, and paradoxically, the failure to bring to a successful conclusion all the collective projects that would have been possible had the settlers made a more radical use of the enormous natural resources at their disposal: for all practical purposes the *ejido* system has been abandoned and each of the *ejido* settlers works their land parcel individually. The influence of the official institutions has not been foreign to the gradual loss of the location's collective character. Officialdom consistently treated the *ejido* members as if they were individual, private producers.

Second, the enterprise charged with educational services, with its different commissions, which were among the important achievements of the original OW, were allowed to disintegrate. No alternative structure capable of dealing with community problems has taken its place. Existing structures are the usual official ones: the Assembly for Improvements, presided over by a judge, has authority to act in an auxiliary capacity to the Local Committee of the Union for Regional Ejidos which, in turn, forms part of the Alliance of Peasant Producers of the Bay of Potosí. In actual fact, none of the official bodies in Potosí is controlled by the founder members, but is rather in the hands of the new generation of leaders who arrived in Tampaón post-1978.

A number of factors explain the lack of continuity in the organizational processes that came out of the original OW. These include:

- The absence of a consistent, continuing capacitation programme for both founder members and new settlers, which would have allowed the setting up of new enterprises in response to shifting situations.
- The constant influx, over the years, into the *ejido* centre of Tampaón, of newcomers with an almost infinite range of backgrounds and expectations. In the absence of an integrating factor, the community spirit has suffered, social ghettos have been allowed to creep in and there has been a marked decrease in social participation and initiatives taken in common.
- In the opposite direction there has been a constant outflow through emigration, especially to the USA, especially of younger members of the community. It is estimated that about 45 per cent of all the youngsters born in Tampaón have gone to work in the USA.
- Article 27 of the 1992 Reform Law, which legalized the renting and outright sale of *ejido* plots, inevitably allowed land to be concentrated in the hands of a new type of private farmer who, little by little, introduced improved stock, artificial pasturelands and big cattle-fattening practices involving thousands of head of cattle, while, at the same time, the *ejido* production continued as before, with its outdated practices and technologies, not capable of providing a real employment-generating alternative.

Interlude: Official Recognition by the Mexican Authorities

Seven years after the OW event, Clodomir Santos de Morais, then guest lecturer at the University of Rostock, Germany, where he was finishing his doctoral thesis, received an invitation by Fernando Gonzáles Vuillareal, of the SRH, who was the PRODERITH counterpart in 1978, to come to Mexico for the occasion of the signing of a new financial funding convention by the World Bank in support of the PRODERITH projects. On 15 January 1985, Dr de Morais was officially welcomed at the airport of Benito Juárez, Mexico City. The following day, in the central offices of PRODERITH, they showed him the video of the original

Tampaón organization workshop, immediately followed by a colour film on the new Tampaón illustrating all the important advances in urban installations of the *ejido* centre. In the evening of the same day, Dr Clodomir participated in the solemn signing of the Financing Convention of PRODERITH by the World Bank, realized thanks to the resourcefulness of the then secretary of agricultural and water resources. This was an apt gesture and a way of paying tribute to the creator of the mass capacitation method.

The Enterprise Workshop and Entrepreneurial Management Workshop (EMW) in Huatusco, Vera Cruz

In February 1996, Msc. Miguel Sobrado Chaves of the National University of Costa Rica was invited to Huatusco, Vera Cruz, to investigate in a direct fashion the feasibility of a workshop there and to determine which type of capacitation methodology would best apply here. Sobrado's subsequent report indicated that such an event was indeed feasible, based on a number of existing associative enterprises that shared a number of production resources in common, but which, at the same time, in the new context of liberalization of the Mexican economy, would not necessarily be able to respond to the new challenges in terms of competencies needed in an era of the open capitalist market economy. The main problem in the region of Huatusco, Vera Cruz, was the urgent need to capacitate the coffee producers, in the light of the recent presidential decree abolishing the Mexican Institute for Coffeegrowers, a federal government organism, formerly in sole charge of coffee production and marketing matters. All the infrastructural functions (plantations, coffeehouses, machinery, transport, etc.) of the now defunct institute were to be transferred to the producer organizations, who lacked the basic management know-how and skills – they were not adequately prepared mentally, socially, economically or administratively to manage an enterprise. The need for rapid and practical capacitation, in which paternalistic and dependency-creating structures could be overcome, imposed itself.

A workshop for entrepreneurial management (TGE – taller de gestión empresarial) was run in May 1996. One of the crucial moments of the workshop was the so-called 'weaning' exercise, lasting three days. This was found particularly necessary as the attendants at the course manifested a great resistance to thinking for themselves, taking responsibility, making decisions. Workshops were run at area level and the participants transmitted to their local organization or institution the methodology they had learned at the TGE. The General Union, set up in 1990, had remained, until then, virtually a letterhead organization. Its membership has now reached

1,800 producers in 45 communities. The union produces a quality organic coffee known under the trade name 'Genuine Huatusco'. The union runs an original collective harvest gathering system. A new ecological awareness has emerged about the possibilities of growing coffee in more environment-friendly ways. Vertical, hierarchical, army-type command structures have been done away with and decisions are now reached by collective decision-making. Power relationships in the enterprise also underwent a sea change, thus laying the foundation for a more collectivist culture and an economy of solidarity. The union is, however, still discriminated against by private banks, which feel that social organizations are 'not creditworthy'.

Conclusion

The Mexican experience with the OW can be divided into a pre- and post-1996 period. The first wave of OWs in Mexico did result in an autonomous movement covering the whole nation, but a long history weighed down by clientelism and corporativism in Mexico seems to have been too great for the entire potential of the method of mass capacitation to come into its own in our country. Added to this must be the non-participation of the great majority of Mexican universities: this has severely limited a more widespread knowledge about and systematic analysis of the method.

The events of the 1990s are still in full evolution. They are taking place against the background of a democratic transition and a keener interest, in academia, especially on the part of the Autonomous University of Chapingo, all of which seem to justify new hope. In retrospect, it would appear that it was the solid results obtained by the agrarian reform in Honduras that were the determining factor in making the Mexican authorities realize the unique value of the de Morais workshop methodology. In 1974 for example, Lic. Sergio Reyes Osorio, then minister for Mexican agrarian reform, decided to send a 30-strong delegation, all members of the human settlement project of the Rio Papalápan, to learn capacitation methods in the Guanchias Cooperative in Honduras so that they could reproduce the method in Mexico. The political atmosphere under President Luis Echeverría (1970–76), however, became less favourable to this approach. Things improved under the presidency of José López Portillo, when the capacitation events of the Lacandona forest and Tampaón took place. On balance, the Tampaón and Selva Lacandona experiments can said to have been successful in that they managed to integrate new population centres with settlers from disparate origins in a terrain originally not very favourable to agricultural activities. In both experiments, the 'common pool' around which self-capacitation developed consisted – beyond and above, of course, the land itself – of the production plots allocated to the new settlers, the audio-visual teams, the sound and image reproduction equipment that allowed, for example, for the production of manuals and newspapers and also the educational installations and materials.

A clear lack of continuity in the capacitation effort, however, has to be deplored. A nationwide SIPGEI, with its national economic development specialists (TDEs), on the model first set up by de Morais in Portugal, is the missing factor here in Mexico. Self-managing enterprises, and the economic autonomy they bring to ethnic groups in the land, went against the grain, in particular, of the National Institute for Indigenous Affairs (INI), known for being set in its protectionist and clientelist ways. The PROCCARA programme, directed by Clodomir Santos de Morais, lasted a total of 46 months. During that crucial period of 1974–76, on top of the significant achievements obtained in Honduras, where 25 members of the Honduran armed forces also took part in the OWs, very positive effects were also recorded in other Latin American countries because the 'centre' workshops in Las Guanchias in Honduras had also been attended by rural development workers from Nicaragua, Guatemala, El Salvador, Mexico, Costa Rica, the Dominican Republic, Venezuela, Colombia and Peru. The mass capacitation experiments set up by PRODERITH in Mexico, influenced by the success of the Honduran model, can be seen as, *de facto*, the initial stages of SIPGEIs. Because of inertia and internal friction these were inhibited in their further logical development.

Note

1. *Ejido*: Mexican term, meaning land held and cultivated in common.

8

The OW in Panama, Colombia, Venezuela, Ecuador and Peru

Miguel Sobrado[1]

The Agrarian Reform in Panama

The agrarian reform in Panama pushed through by General Torrijo, after the nationalist coup of 1969, only reached the conflict zones of the country, where large estates were expropriated and landless agricultural labourers settled instead. The head of the Panamanian Agrarian Reform Board, who became later the minister of agriculture and livestock, Eng. Nilson Espino, adopted the 'Honduran model' of rural development, which implied large-scale land settlements based on collectivist ownership and production. The 280 enterprises of that type banded together in CONAC (National Confederation of Campesino Land Settlements) under the leadership of the agricultural worker Julio Bermudez. In the capacitation centre in Divisa in the municipality of Penonome, Cocle Province, and in other locations in the republic, more than 2,000 learners took part in the OW learning events organized by CONAC. The Honduran academics Carlos Tovar and Oscar Leivas Cerrato were respectively field workshop and centre course directors here.

Colombia

The agronomists Nemesio Porras and Luis Porras, during the 1980s, introduced the massive capacitation method in the Darien, an area near the Colombia border, where they organized a large-scale field OW among the population of the Pacific coast, in Guarachine, financed by the ILO's PREALC representative (Regional Employment Programme for Latin America and the Caribbean), Lic. García Huidobro, and by the representative for the IICA (International Institute for Cooperation in Agriculture). Also extending a helping hand in the massive capacitation effort were Costa Ricans from the team of the Universidad Nacional of Costa Rica (UNACR) as well as Iván Labra, who was in Panama at that time. As a result of this workshop, numerous enterprises, as well as a monthly newspaper, were created. Professor in sociology at the National University of Costa Rica Jorge Mora Alfaro (now rector at that same university) was the principal initiator of the mass capacitation methodology in Colombia in the 1970s. In the 1980s the Hondurean university professors Carlos Tovar and Leivas Cerrato went to conduct several field OWs in Colombia. In both cases IICA was the sponsoring institution of the OWs in their various forms, conducted by the two aforementioned academics in different locations in Colombia. When a sufficient number of counterparts of the different institutions had been formed, the methodology was further disseminated throughout the principal rural and urban areas of the country, and in total more than one hundred workshops were realized as from 1979, when the national training service, SENA (Servicio Nacional de Aprendizaje – the agrarian learning centre of the region of Córdoba) made its premises available for the purpose.

The first OW in Colombia took place in El Povenir. This was followed by the OWs organized in San Rafael de Cortina, Magangue and Bolivar; there were also the OWs in Carmen de Bolivar, San Jacinto, San Juan and Cartagena from which a number of medium-sized entrepreneurial structures, which grouped dressmakers, iron-workers, electronic specialists, etc., ensued. In all, an estimated four hundred mass capacitation OWs were held in Colombia. The workshops were led by teams made up of the following highly competent professionals: Maria Cadena, Rafael Morales Marin, Jesus Martinez Zuñiga, Omar Gonzalez, Raimundo Guardo Puello, Hernan Gonzalez Londoño and Hugo Escobar Melo. Recognition has to be given to the fact that this was the only team that set out to produce the first manual on the OW method, entitled *Experimental Organization Workshop. A Methodology for Capacitation and Organization*. It is a very substantial document of 208 pages published in 1986 by SENA, and offers a fundamental analysis of Clodomir Santos de Morais' Theory of Organization.

Venezuela

Two outstanding Venezuelan institutes paid great attention to the rural and urban applications of the Mass Capacitation method in Venezuela, namely the National Agrarian Institute of Venezuela (IAN) and the Foundation for Applied Capacitation and Research for Agrarian Reform, better known as the CIARA Foundation (Fundacion para la Capacitación e Investigación Aplicada a la Reforma Agraria), as well as the International Institute for Cooperation in Agriculture (IICA – see Chapter 9 by Leopoldo Sandoval below). The Honduran Oscar Leivas Cerrato and the Chilean Ivàn Labra Moya were the principal pioneers in the introduction of the

OWs in Venezuela. However, present at the first international OW which took place in 1975 in the famous capacitation centre David Funez Villatoro of Guanchias, municipality of Santa Rita, Department of Yoro, Honduras, were several students from Venezuela, prominent among them the agronomist Orlando Sosa Moreno of IAN and Magada Y. and Perozo V. of the CIARA foundation.

At the Seminar on the Method for the Development of Community Campesino Enterprises and Organizational Workshops, which was organized by the CIARA foundation in Caracas in 1980, the IICA, the Institute for Agrarian Capacitation (INAGRO) and IAN, notes and ideas were exchanged on experiences in the application of the mass capacitation method in the Central Western, Central, North Eastern and Andes regions of Venezuela. According to the *Seminar Report on the Method for the Development of Community Enterprises and Organizational Workshops*, published conjointly by IICA, INAGRO, CIARA and IAN, these institutes allowed 96 OW directors, in all, to be actively involved in the running of 286 workshops from which 11,440 campesinos benefited. It concerned a three-pronged strategy: during the initial stage of the plan, from April 1981 to March 1982, 32 workshops were organized in which a total of 1,280 participants took part. During the second stage, 77 workshops benefited 3,080 persons while a third, again, saw a total of 97 OWs with 3,880 beneficiaries.

During the 1980s, just as in the neighbouring Republic of Colombia, a movement promoting the organization of the rural populations around production issues and the generation of employment by means of self-managing community structures spread like wildfire. In some regions in Venezuela where the institutional frameworks were still very backward, 'organization for struggle' was perceived to be the only alternative allowing people to survive in hostile conditions. It was indeed an era very much marked, in both Colombia and Venezuela, by violence in the countryside. It is worth reminding the reader that, back in 1969, the ILO in Geneva, probably exasperated by all the talk about the then 'Social Participation' buzzword (in Clodomir's words, a kind of 'gaseous vertebra' term, but copiously parroted by the various United Nations agencies especially from the 1970s onward), had decided to convene in each continent a symposium in which the idea of social participation was to be thoroughly discussed in order to clear the air. Those called by the ILO to the Latin American continent meeting were thirteen sociologists who stood out for their expertise in social participation matters. They were the Mexicans Paulo Gonzalez Casanova and Rudolfo Stavenhagen; the Argentinians José Nun and Torquato Di Telaq; the Brazilians Fernando Henrique Cardoso, Almino Affonso and Clodomir Santos de Morais; the Chilean Hugo Semelman, the

Colombian Fals Borda, the Peruvian Anibal Quijano, the Haitian Jean Casimir, and the Venezuelan José Michelena.

The symposium carried over into an interminable discussion, followed by yet more discussions by correspondence, lasting several months, until the same group met again for yet another five days of hot debates. The upshot was that the specialists, gathered in the Colegio de Mexico, clarified the correct use of social participation parlance, what it was being used for, how and in what conditions it ought to be used, and also what the 'essence' of the 'social participation' phenomenon was. In the end, the key discussion gravitated around the question as to whether the concept was of any practical use at all, or whether we were not getting lost, yet again, in some academic hall of mirrors. Whatever the case may be, the symposium was an occasion to get to know each other better socially, because the mystification spun around the concept by the United Nations agencies and the Organization of American States (OEA) was enormous. Nevertheless, we had to wait another 30 years before Raff Carmen would call a spade a spade and expose the mystifications (and manipulations) around participation as 'participulation'. Among the more unusual research projects at that time, in the wake of this scientific 'conclave', was the field work done by Orlando Fals Borda, on social participation in the violence-riddled areas of Colombia, and José Michelena's project called 'Social Participation in the Venezuelan Guerrilla Movement'. This only goes to show that even in countries rife with armed conflict it is still possible to disseminate organizational structures based on 'social participation'.

Peru

Peru, under the government of General Alvarado, devised the most radical agrarian reform Latin America saw in the twentieth century. With one stroke of the pen, on 14 June 1969, all the great capitialist enterprises along the Peruvian coast, the majority of which were owned by absent landlords and transnationals, were expropriated. Once the expropriation was complete, the state set out to prepare its workers, employees and salaried agricultural labourers for assuming the task of managing those enterprises. In the maelstrom created by the Peruvian agrarian reform, however, groups of litigants fell out with each other, among them groups of reformers themselves. In any case, amid all these conflicts, there was one constant that kept nudging the agrarian reformists towards collaborating with each other, namely, the urgent need to prepare cadres that ought to guarantee the successful outcome of the reform process. The government applied to the FAO for help in setting up, in Lima, the Centre for Agrarian Reform Capacitation and Research (CENCIRA), while taking a cue from

ICIRA (Capacitation and Research Institute for Agrarian Reform), sponsored by the government of Eduardo Frei in Chile at the beginning of the 1960s.

In contrast to the great contribution to the Chilean agrarian reform by ICIRA, initiated by Frei and later on pursued by Salvador Allende, CENCIRA limited itself to locking up a dozen experts in a room for several years, keeping them sweet with fat international salaries so that they would keep out of the way and not interfere with what the Peruvian revolution considered to be 'its' agrarian vision, based on collectivist principles ranging all the way from the agro-industrial to the industrial sector. Of the entire CENCIRA project's achievements the government allowed only the audio-visual paraphernalia – very avant-garde in those days – to be used in agricultural training. Ten years on, we see the FAO duplicating the same audio-visual programme in its Mexico Project. Because of its novelty value, the technology spoke to the imagination of institutions while the gist was being overlooked, i.e. the need for entrepreneurial capacitation in modes of self-management.

The vogue for Super 8 films and closed circuit TV, about which so much noise was being made just then in the context of space shuttle flight simulators, was then the flavour of the month. As an epilogue to this period it suffices to mention a proliferation of campesino training workshops in the use of audio-visual systems and the simultaneous erection, in some communities, of so-called 'communication centres', which usually consisted of a number of loudspeakers, music centres, and the dissemination of local news provided by means of the amplification systems put at their disposal, usually stored in a small office that also had to serve as the women's regular meeting place. It was not until 1971, when Colonel Basurto, director-in-chief of the National Institute for Cooperativism, inspired by the Gerardo Cardenas Falcon model, accepted the project as proposed by Clodomir Santos de Morais (acting on behalf of the ILO and financed by the Special Fund of the United Nations that specialized in the formation of specialist cadres in knowledge and skills of self-management) that, at long last, the institutional conditions for the application of the methodology, so long postponed in the Peruvian agrarian reform, could be realized. Unfortunately, by the time this project had been approved by the UN fund, Clodomir Santos de Morais had already been appointed director of an identical project in Honduras, namely the PROCARRA programme (see Chapter 6).

The solution adopted by the ILO was to appoint the anthropologist Darcy Ribeiro as director of the Peruvian project, also known now as 'Project SINAMOS' (National System of Social Mobilization). His counterpart was the famous anthropologist Carlos Delgado. In the end, the

SINAMOS project limited itself to 'critical consciousness-raising' projects among the rural producers, without introducing them to the necessary 'organizational consciousness', too, the only way in which the efficient operation of the gigantic enterprises in the Andean Cordillera, run by the former day-labourers, could be assured. Neither did SINAMOS take advantage of the opportunity to foster organizational structures inside INCA PLAN which, (em)powered by the radical Agrarian Reform Law, constituted the political and ideological backbone of the Peruvian military's revolutionary discourse of that time. That is how, when retrograde forces in the Peruvian army organized a coup against the government of General Alvarado, there was neither a party structure nor a national structure for national social participation sufficiently firmly rooted (as might have been the case) in the thousands of distinct forms of self-management, capable of defending the achievements for which the government of Alvarado had taken the responsibility. The consequences, therefore, were very grave. The first thing the right, once in power, did was to dismantle the advances made by General Alvarado's agrarian reform and return the expropriated farms, which had been transferred to the workers, to their former owners.

We cannot even say that the socialist agrarian reform had been cut short. The reform, once destined to change the history of the Peruvian economy, had hardly taken place at all. What had happened was that the former owners had been compensated for the expropriated properties, receiving massive bonus payments, monies they then were able to use to set up new enterprises, industrial sites, or service industries this time. This means that the government had paid them for the import of machinery and back-up credit to finance their new industries. What it all amounted to, in the end, was that what went under the name of agrarian reform consisted of no more than the transfer of agricultural capital to the industrial or service sector. The lack of a properly organized popular base, be it in the Peruvian Revolutionary Party (which SINAMOS never aspired to nor had the permission to set up) or of a great national system of participatory self-managing enterprises, meant that it was not difficult for the right to engineer the total collapse of the revolution and the agrarian reform of General Alvarado. The broad masses of rural and urban producers found themselves therefore orphaned, abandoned and frustrated while hunger devastated the hundreds of thousands, even millions of ex-beneficiaries of the agrarian reform. This resulted in a large void in Peruvian society, which, after ten years, was overrun by militaristic rural movements of urban inspiration such as the Sendero Luminoso or the Tupacamaru.

The Peruvian institutional framework, as from the fall of General Alvarado in 1976, therefore became very thinly based and the great masses of the disinherited in the countryside and in the miserable slums of Lima remained without any organizational perspectives whatsoever. The ALEA (Latin American Association of Self-managing Enterprises) was then created in Lima and managed to realize, in 1980, in the town of San José de Costa Rica, the first continental meeting, with the financial and political backing of the IICA (an OEA organization). At this meeting a board of directors was elected, among them the self-management practitioner Willian Moreno from Peru and the Brazilian Joaquin Lisboa Neto, who had learned the skill of directing the field OWs with Nemesio Porras Medieta in Nicaragua. The application of this methodology led Joaquin Lisboa Neto to found the self-managing enterprise association ADERI (Association for Integrated Rural Development) in Santa Maria de Victoria, in the state of Bahía. Willian Moreno, meanwhile, became the head of ALEA, with its headquarters in Lima, responsible for the formation of many cadres, directors of OWs and initiator of hundreds of events of this type, notwithstanding the institutional limitations imposed by a government hostile to popular movements. Thus it was possible to generate hundreds of new self-managing enterprises in Peru and the way was opened for the generation of workplaces and income generation benefiting the excluded of the countryside and in Peru's towns.

Note

1. This chapter is based on the personal recollections of Clodomir Santos de Morais.

9

Three Decades of Work with OWs in Latin America

Leopoldo Sandoval

Many thousands of millions of dollars have been spent in Latin America and around the world on rural development research and projects financed by the international development community or by individual countries, with, in the end, hardly anything to show for it. This is principally because when enormous sums of money have been poured into shoring up the local infrastructure, in boosting production or social development, the intended beneficiaries have not consciously participated in the problem diagnosis, or in the management of those projects. They therefore have no real ownership or control of the projects and have not been able to use them as stepping-stones for an autonomous and sustainable development. In my opinion the root of all this failure lies in the organizational methodologies that are being promoted. Every person and every development institution worth its salt knows that organization is indispensable and they therefore try to organize people, albeit with traditional and wholly inefficient methodologies.

One of the few methods, if not to say the only one, that has proved again and again its efficiency and, in my personal experience, has the additional qualities of mass application and low cost, is the OW and its related enterprise management workshops. In 1966, as president of the National Institute for Agrarian Transformation (INTA) in Guatemala, I proposed, promoted and initiated rural production cooperatives with the workers of a group of 28 coffee, sugarcane and cattle-producing national estates, which were all that remained of over one hundred estates expropriated from their German owners after the Second World War. In those days we did not know about the method that is the subject of this chapter, and the experiences in collective production in Israel, the USSR or China did not really suit our Guatemalan conditions.

Because of backstage political shenanigans I was obliged to leave my post at INTA prematurely without having been able fully to realize my objective of developing the aforementioned cooperatives, but I remained firmly convinced that this model would be valid for agrarian development in Guatemala and Latin America in general. After my resignation from INTA, in 1968, I joined the International Institute for Cooperation in Agriculture (IICA) where I continued to work for fourteen years on agrarian reform and rural development promotion and capacitation programmes for Central America and Latin America as a whole. I encountered situations that allowed me to develop my concerns and enrich my experiences. In particular there was the thrust given to the idea of the campesino community enterprises as the principal strategy of the agrarian reform programmes advanced by the IICA and 'Project 206' of the Organization of American States, in the course of which I was privileged to meet people endowed with considerable vision in rural development matters, such as Victor Gímenez Landinez (Venezuela), Enrique Torres Llosa (Peru), Armando Samper (Colombia) and José Emilio Araujo (Brazil). Those campesino community enterprises were the exact equivalent of what I had envisioned with the cooperative rural estates I had been planning to develop in Guatemala.

Also extraordinary was meeting, in the same period, Clodomir Santos de Morais and Miguel Sobrado, to mention just the two most important personalities. My subsequent responsibilities as minister for agriculture of my country and functionary of the FAO for Latin America allowed me to promote the development of the method. The above-mentioned events allowed the coming together, in one fortunate historical moment, of the persons, the method, the political and institutional opportunity (at the level of my own country and of the continent at large) to champion and initiate an idea, a methodology and a movement that meant a real chance to reach not only the elusive objective of rural development but also of development, full stop, in the countries of the Third World. It is beyond the bounds of this short chapter to explain the concrete experiences and achievements with the method in Honduras, Mexico, Costa Rica, Brazil, the Dominican Republic, Colombia, Nicaragua, Panama, Guatemala, Zimbabwe, Botswana, Mozambique and other countries, all of which constitute a living testimony to the efficacy of the method.

However, I cannot fail to refer, in general terms, to the concrete experiences I had the privilege to witness or to live through myself. Outstanding among those is the work with groups of illiterates in Guatemala who, moreover, speak only their own native language: the members of the cooperative estates that currently belong to the FEDECOVERA, whose language is *Keckchí*, in the north of Guatemala, as well as a *Tzutuhile* women's group in Santiago Atitlán, on the shores of Lake Atitlán, in the centre of the country. Other experiences, such as those of Guanchías and COAPALMA and HONDUPALMA in Honduras and the cooperative El Silencio and others, which form the production cooperative FECOOPA in

Costa Rica, are achievements that have endured more than 25 years, each one representing a living testimony to the method's efficacy.

As for the case of Honduras, the work realized by PROCCARA under the directorship of Clodomir Santos de Morais has already been amply documented in Chapter 6. Between 1978 and 1982 the IICA, as part of the programmes of which I was in charge, developed a project called 'Development of the Campesino Community Enterprises' for Central America and the Dominican Republic. One of the principal offshoots of this project was the formulation of a methodology specifically for the training and development of those enterprises, in which the workshop was included as the first stage and the entrepreneurial management workshops as consecutive stages.[1] Unfortunately, because of a change of personnel and institutional policies at the highest level in the IICA in 1982, this methodology was put on ice and eventually disappeared in the IICA archives. Due credit must be given to the financial support provided for this project by the Dutch government, with particular thanks to the minister of development cooperation of that time, Peter van Ginneken, a rural development expert who was aware of the exceptional efficacy of the method and who tirelessly supported its development on other occasions from the different government positions he held. Also important was the research work of Cees van Dam (see van Dam 1982).

One concluding statement I want make, based on four decades of institutional work in the field of rural development, and with all the force of conviction I am able to muster, is that the application of the OW method constitutes a real, genuine hope for the rapid transformation, on a massive scale and at very low overall cost, of the large groups of the excluded, especially in the countries still referred to as underdeveloped. The method has, moreover, the potential to achieve conditions conducive to democracy, freedom and fellowship, security and social justice.

Note

1. The team working on the elaboration of this methodology consisted of Jaime Llosa, Jorge Sariego, Marco Tulio Araniva, Pedro Urra, Julio Gil de Muro and Sergio Mollinedo.

The OW in Africa

10

'Doing Enterprises' in Wartime and Post-war Mozambique

Isabel Labra and Iuàn Labra

On achieving independence on 25 June 1975, Mozambique shared many of the characteristics of the other newly independent former Portuguese colonies, particularly as regards the dearth of people qualified to take up the jobs left vacant by the Portuguese who had left *en masse*. During the colonial era, education was a privilege reserved for Europeans; 'natives' had access only to mission schools and later to the priesthood. From the very first year of Mozambican independence, direct military attacks from the racist neighbouring regimes (South Africa and Rhodesia), and later on RENAMO attacks, sponsored by the same regimes, kept the newly independent country busy. Mozambicans were trying to defend their newly acquired independence, setting up government structures without adequate human resources, setting up new economic structures and at the same time tackling the inherited inequalities left by the colonial regime. A mammoth task, indeed.[1]

The OW came to Mozambique in two separate waves: in the 1980s and early 1990s, Clodomir, then at the ILO in Geneva and IATTERMUND in Brazil, was invited on different occasions and by different agencies to run workshops for Mozambicans and in Mozambique itself. The authors of this chapter, working from their Zimbabwean base (see Chapter 12) were involved in a second wave of OWs in the mid-1990s, mainly at the invitation of international NGOs.

First-wave Involvement in Mozambique[2]

Most of the Mozambicans who attended the ILO Geneva OW centre run by de Morais there in 1984 were upper-level officials and trade union leaders with little time to spare for a workshop that fully occupied their time for at least a month. That is why the Mozambican government asked the ILO to replicate the Geneva workshop in-country, with the strengthening of their trade union central officers in mind (on the Guinea-Bissau and São

Tomée Príncipe model), and also to enhance their organizational capacity.

The day Clodomir arrived in Maputo, the 60 recruits from the different provinces preparing to attend the OW were already at the OTM (Mozambican Workers' Organization) Formation Centre in Matola, 30 km south of Maputo. The participants had not quite settled in yet, because the night before the inauguration of the course the apartheid forces had conducted an attack with grenades and machine-guns, pock-marking the wooden walls of some of the dormitories with bullet-holes. The OTM and the Ministry of Labour wanted to suspend or postpone the workshop, especially as they did not want an international consultant to be exposed to that kind of risk. Clodomir himself, however, managed to persuade the local authorities to allow the OW to go ahead, and with only two days' delay the go-ahead was given for the workshop to be held in the very centre that had been damaged by the terrorists.

During the first week the apartheid forces launched another assault, but this time with devastating results for themselves. From the very first day of the OW participants had set up a vigilance committee as their first enterprise, with the task of keeping watch, especially at night. The upshot was that at the next attack the assailants, few in numbers, left four dead and fled carrying another four wounded with them in the night. After 30 days, the participants went back to their respective provinces to duplicate what they had learned there, thus boosting the organizational level of the trade union sector.

When Clodomir Santos de Morais was asked again to come to Mozambique, the whole climate had changed. By then, all the Mozambican towns were packed with thousands of internally displaced people fleeing from RENAMO attacks. Unemployment had become endemic in both countryside and towns. The only means of transport within the country was by aeroplane and/or vehicle convoys protected by tanks and army personnel. This, however, did not necessarily convince either the Ministry of Labour or the trade unions that a mass organizational capacitation programme would allow the great numbers of unemployed to set up membership enterprises and thus generate new jobs and income. The OTM itself was facing bankruptcy as the rug of state paternalism was being pulled from underneath it. With its lack of expertise in running a modern enterprise economy, its proposal that some parastatals be syphoned off to it spelled sure disaster for both.

The CRS invites IATTERMUND

In the end the Catholic Relief Services (CRS) and Caritas Mozambique sponsored the first IATTERMUND mission to Mozambique. The CRS request came about partly as a result of an interchange between Clodomir and the CRS representative for southern Africa, Palmari de Lucena. When asked what kind of work IATTERMUND was involved in, Clodomir replied that, at IATTERMUND, 'we do not work'. Organizations that 'do work', Clodomir was anxious to explain to the by now mystified representative, usually try to stretch out the 'work' or the 'job' as long as they possibly can, because, once the task is finished, the 'doer-of-work' is out of a job, too. At IATTERMUND, by contrast, we 'do enterprises'. Our large-scale capacitation activities start on a certain date and finish within, at most, 40 days: we have to stop then as, within that period, an enterprise has already germinated and the professional formation (training) this enterprise and its initiators requires (mechanics, electricians, typists, tailors, accountants, builders, manicurists, painters, and so on) has already been done. That is the moment when the technical cooperation of IATTERMUND is completed. Its intervention is such that it does not create any form of dependency among its participants. Impressed by this highly original and as yet unheard-of approach to development aid and job creation, CRS invited the IATTERMUND team to introduce the OW in their work and with their workers in Mozambique. After the usual preparations, Clodomir Santos de Morais and Paulo Roberto da Silva (the current IATTERMUND president) arrived in Harare, capital of Zimbabwe and CRS HQ for southern Africa, for a preliminary briefing and to arrange for the CRS/Caritas contract.

The Polana Canizo OW (1991)

After the Harare briefing, Clodomir Santos de Morais and Paulo Roberto da Silva set up a capacitation event in the wretched township of Polana Canizo II in Maputo. Canizo II, one of the capital's most miserable townships, was next to the rich residential area, which also contained the luxurious Hotel Polana.[3] Because the area is little more than a helter-skelter collection of dwellings made of old sackcloth, tin and thatch, it was nicknamed 'Polana Tin Town One'. There was not a single house with upper floor or tin corrugated iron roof, normally standard fare for cheap township dwellings, in sight. As the war and unemployment situation worsened, Maputo TV started carrying almost daily images of 'human torch' incidents – rustlers or robbers, unemployed like the rest of the township residents, being lynched and set alight by the mob. Something needed to be done and it has been proved over and again that the poor and unemployed, when given only half a chance, always find solutions by themselves.

More than four hundred people participated in this first Polana Canizo

Field Workshop, the majority of them women. The Apostolic Nuncio and civil society representatives attended the inauguration, but sadly no one from the government was there. The workshop achieved the formation of more than two hundred pre-professionals in dressmaking, food preparation, typing, mechanics, bricklaying, and so on, organized into 20 pre-professional groupings. Some of the participants set up three socially owned and managed enterprises. One of these was called Sopão, in direct reference to the soup sold by 20 women each day in Canizo I and Canizo II. They prepared thousands of bowls of soup made of greenery, vegetables and meat each day. These otherwise dirt-poor women did not need one single cent in start-up capital from the CRS. In the first week of their enterprise, they managed to borrow a few big cooking-pots, collecting the left-over vegetables, greeneries and meat at the local bazaar. Long queues would form each day for that famous soup out of those famous big pots, sold at 20 centavos a bowl. Just a week later the women were already in a position to buy their own cauldrons and all the other implements needed for their remarkable business, literally created out of nothing, thanks to the organizational consciousness they had acquired during the OW. Men's enterprises started buying and selling construction materials (planks, sticks, poles, ladders, tiles, zinc and the like) and others engaged in vehicle maintenance and painting.

The Caritas Mozambique 'Course' OW for TDEs and the First PROGEI/SIPGEI

In September and October of that same year, 1991, after another stopover in Harare for a new briefing, Clodomir de Morais and Paulo Roberto da Silva proceeded to Maputo. After a quick interview with the IATTERMUND representative in Mozambique, the economist Pedro Chaves, they began by securing the cooperation of some instructors. The 'course' OW for the formation of economic development experts (TDEs) was to become the core of the Mozambican employment and income-generation project (PROGEI).

A good number of the 42 participants had had some prior training as Christian catechists, among them a young Mozambican woman called Sister Tereza, of the northern diocese of Pemba (Cabo Delgado province), who turned out to be one of the most brilliant graduates. Luis Duarte Langa, of the diocese of Xai-Xai, and Filipe Sales were among those who had attended the Canizo field OW. At the end of the event the graduates were transported back to their respective dioceses where they would now initiate the formation of local investment project assistants (APIs). APIs are expected to identify, in their communities, employment and income-generating projects. Having gained critical mass serious thought could be given to the build-up of the first SIPGEI in this part of the world. The TDEs had to cope with strong institutional resistance, both from their own government and churches and from the numerous NGOs that were professionally wedded to 'relief' work as they understood it. They created an enterprise called ECOMAL (Enterprise for the Provision of Construction Materials), which provided employment and income to 1,500 families, even though it did not carry the official stamp of approval. *Pinto Pilão*,[4] which was the creation of TDE Sister Tereza, was an enterprise that was subsequently held up as a model for other regions. *Pilão* produced and sold cornflower for the poultry industry in the province of Cabo Delgado. In the port of Inhaca an 80-member fishing cooperative built their own fishing-boat; this was the brainchild of the TDE Filipe Sales of the diocese of Quelimane. He also was the initiator of a famous integrated workshop for the disabled, in the course of which the participants set up a tin bucket production enterprise and another one for the manufacture of prostheses, in which subsequently a lot of interest was expressed from abroad.

Second-wave Involvement: Matzinho, Munguine, Boroma and Nhatambala

The OWs described below, in which the authors were involved as directors, took place between 1992 and 1995. Each of these OWs, in our opinion, provided an answer to some of the most pressing questions development and relief NGOs operating in the region were asking themselves at that time:

- Where and how to find new approaches better suited to the construction of civil society in the new climate of the peace process?
- How to switch from assistance and relief agents to development agents?
- How to get genuine participation?
- How to put a stop to never-ending cases of embezzlement and theft and give participants a real sense of ownership?

The Matzinho Village Enterprise in War-torn Mozambique

The Norwegian NGO Redd Barna Mozambique (RBM) in April 1992 invited the authors to come and facilitate an OW in Matzinho, Manica province, a settlement of people displaced by the war. The productive activities selected by participants and around which the OW was eventually organized were vegetable production, sewing, brick-making and small-scale construction. Other activities were book-keeping, tree planting, literacy and nutrition. Instructors and materials were supplied by both the NGO and the government. A military escort and constant radio contact provided by the Zimbabwe National Army gave the proceedings the aspects of a military-style operation complete with an 'in case of ambush' plan. Camp was set up in an old abandoned house dimly lit by paraffin lamps. The conversation was dominated by accounts of previous attacks on RBM staff. With a 25-strong platoon constantly on watch, every bird call in the night sounded in our imaginations like a guerrilla signal for an imminent attack.

The next day 750 participants did turn up: they spoke nineteen local languages between them, with only 3 per cent managing some Portuguese and up to 90 per cent illiterate. The opening motto of the OW, 'Organize Yourselves into Enterprises', originally did not make much of an impact on an audience who would have turned on their heels at the very mention of the word 'cooperative', so disastrous was their past experience with those government-induced ventures. OHP transparencies explaining the difference between people working individually and in groups did manage to convey the main message all the same, after which the participants were left to get on with the job.[5]

Very quickly, no doubt because of previous experiences with food-for-work schemes, participants divided into groups: sewing, brick-making, construction, bee-keeping, pre-school, nutrition, health, water-pump repairs, horticulture, firewood, herbal medicines, carpentry, literacy and others. Each group elected its representatives, with the general assembly appointing the committee in charge of overseeing the entire enterprise. The leadership learned how to manage the rationing and measurement of food, and each branch did receive its share according to membership. Food distribution was now firmly in the hands of the refugees themselves. But problems with the grinding of the maize, combined with the lack of sufficient cooking-pots, delayed the cooking activities sufficiently to jeopardize the whole experiment: as late as five o'clock, after the end of the capacitation courses and after the instructors and soldiers had left, hundreds were still waiting for their meal. Food distribution was not only slow and frustrating, but some managed to grab double or triple rations, while the poorest women, who had contributed large piles of firewood, received nothing at all. Proceedings deteriorated further, and, amid loud shouting, ended in a general free-for-all. The women refused to contribute any more firewood, and with men carrying axes slung over their shoulders trying to re-establish order, things started to look ominous. An old man eventually managed to calm down the infuriated women and persuade them to talk it over.

The crowd had now started gathering around the OW directors. 'We are very disappointed in you,' we said. 'If you are, as you demonstrate, unable to organize yourselves, you do not deserve any help. Tomorrow we will see what measures you have taken to take control of the situation and see whether you decide to stop carrying on in this way.' Peace was restored and the crowd dispersed quietly. Next morning the enterprise discussed the events of the previous day. A lecture on 'bad habits' arising from individualized patterns of work could not have come at a more opportune moment.

The leadership picked out nine of the worst troublemakers. Their expulsion was decided on a somewhat hesitant show of hands amid random clapping and shouting. One of the expelled took the floor and denounced the leadership. The enterprise eventually decided that every workgroup should have its own kitchen, and the exercise was able to proceed. Thereafter, the work picked up markedly in all sections. Maria Piedosa, the sewing instructor, managed to organize a 'factory under the trees'. A previous employee of a large textile factory, she had internalized the principle of the division of labour: a 20-section production-line made patterns, cut material, did the sewing and controlled quality. And all this by hand! They kept on producing clothes until an influx of second-hand clothing ruined the business, whereupon the group branched off into other ventures over a period of another two years.

The water-pump group carried out six repairs in total. The bee-keeping group made 50 hives, some out of tree bark. But when the Ministry of Agriculture sent them as instructors to other parts of the country, the business understandably collapsed. The firewood group planted thousands of leucaena trees. The fruit-tree group planted mango, paw–paw and litchis. Carpentry, horticulture, brick-making, pre-school and nutrition also did well. The remaining five old medicine men gathered and transplanted medicinal herbs, passing on their wisdom to 25 youngsters who kept producing herbs and roots for sale for more than a year. The literacy group comprised more than three hundred students and some eighteen monitors working on a voluntary basis. Each workgroup requested to learn the technical vocabulary of their chosen trades. The Ministry of Education eventually took over and kept it going for several more years.

Seven months on, the Matzinho enterprise numbered around four hundred members divided into several branches. One meal a day continued until harvest time. The leadership was changed because of embezzlement of funds. The latrine production group diversified to pots and grass mats. The fruit-tree group tilled and planted ten hectares of maize and sorghum by hand, while the health group engaged in cholera prevention measures. Unfortunately a proper evaluation of Matzinho never took place. What we do know is that the peace process allowed the majority of Matzinho refugees to return home. After two years the women's brick-making group was the only one still in operation.

The Munguine OW in Post-war Mozambique (January 1995)

The Munguine Union of Cooperatives and Peasant Associations comprised ten associations and six cooperatives and had a combined membership of 2,232. About twelve thousand people cultivated 1,237 hectares.
Before independence, Chinese and Portuguese settlers had dug irrigation-
drainage canals, drawing water from the Nkomati river during winter and
draining it in summer. After the departure of the Portuguese the canals
had been allowed to silt up, rendering them useless. A mere 10 per cent
of a potentially rich cultivation area was in actual use.

Ursula Semin-Panzer, an employee of an international human rights
NGO, had been working, at the risk of her life, for and in Munguine for
some time. Funds for a primary school had been raised, as had funds for
finding new foster-parents for abandoned children. Tractors, ploughs,
pumps, irrigation pipes, irrigation sprays, hand tools and seeds were all
included in the original aid package. But with the equipment left unused
for years, Ursula thought that an OW would bring new life to Munguine
and break the paralysis.

The Munguine Union leadership was paternalistic and authoritarian,
with all functions concentrated in one person. Members were used to
waiting for handouts and because of the way it was structured, diverting
resources was relatively easy, but it did appoint a team of eleven facilitators,
four of them women. Registration of participants, labour control, records
and costing, infrastructures, logistics, accounts and purchases, Portuguese–
Ronga translation, skills courses, coordination, files and documentation,
literacy and culture were all in the hands of community members, with
little or no involvement from NGO officers being requested.

Living up to pre-OW agreements, the union had also organized the
water supply and bought tools, building materials, basic bedding, food
and water containers. Fixed pit latrines, shelters for the cooking, a lecture
place, store-rooms and lodgings for outside participants were also prepared.
These preparations had themselves triggered a complex logistical operation
that became an integral part of the organizational capacitation exercise.
The participants took about four hours to elect a president and two representatives. But a treasurer could not be found. 'Money is tricky,' they said;
no one wanted to get involved in the job. This meant that they were going
to continue to depend on the facilitators. Apart from the lectures and
meals overseen by the facilitators, no activities took place during the first
days. At mealtime 350 participants gathered, then wandered off for the
rest of the day. The leadership did not ask for either an inventory or a
start-up grant and did not organize any work. However, when a cholera
epidemic threatened, the facilitators helped with the isolation of suspected

cases so as to prevent the disease spreading. This event also proved a turning-point in making the leadership face up to their full responsibility for the affairs of their enterprise. The sick were sent to hospital and the leadership began a series of meetings that ran well into the evening, trying to put their act together. But the general malaise continued.

On the fifth day a group of angry women were arguing: it appeared that the representatives of the participants' enterprise were self-appointed. One of them had a history of misuse of money, and had been sacked at least three times from previous jobs. Being soft-spoken and far more educated than the average person, he had continued to cheat his way into community organizations for the sole purpose of diverting their resources. After strong representations from the community he was promoted sideways as secretary. A reshuffled leadership eventually managed to put people to work. Three offices were constructed from local materials, with 'Health', 'Human Resources' and 'Secretary' painted on the outside. Different groups undertook construction work, one team for each canal, and did the cooking and cleaning. They appointed a store-room keeper, fixed handles to tools and visited the work sites. The construction group demolished walls that were beyond repair and cleaned up the whole building site: this marked the end of the 'installation' phase of the workshop.

The group, now in possession of the means of production, had already achieved some form of organization, and production had started. The leaders, however, remained aloof, hiding in their newly built offices. From the second week onwards, a lot of work took place and logistical short-comings became apparent: the money of the participants' enterprise had run out, the start-up grant was exhausted and the enterprise was not yet able to put a proper labour remuneration scheme in place. There were other problems: the participants' list was artificially swollen, the enterprise was buying more food than it needed, and cooking oil and bread never reached the participants. Right on cue, the food and some of the stationery had started to find their way to the secretary's house. The poorest women were angry but powerless. By noon, when the participants were coming back from a hard day's labour, there was no food for the workers, but the leaders were quietly eating their meals behind the doors of their offices. The malpractice of swelling the lists so as to get more rations was denounced by the director, and the angry women protested vociferously in a disorganized meeting that lasted the whole afternoon. There was more shouting and running about, but otherwise nothing much was happening. The leadership managed all the same to put in place some membership control procedures and food distribution measures. Inefficient and bureaucratic leaders' functions were allocated, instead, to workteam coordinators. The lectures on Theory of Organization discussed management distortions created by the artisan form of labour and the participants were able to identify these in their own ongoing social practice.

By the third week, an ambivalent situation had developed: work was progressing very well in every section, but the malpractice of swelling labour records continued. The leadership, all ex-miners, organized the cleaning of the three main as well as the secondary canals that brought water directly to their own individual plots. The remaining three canals that fed the plots of the poorest peasants, some of them women with children, were the longest and toughest to clean. They were only allocated a few people, in some cases exclusively women directed by one man. The ex-miners, used to operating within a large, capitalistic enterprise, typically exploited the labour force of the poorer, less developed small peasant farmers.

The Theory of Organization prompted the group to address these and other management distortions. Each works committee took charge of the workplans and the critical analysis, which eventually led to the replacement of male coordinators and the election of people who truly represented the groups. This resulted, for example, in an illiterate woman being elected onto the leadership board. Every evening she would ask her son to write out the group's workplan and critical analysis for her, which she then competently submitted for discussion. The team of coordinators made up the coordination committee, which met daily, reviewing past work and laying plans for the following day. They managed to put an end to the deviation of the labour force towards private plots and to reallocate it to the neglected, more difficult canals. This way, the group managed to clean up all six canals within the duration of the workshop. The 20 non-working persons of the leadership were left without any members to lord it over and were thus reduced to a kind of 'clerical duties' committee, whose coordinator was president of the enterprise.

Unemployed youngsters with the reputation of being drug-users and thugs were invited to join the construction group so as to introduce them to an organized socialization process, with the prospect of a future vocational training institute in mind some time in the future. Towards the end of the third week, the youngsters went on strike demanding jobs rotations, protective clothing and some form of monetary allowance. Those demands prompted the canal-cleaning groups to ask for protective footwear. The gradual realization that the workshop was not in the business of providing actual jobs disheartened some and productivity nose-dived. After work intense discussions took place in the daily general assembly and members of the construction group willing to resume work were physically prevented from doing so. Work in all sections picked up, however, towards the end of the OW. The coordination committee met regularly and effectively managed the enterprise.

Summing up, the Munguine Union achieved a small organic agriculture demonstration plot and cleaned more than seven kilometers of canals. The roofing of the community building was about 70 per cent completed and the participants had gained experiential knowledge of participation in a large and complex organization. The organizational framework had been understood and applied. A structure had been put in place allowing activities in areas of literacy, organic agriculture, carpentry and construction to continue in the future. The Union's paternalistic leadership was eventually replaced, too. Unfortunately, and as in so many other instances, the sponsoring agency did not provide any funds for an evaluation and follow-up.

Boroma and Nhatambala (October 1995)

The Integrated Rural Development Project at Degue-Boroma, funded by Weltfriedendienst, a German NGO, had been in operation in Tete province for a number of years. Originally an emergency aid project, it had gradually shifted to food production, using five irrigation schemes along the Zambezi river. Irrigation had been seriously hampered by continuous thefts of equipment from the project. Technical solutions, not always well thought out, were preferred to empowering participatory approaches. A General Peasants' Association and Management Committee drawn from each of the irrigation schemes did exist. There also were buildings, office furniture, a small lorry, a grinding mill, a fence-making machine and a huge (but unused) diesel tank. More community-friendly and capacitating approaches, such as participatory planning meetings between the provincial agrarian officers and the beneficiaries, gradually came into vogue. A new leader had also managed to mobilize a core group of members, which had resulted in a revitalized Boroma.

Cassica and Degue 7 de Abril were completely paralysed. Degue Samora Machel had only a very small group of members, who took the fence from the perimeter of the scheme to fence off their own small plots. Nhatambala, composed of poor women, had an operable electric water-pump. Their fields were in a sorry state, though, but still provided vegetables for sale and consumption. In all places infrastructures were in various states of disrepair and the soil was severely threatened by erosion.

The Boroma OW

The preparation phase of the OWs began with a seminar for four project staff, plus seven elected representatives from the irrigation schemes. Together they made up the Facilitators' Enterprise: their expertise included canal building, organic agriculture, windmill repairs and maintenance, tanning and leather work, and labour records and costings. The Boroma OW began on 24 July 1995, with the facilitators still ferrying tools and materials to the site. The opening took place under an old tree surrounded by canvas. Lectures and meetings used the same space throughout the workshop. The director delivered the opening speech to 110 participants, 70 per cent of them women. After three days, participation stood at 165 (118 women and 47 men), most of them not members of the association. Women were accompanied by 145 children and under-fives. Thirty-five women and twelve men were illiterate.

Five hours after the opening, the technician from the Provincial Direc-tion of Agriculture (DPA) announced to the director: 'I have already organized the participants and divided them into three groups: the canal construction group, the agriculture group and the tanning and leatherwork group.' The director, deputy director, secretary and heads of each group had already been appointed, too. The enterprise would be called the Boroma Agricultural Development Company. He concluded: 'This is how I have organized everything.' There was nothing unusual about this decision-making from above: in a civil war situation civil society, for people's protection, had been structured around adherence to instructions delivered from on high by government instructors assisted by party officials all the way down to neighbourhood level. Expatriates were seen as decision-makers and were usually only too willing to oblige. The population had grown accustomed to sitting and waiting for instructions and resources. Self-organization was out of the question: even cooperative ventures were strictly structured from the top down. The recent general elections apart, there was no genuine culture of democratic participation. The director asked for a meeting with the leadership, congratulated them, and pointed out that their enterprise would need somebody to handle the money, and to take care of the children and of the overall discipline. The following day a treasurer, a book-keeper and a head of discipline had dutifully been appointed. The facilitators spent the rest of the day on sorting out adminis-trative matters.

Meanwhile the participants sat around, not having been provided with any tools: the facilitators clearly were not facilitating. The workgroups they agreed upon were canal construction, chiteta-digging (a root tradi-tionally used in tanning), organic agriculture and leather-work. The first days most women did little more than wait for meals and chat, without any apparent sense of urgency. After a few days work did start in all the areas mentioned. It was only gradually that it dawned on us, that in an area of extreme deprivation, regular meals for three days made a world of a difference, and strenuous work became possible.

The first lectures highlighted the poor level of division of labour the group had reached so far and showed up the tasks still left unattended. The group had run out of money and there was very little food left. No payment claim had been submitted yet by the enterprise. To prevent a crisis, the facilitators unilaterally decided to give the group an advance. There were few prospects of a better leadership than the one in place and no noticeable deviation of resources was taking place, so little risk was run with such a stop-gap measure. At the same time it allowed the leadership some breathing space. When work did start to improve, discussions centred more and more on the development fund, on costing and on how to get as much money as possible. But trouble was brewing, fomented, apparently, by the government official, the Boroma old leadership and outside participants. At the end of one of the lectures, three or four people started shouting for money. The director of the workshop explained that no claims had been received so far, and nobody had turned up to attend labour costing training sessions. The meeting was in turmoil. The leadership explained that the calculation of the labour quotas was in hand and that a training session would be held the following day.

The agriculture group, led by two or three women who were related to some of the wealthier peasant farmers, would not have any of it and accused the facilitators in particular of being 'slave-drivers'. Any proposals for discussion or explanations of the calculation of work hours on the prevailing market rate were rejected out of hand. It soon became clear that little information was filtering down from the leadership. On the surface, the leaders were an understanding, cooperative bunch who took a dim view of the participants' perceived unrealistic ambitions, but in reality they were not leading, and did not hold any general assembly meetings or organize any other form of dialogue. They seemed to rely on the participants' opportunism and got involved as little as they could.

The last day of the second week, when the facilitators had had just about enough and were ready to leave, a group of outside participants trying to board the project's pick-up were prevented from doing so. The enterprise of the participants had already one car and a driver at their disposal, but had failed to organize any transport to take the outside participants home for the weekend. The unexpectedly firm attitude of the team frustrated the participants, who, perhaps for the first time, understood the need to organize themselves rather than wait for things to be done for them. The incident developed into a shouting match with the facilitators. After a tense hour or so, it was agreed to charge the transport cost to the development fund.

In the middle of the third week, at six o'clock in the morning, a participant requested machetes from the security guards and made straight for one of the instructors' tents demanding money: 'You wake up the

Wazungu [Europeans] – I want money now.' He ended up assaulting the book-keeping instructor with several machete blows. Three team members managed to ward him off and run for their lives to the river, where they boarded a canoe and escaped downstream, from where they eventually made it to Tete. By then a crowd had caught up with the assailant, beaten him up badly, and brought him to the police station. The man in question, it turned out, had spent years in RENAMO camps and was obviously mentally ill. During the first two weeks, he had perhaps been the hardest worker of the channel construction group, and had shown an increasing involvement in the whole exercise. After this incident the facilitators' enterprise moved to town on a daily basis.

By the fourth week activities had returned to normal, even though the development fund problem still remained unresolved. The group realized that the OW was drawing to its end, and asked for a one-month extension, with individual wages rather than further developmental activities in mind. The facilitators agreed on one more week. The day before the closure, the inventory was handed over by the participants. After stock-taking it was agreed that missing items were to be subtracted from the development fund. The leadership, however, could not work out participants' shares according to labour contributed.

When the facilitators were about to send the first load of project tools to Degue, a small crowd blocked the gate of the newly constructed fence around the irrigation scheme with tree branches. Fearing that the leadership might pocket their money, they logically did not want any car to leave the place before the development fund had been paid out. The coordinator of the project and the OW director spent a whole afternoon and part of the evening in virtual captivity, helping the participants to work out the list of participants and the number of days' work, and to allocate the corresponding sums to each. The distribution of the individual payments ended a 21-hour siege and the gate was opened.

The distribution of certificates was set for ten o'clock the next day but, unusually, no celebrations were prepared. Instead, there was a complaint that no food had been forthcoming that day. The director handed over the certificates to the leadership and began dismantling the tents and packing up, the leadership handed over the certificates; thus a training course had finished without any dancing and singing, perhaps for the first, and, we hope, for the last time in Africa.

The Nhatambala OW

Nhatambala OW benefited from its predecessor in every respect. Early in the morning, long before the opening, a group of 30 women was already working, using their own tools, repairing parts of the existing fence. The opening speech took the form of a lecture. The participants kept busy the rest of the afternoon and the morning of the following day. The Training Enterprise Eduardo Mondlane Association of Nhatambala announced its elected leadership and workgroups and declared its readiness to receive the inventories. From then on matters relating to food, the development fund, investment in the house, rules for use of the lorry and other issues were settled in a number of meetings between organizers' and participants' enterprises. Decisions were reached by consensus. The elected leadership consisted of four women and four men, often members' own young daughters or sons. The Nhatambala Association elders took up the leadership of the workgroups, which resulted in a highly productive use of the working time. Whenever a problem arose the leadership was careful to consult the general assembly; it also invested a lot of energy in clerical duties and meetings as well as in visiting and monitoring the workgroups, organized by the leadership and heads of groups conjointly, on a daily basis. Misbehaviour was penalized by changing the transgressor to another task with stricter control. The Nhatambala workgroups (number of workers in parentheses) were: fencing (37), agriculture (19), fencepole cutting (19), canal building, (38), stone and sand collection (18), kitchen controllers (2). Eight of the more educated young people acted as part-time literacy monitors of their workgroups. A crèche took care of 109 children.

The shadow of Boroma was never far from either participants or facilitators. Throughout the Nhatambala OW, participants were keen to 'avoid Boroma mistakes' and on 'not behaving like those of Boroma'. This was not so much a criticism of Boroma as a warning of what may happen due to lack of knowledge and experience. When several OWs are run in the same area it is amazing how quickly stories about previous 'mistakes' travel and how constant reference is made to them, a form of 'horizontal learning'. The work at Nhatambala went well with high productivity levels achieved, with well-attended lectures and a high level of participation. Outside interference from the Provincial Directorship of Agriculture did not affect the unity of the group or the capacity of the elected leadership.

Nevertheless, the settling of the development fund did cause some last-minute disturbance. Some youngsters started shouting that they did not accept the settlement, and incited others to do likewise. The leadership thereupon instructed those in agreement to stay inside and ordered the others out. Facilitators trying to intervene were told that the quarrel was not with them but with the leadership. In the end, it all came down to a desire for more transparency in the accounts. The next day, all 160 participants in a carefully planned and organized joint operation moved half the fence and fixed it in a permanent location, to protect young saplings and cultures against invading goats. It all was done with speed and efficiency.

Unlike Boroma, Nhatambala OW ended with a well-organized closing ceremony, with the facilitators contributing food and the participants traditional drinks for the ensuing celebrations.

Conclusion

Both the first- and second-wave involvement of the OW in Mozambique demonstrated that, given half a chance, people are perfectly able and willing to organize themselves and get enterprises going. Institutional resistance, be it from government, churches or the sponsoring NGOs themselves – none of them is used to people taking matters in their own hands and acting autonomously – was a recurring theme. The OWs also cast in a sharp light the dramatic shortcomings of mainstream relief and development work. In Boroma participants were only too aware that mainstream projects had cheated them for years – for instance, by allowing huge electrical pumps and kilometres of cables to lie idle in project store-rooms. The violence in Boroma was not foreign to this: people did not want to be cheated yet again.

Nor are the conditions of service and affluent lifestyles of European experts and volunteers any help: such apparent profligacy grates with the surrounding conditions of abject poverty, only made worse by the extremely modest results delivered by such projects to those most in need. The OW, by contrast, gave the participants the freedom of organization within the law and genuine freedom to express themselves and allowed them to hold facilitators accountable for years upon years of failed projects.

The OW showed its capacity to cope and operate in extreme conditions, i.e. a sixteen-year civil war and post-war chaos. It provided invaluable insights in the social psychology of large groups of relatively uneducated and often illiterate people and on the potentially positive aspects of the apparent rebelliousness of youngsters, victims and also survivors of that civil war (see also Chapter 12).

As John Wilson, who acted as facilitator at the Munguine OW, stated in his diary of the Munguine OW: 'The approach brings in social conflict and shows how to deal with it.'[6]

Notes

1. For a more detailed account of this period see: Christie, I. (1988) *Machel of Mozambique*, Harare: Zimbabwe Publishing House.

2. Clodomir Santos de Morais provided the field notes on the ILO/IATTER-MUND part of the chapter from his personal reminiscences.

3. *Canizo* means 'cane' in Portuguese. The rich Polana neighbourhood is popularly referred to as Polana Cimento (Cement Polana), and the poor area is called Polana Canizo (Cane Polana).

4. *Pinto* and *pilão* for the traditional home grinding-stone for cereals.

5. On the use of OHPs see Chapter 12, p. 122.

6. J. Wilson is a Zimbabwean permaculture specialist who brought to the OW approach the techniques of organic agriculture and of participatory rural appraisal (PRA).

11

In Angola, Guinea Bissau and São Tomé e Principe

Paulo Roberto da Silva[1]

Clodomir Santos de Morais was called in in the early 1980s by the Workers' Education Programme of the ILO, Geneva. In that position he directed several large-scale organizational capacitation courses either in or intended for the former Portuguese colonies. One was held in Geneva, and the others in Angola and Guinea Bissau.

Angola: An Abundance of Jobs But No One to Fill Them

The first experiences with the large-scale capacitation method in the new Portuguese-speaking popular republics of Africa happened in rather peculiar circumstances, in that the need for the generation of new workplaces there was hardly felt. The real problem in those newly independent territories was one of an abundance of jobs, with not enough professionally qualified people to fill them. One of the more telling examples of this paradoxical situation was Angola. Angola's victory over colonialism (1975) had meant that the Portuguese had precipitately left their former so-called 'Overseas Province' of Angola, where the Portuguese dictator Salazar had been planning to install the seat of his future empire in a new town in the centre of the country, then called 'Nuva Lisboa' (New Lisbon), known today as Huambo.

The situation was very similar in the former Portuguese territory of Mozambique (see Chapter 10). When Clodomir met two Mozambican officials, for example, in the 1970s for an evening meal at the famous Alto de La Trinidad in Upper Lisbon, a customary watering-hole for hundreds of visitors from late evening till the early morning, all unemployed and part of the local 'small left' or 'leftish' intelligentsia, his guests could not supress their comments about the extraordinary concentration of qualified people in that place, whereas there was such a crying need for qualified personnel in their own home country.

Offering, in situations such as these, a nationwide capacitation

programme 'to fight against the scourge of unemployment' was not among
the most urgently felt needs in the new Angola. On top of this, in the
constitutional style of the Eastern European socialist republics, the state
set out to provide jobs for all its citizens: whether you were a simple
barber, a shoeshine boy, or a newspaper seller on the streets, all, down to
the most petty occupations, were state employees, a fact that did not
prevent a profound social diversification in the country at a later stage,
with the appearance of *nouveaux riches*. In the first years of its independence, Angola therefore genuinely saw itself as a country with a fully
employed citizenship, with the State as grand patron of all and sundry. A
programme to fight a non-existent unemployment problem was therefore
not on the cards. Nor had it been possible to interest the Angolan government in a literacy programme, such as the one offered by Paulo Freire and
his wife Elza. Matters pertaining to education and literacy were considered
to be the proper domain of the Ministry of Education and of their own
National Workers' Union of Angola, whose general secretary, Pascual
Luvualu, held the rank of government minister and was a member of the
Central Committee of the party in power, the MPLA.

Faced with the workplace inflation in professional jobs, the government
did see the merit, though, in providing a modicum of professional training
for those who were going to fill the posts or, at the very least, in trying to
extract a better performance from those now doing those jobs. One example
that perhaps typifies the job situation more than any other is the case of
former male nurse Mendes de Carvalho, who was put in charge of Luanda
hospital even though he had never run a small clinic, let alone a hospital,
before. His main credentials were having suffered for many years in prison,
at the concentration camp of Tarrafal, in the Cabo Verdian archipelago in
the middle of the Atlantic Ocean, where the Portuguese dictatorship used
to cage its political enemies. Mendes was elected mayor of Luanda and in
quick succession rose to the position of minister of health and ambassador
to the (East) German Republic.

The brain drain of the few qualified personnel the country possessed
compounded the problem: only half of the representatives of an Angolan
delegation headed by de Carvalho to the HABITAT World Conference in
Canada in 1976, for example, were still Angolan residents two years later.
All the others had left the country. This did not just mean the loss of half
a dozen professional people: however small their numbers, in view of the
extreme dearth of people with university training, the impact of their loss
was massive.

The Angolan National Trade Union, with a membership of over fifty-
thousand workers, for its part, was only ever interested in trade union
education, more specifically courses in trade unionism and trade union

administration, as well as courses in TU politics given the new environment of a burgeoning African socialism. Many of them were registered on workers' education courses at the gigantic Centre for Trade Union Education in the city of Malange. The courses in professional training for the industrial and service sector were the responsibility of a section of the Ministry of Labour, while the courses in hygiene and safety at work were the responsibility of yet another department.

Pascual Luvualu exercised an extreme vigilance over the ideological purity of the Worker and Peasant Education Programmes – understandable, to a certain extent, in a country where religion, i.e. Catholicism, had become so fused with colonialism. For many an Angolan revolutionary, Salazar and Cardinal Cerejeira (who was known to be in the engaging habit of blessing the government troops before they went into battle against the nationalists), were hand-in-glove associates in the same colonialist venture. So a literacy programme led by Paulo Freire, then at the World Council of Churches (WCC) in Geneva, had little chance of being welcomed by the Angolan government, even less so after the intervening but failed coup attempt by Nito Alves, the death of the 'father of independence', Doctor-President Agostinho Neto, and the gathering struggle for power between the two cultural majority groups in the country, the Kibundos and Mobundos.

The OW Called in by the Angolan Trade Union Movement

The only technical cooperation assistance from the ILO that, as already mentioned, Pascual Luvualu was interested in was strictly limited to trade union education. It so happened that the Angolan National Workers' Union, with its gigantic membership structure spread over the entire country of more than 2 million square kilometres and 10 million inhabitants, was in urgent need of courses in trade unionism, trade union administration and trade union politics, given the context of the promising new vistas for African socialism. Of the over fifty thousand workers who participated in the 1987 May Day celebrations, singing the *International* while marching past the official stand, no one was unemployed, as the constitution gave the right to a job to everyone, even though that job may have been extremely poorly paid, not sufficient to feed themselves, let alone their families.

The courses in professional training for the industrial and service sector were the responsibility of a section of the Ministry of Labour, under the directorship of a certain David Gove Lussoke, while the courses in hygiene and safety at work were in the hands of the department directed by Augusto Lot, another former prisoner of the colonial regime. Partly in recognition of past support and services rendered to the Angolan Trade Union Movement by Césare Poloni, former Italian Socialist Party militant and director in charge of the Workers' Education Programme (ILO EDUC), Pascual Luvualu agreed that the external consultant Clodomir Santos de Morais be called in to run the first OW planned by the Angolan Trade Union headquarters, then located at 23 av. Rainha Ginga.

Fifty people participated in the workshop, the majority of them trade union leaders from the capital Luanda. Manuel Augusto Viage, aka 'Rivas', the trade union director of training, inaugurated and closed the first four-week OW run specifically for the formation of specialists in organizational matters and to strengthen the national trade union teams. The Workers' Education Department subsequently made good use of those specialists in most regions of the country. The other ILO missions Clodomir Santos de Morais was entrusted with by the ILO in Angola were fact-finding missions into urban drift (of the labour force), facts that were relatively easily verifiable by interviewing the provenance of the newcomers to the enormous *musseques* (townships or slums) that had started mushrooming around the main urban centres. In the course of these investigations Clodomir also became involved in the large ILO mission entrusted with the investigation of the Workplace hygiene and safety needs of Angolan workers.

Guinea Bissau and São Tomé e Principe: The 'Course' OWs in Guinea Bissau

The first intensive 'course' OW run in Guinea Bissau for the formation of trade union leaders took place in January 1985 at the headquarters of the local UNTG (the Guinea Bissau Trade Union HQ). The problem was that this institution represented little more than its banner name, which made the task of covering this country of one million people all the more daunting. Paulo Freire, five years earlier, had conducted an literacy project there that was never concluded for lack of financial support. Two of Clodomir's local counterparts were graduates of the Geneva Centre OW, Fernando Fonseca and Salvador Fernandes, who were also expected to be spearheading the setting up of the UNTG structure. The latter, Salvador Fernandes, was the former director of the School for Political Education of the Revolutionary Independence Party of Guinea and Cape Verde, which had operated clandestinely from the neighbouring country of Guinea Conakry and which was also the launching pad for the national liberation army.

During the last two weeks of this OW, the specialists being formed there conducted three 'lightning courses' in Bissau, a town of 100,000 inhabitants, for the formation of trade union leaders. These lightning courses were attended by almost a thousand people, 250 of them dockworkers at the local harbour (stevedores, dock operators, warehouse-keepers, etc.), 230 women belonging to the local horticultural and animal husbandry co-operatives and another 500 or so residents of a former colony with widespread misery. A service enterprise for trade union capacitation – the so-called Amilcar Cabral Brigade for the formation of assistants in most of the villages of the interior – was set up by the same specialists formed during the course. The ILO Workers' Education Service had financed the proceedings and Clodomir Santos de Morais had the overall direction. From 1983 onwards, Clodomir embarked on research in Africa to extract comparative criteria and theoretical frameworks on the capacitation method he had experimented with during the seventeen preceding years in Latin America. This was to become the principal scientific research theme of his thesis at the University of Rostock. The second big capacitation event conducted by Clodomir in Guinea Bissau was another centre workshop with a 40-plus attendance. The aim was a refresher course for new trade unionist cadres from the interior and capital city alike in the context of workplace creation. One of the outcomes was the creation in 1987 of a small clothing factory named (in Creole) No Na Cose (We Have Sewn It Ourselves), which provided 20 workplaces.

Unemployment in Bissau: 1989 onwards

After the fall of the Berlin Wall, more than one thousand students and professionals with university degrees obtained in various Eastern European countries returned to Guinea Bissau. This resulted in a worsening of the chronic unemployment situation, which reached epidemic proportions for the Guinean people from the moment the Portuguese colonialists left the country, taking with them financial and capital resources (machines, vehicles, boats, etc.). On top of this, the colonialists left the country devoid of any higher education institution. They also left behind an illiteracy rate of 85 per cent, which Paulo Freire, assisted by his wife Elza, managed to bring down to 70 per cent. In a capital with 100,000 inhabitants, barely one-third of the buildings were in brick. The remainder were made from palm leaves or cardboard and tin. The public electricity supply had been down for more than two years: in one of the poorest countries in the world, there were no funds for a new electricity plant. Clodomir was sent on a second mission to Guinea Bissau at the invitation of the ILO in 1989 with the purpose of forming cadres for the fight against urban and rural unemployment.

Back to Brazil

However, the time had come to start thinking of returning, at long last, to his home country, Brazil, to pick up where he had left off, back in 1964, when he was exiled by the military junta. The sequence of events as from 1988, when Christovam Buarque, vice chancellor of the University of Brasília, who had been one of the principal sources of inspiration behind the elaboration of the 'course'-type workshops for the formation of the TPIs in Lisbon (see Chapter 15), invited Clodomir Santos de Morais (then in Rostock) to come and work once more in Brazil, is recounted in Chapters 17 and 18 of this book.

Note

1. This chapter is based on the personal recollections of Clodomir Santos de Morais.

12

Hard Learning in Zimbabwe (SADET) and in Post-civil War Mozambique

Isabel Labra and Ivàn Labra

'Why Zimbabwe, of All Places?'

This is the question Raff Carmen put to us at the start of our twelve years of contact. Raff, searching for Third World approaches to organization and management, had come upon the method in the magazine *Workteam*, published by the NGO Cooperation for Research, Development and Education (CORDE), in Botswana, and had obtained our address from the Netherlands Institute for Cooperation with Developing Countries (HIVOS). Gavin Andersson, then editor of *Workteam*, had heard about the method from Ian Cherrett, and had become one of the essential people for its introduction and adaptation to southern African contexts.[1] In his capacity of HIVOS representative to Central America, Ian Cherrett learned about the organization workshop method, and was instrumental in the creation of the Honduran Institute for Rural Development (IHDER).

This institution, in turn, attracted the staff of a just-terminated FAO project headed by Clodomir Santos de Morais, and has managed to continue to work until today for the capacitation of the peasantry in Central America, mainly in Honduras. In the early 1980s, Ian, then still in Central America, was appointed HIVOS representative to southern Africa. After several hours of in-depth consultation on the technicalities of the approach, we outlined our potential involvement in the introduction of the method to southern Africa. While this was taking place in Central America, on the other side of the Atlantic Ocean, in landlocked Zimbabwe, Cephas Muropa, another key figure in the introduction of the method to southern Africa, reminisces:

> When Zimbabwe attained its independence, in 1980, I was a member of Cold Comfort Farm Society, an agricultural collective cooperative formed in 1964 and later closed down in 1970 by the Rhodesian authorities. This experience convinced me that the collective ownership of the means of production was

the only answer to the problems our black population was subjected to by the colonial masters. The closing down of our cooperative by the illegal authorities strengthened our spirits even more. When we finally attained independence, our new government set up a department responsible for cooperative development, under the Ministry of Agriculture. The minister, at the time, was Moven Mahachi, one of the members of our cooperative and a prominent cadre of Zimbabwean struggle for independence. Our government was facing the big task of resettling tens of thousands of refugees, ex-combatants and displaced people, and several thousand hectares of land were acquired for resettlement purposes. Under the resettlement 'A', a family was allocated 5 hectares of land to be individually cultivated and collective grazing pastures. Those who were interested in pooling their resources together and form cooperatives were allocated big farms under model 'B', to be cultivated collectively. The history of Cold Comfort and its contributions to the armed struggle was still fresh in the minds of many people and the new cooperators started to come and seek advice on co-operativism. Thirteen agricultural cooperatives met at Cold Comfort Farm in January 1982. This meeting was followed by another one that was attended by 33 cooperatives, and by a conference, where 76 cooperatives created the Organization of Collective Cooperatives in Zimbabwe OCCZIM. I became the first chairman. (personal recollections of Cephas Muropa)

The answer to the question 'Why Zimbabwe, of all places?', therefore, is that Zimbabwe holds a lot in common with those Latin American countries that went through land redistribution processes. Even before independence, Zimbabwe developed its own cooperative experience. Cold Comfort Farm Society was a commercially viable cooperative, operating under the difficult conditions imposed on the black population by the successive colonial and white settler rule. Its profits went into funding the struggle for independence, taking care of the families of the jailed freedom fighters, sending recruits to Mozambique for training, and posting them to the war fronts thereafter. Zimbabweans thereby demonstrated their ability to organize both the political-military and the productive, market-oriented side of an enterprise. Farm operations provided a convenient cover for people's participation in the armed struggle under the strict principles and procedures that looked very much like the principles held dear by the OW approach:

Cooperatives urgently needed management training and financial resources, and OCCZIM's Executive Committee embarked upon a successful fund-raising campaign and opened training opportunities, even abroad, for the membership of the collective cooperatives. We soon realized, though, that newly trained co-operators, once equipped with certificates, would leave the cooperatives and join private enterprises. That is when Mr Ian Cherrett, then HIVOS representative to southern Africa, told me about OW-EWTO. (Muropa ibid.)

The First OWs in Southern Africa

Ian Cherrett and Cephas Muropa, with the help of HIVOS, Glen Forest Training Centre (a local NGO) and OCCZIM sponsorship, ran the first field OW ever in (anglophone) southern Africa. The place was Rujeko Cooperative (Makoni District Union, Zimbabwe) and the year was 1986. This was followed by another OW in Serowe, Botswana. Cephas Muropa gives us the following 'before and after' account of this workshop:

> The situation at Rujeko Cooperative before the OW was very bad indeed. The leadership was using the co-op's property to their own private advantage and a lot of embezzlement was taking place. The chairperson, for example, took over one acre of land as well as the borehole, meant for the cooperative vegetable garden, and started cultivating for his own account. The leadership used some of the buildings to rear their own chickens and distributed fertilizer belonging to the coop among those members who supported them. This practice led the rest of the members to demand their own pieces of land for individual cultivation. It was striking to see very healthy individually cultivated plots next to the wilting collective ones. The members thought that the leadership were into witchcraft to keep their positions, and hoped for outsiders from the Ministry of Agriculture or donor organizations to redress the situation. One expatriate had spent three years there, without much visible success. Superstition, allegations of witchcraft, gossip, indiscipline and confusion prevailed. The success story of the Rujeko OW, though, was short-lived. Training institutions failed to come up with the complementary skills and managerial training needed. There just was no follow-up, and the newly acquired democratic decision-making procedures, namely the Critical Analysis and the Work Plan, had not yet become a deeply established routine. New members brought new ideas and the coop went back to its pre-OW vertical, authoritarian ways. (Muropa ibid.)

The results of the Rujeko OW, though, made a great impact on further developments in the southern African cooperative movement. The first issue of *Workteam* (1986: 1) reported on the Rujeko workshop and thereafter carried stories of others that took place successively in Botswana, Zimbabwe, South Africa, Namibia and the Caribbean. *Workteam* also published a cartoon series on the de Morais Theory of Organization. Between 1986 and 1988 OWs took place in Serowe, Otse, and at a salt production workshop in the desert, in Botswana. In South Africa, the NGO Akanani, in the then northern Transvaal, built part of its training centre through an OW event. The Rujeko and Serowe workshops, in turn, led to an invitation to the authors, who were brought to Zimbabwe to develop the approach further. The Glen Forest Training Centre, a rural vocational training centre hosting the approach, would soon prove to be not up to that task.

Hard Learning

Once in Zimbabwe, we started by creating the conditions to run an OW at Glen Forest Training Centre. Only the centre's director had been exposed to the method, at the 1986 Rujeko workshop, and the rest of the staff was completely new to the exercise. It was just like trying to stage an opera with people who did not know either music or drama, let alone the combination of both. A new intake of trainees was coming to attend several rural vocational training courses, and we thought we could run the workshop by handing over to the trainees all the facilities of the centre, plus all the training staff and food for the first days. The enterprise formed by the trainees would have to organize all training activities, plus catering, recreation, sports and whatever the group could think of. It was clear to us that we were not achieving the right social composition of the group, but this seemed to be the only possible way to get started. We had drafted in some teaching aids to illustrate the Theory of Organization. They were a set of flip-charts with drawings that we put on the walls of the lecture hall. Women sat on the floor, the men on the available benches. After the director's speech, time dragged on without the participants seeming able to get organized. Three meals a day were served for the first three or four days, after which the group could not put to use the remaining food that had been handed over to them, let alone organize any other productive or learning activity. People would gather in the grounds, the women with their small babies, waiting for food, running into a second and a third day. The only activity taking place was singing and dancing. The workshop was about to collapse.

During our previous years in Latin America we had begun explaining the changes that occur in the OW by means of Leont'ev's theory of the objectivized activity.[2] We thought that this theory would be able to explain the phenomenon taking place with our 120 participants, and that this understanding, in turn, would help us take the experiment forward. The Theory of Organization has introduced the concept of 'ideological be-haviour' applied to four social strata, namely the artisan (or individual producer), the worker, the half-worker and the lumpen (social misfit). Deep insights had been achieved into the psychological traits belonging to the art-isan form of labour, but research had never been carried out into the psychological traits attaching to the other forms of labour. Therefore, the situation we faced in the Svetaida workshop could not be directly explained by the Theory of Organization and was going clearly beyond what had been termed 'the anomy period', known from our Latin American experience. The facts on the ground pushed us to go one step further in the analysis of how the activity determines psychological reflection, to look into the activities that this particular group of participants used to perform, and explain, thereafter, their reaction to the conditions of the workshop.

The participants were not exactly 'individual, self-sufficient workers'. Although, like tailors or shoemakers, they individually perform all operations needed to produce one article, subsistence farmers do not draw all they need from this one activity, and, therefore, they are far from self-sufficient. The classic self-sufficient peasant farmer obtains the milk and meat from a few cows, meat from pigs, chickens and small livestock, and a variety of vegetables, fruits and cereals from the fields. Therefore the stereotype of the 'artisan' does not account for the context of their activities and cannot explain all the characteristics of their social psychology. On top of seasonal subsistence farming and cattle rearing, hunting and gathering are not a distant past, but something they still resort to. In an effort to explain this particular form of psychological reflection of these activities, we coined the expression 'pastoralism' to define the attitude of waiting for any given situation to sort itself out, with little or no attempt to intervene in the course of events.[3] In the activity of the small subsistence farmer, waiting for the rain shapes the social psychology of subsistence farmers, who resort to prayers, and, in some cultures, to singing and dancing, as the only legitimate 'intervention' allowed in their situation. This explained why the participants witnessed the total disintegration of their enterprise, 'sitting to the death', even when they had run out of food for themselves and for their children. As we said before, faced with the situation the OW had placed them in, the only thing they could do was to engage in singing and dancing, apparently as a culturally determined expression of their defencelessness in a situation that they could not control. At the same time, this could be an expression of hope and a plea for the intervention of external actors to do something for them, or on their behalf.

Some of the participants came to ask for the intervention of the director, saying that the group had failed to organize itself and asking the director to take control of the centre and organize the activities for them. Trying to shake them up, the director addressed the participants in a way that in Latin America would have provoked a violent reaction. 'This would mean that you are unable to organize yourselves, and that you need the white man to come and organize things for you.' The immediate unanimous response was clapping hands, ululating in agreement, and relief. As said before, when designing the workshop, we did not control the variable 'social composition of the group' and we did not include assembly-line workers or people with experience in social or technical division of labour. Their expected 'ideological behaviour'[4] would have made them contribute the organizational framework that is characteristic of their different life experience, assisting other participants to find the way around their problem. So, in order to rescue the sinking Svetaida[5] workshop, we resorted to constitute what de Morais had termed a 'primary structure', to overcome the inability of the group to organize themselves and make progress in the self-sustaining way, as a group.[6] The workshop then managed to meet its objectives. A small group of participants were able to constitute themselves into a small enterprise that undertook construction work at the centre, lasting a few months, but without further follow-up. One of the participants of the Svetaida workshop successfully lobbied for another OW to be held at his cooperative, and Norwegian People's Aid, a donor agency, sponsored a workshop in Mauya Cooperative. This last one led to an interrupted chain of workshops covering a whole district. The method had stepped into the country.

The Adaptation Process

The model of the OW that we took to southern Africa came from the Honduran experience. There, most of the workshops took place in the capacitation centre David Funez Villatoro, which had been specially set up for this purpose. The participants received the property rights over 40 hectares of maize ready to harvest, a chicken-run, cattle, a piggery, orchard, a vegetable garden, tractors with their drivers, one small pick-up truck, secretarial staff, offices and all the facilities of the centre. They would harvest, take the maize to the neighbouring town, San Pedro Sula, sell, and record the sales and the money. The centre would serve food three times a day for three days only, and from the fourth day onwards the participants would buy and cook their own meals from the proceeds of their sales. From the very moment at which the participants gave themselves some form of organization, precarious as it might have been, they received the property rights and managed all productive, service, cultural and sports activities that took place during the workshop. The participants' enterprise was, therefore, a real, though temporary, enterprise. The quantity and quality of the means of production in the hands of the participants, plus the need to generate their own means of survival, was complex enough to prompt the participants to develop a proper management system.

When the authors came to southern Africa, they did not find such conditions in the Glen Forest Training Centre, and had to create in the villages the conditions for the establishment of a real, though temporary, capacitation enterprise. They therefore resorted to a so-called development fund, which was instrumental in concentrating the population around some productive activities chosen by them, and in preparing the set-up of a village enterprise.[7] In 1989, Norwegian People's Aid (NPA) funded an OW at Mauya Cooperative, within the Nyama Resettlement Scheme, Hurungwe District, Mashonaland West, Zimbabwe. Before the workshop, the cooperative was collapsing, despite the large amounts of money granted to it by NPA. In the three seasons after the workshop, the cooperative achieved a significant increase in its tobacco crop, which allowed it to pay back its huge loan to the Agricultural Finance Corporation. The lack of operating capital and the drought hindered the possibilities of overcoming its financial difficulties once and for all, but the continuing relationship with the financial institution allowed the cooperative to remain viable. In this example, it was very clear that the cooperative attained a sound level of organizational strength after the workshop. Other major achievements of the cooperative to date are the establishment of literacy and an adult education programme, which lasted for many years and from which graduated several cooperators. Based on this accomplishment, the next step would have been to turn the organizational strength into economic success. This was not possible due to the prevailing economic conditions in the country, characterized by prohibitive interest rates that prevented an adequate capitalization of the farms.

Three villagers of neighbouring 7B village participated in the Mauya OW, after which they encouraged their own village to request a similar exercise. The village had obtained the services of Zimbabwe's Agricultural Extension Services (AGRITEX), which provided a feasibility study and the blueprint for the construction of a small earth dam. This prompted Catholic Relief Services (CRS) to sponsor another OW that took place at 7B, from 30 June 1990 to 28 July 1990. After that, virtually each and every village at Nyama, Pote I and Pote II resettlement schemes and the communal lands of Mukwichi, Kasangarare and Chundu would request OWs to take place at their villages. The informal grouping constituted by the authors, accompanied by Cephas Muropa and Panganayi Fobo, decided to create the Southern Africa Development Trust (SADET), a non-profit organization that would seek funding and implement the projects. At this stage, it was essential to produce documents that could explain the process. Literature on the method was reduced to a few paragraphs of the Theory of Organization that did not help in spreading the approach, raising funds, or explaining it to the newly recruited local staff. Therefore, all subsequent workshops were documented, and the authors produced a collection of papers on what the OW was all about. Initially, in the NGO community there was little or no doubt that the two expatriates from Latin America could effectively run such workshops, but nobody would believe that local personnel could replicate them. High illiteracy rates made lectures difficult to follow, and put the content beyond the reach of most of the current development workers, even those with university degrees. The role of the director had not been made clear or transparent. It seemed inextricably linked with the personality of the director, taking a cue from de Morais' own personal style. The results obtained in the field seemed to be the work of a 'guru' and his followers, rather than the result of a consistent, systematic, replicable developmental approach. The method seemed to dwell on the director's role, and this role seemed to be non-transferable.

Nevertheless, the results appeared so impressive that the international NGOs (CRS) and terre des hommes Germany (tdh) funded SADET to the tune of US$ 1.25 m. This created an acute need to put together a director's formative process, aimed at building a team able to undertake mass capacitation operations. This process had to take care of the following:

• Development of teaching aids to deliver the Theory of Organization
• Analysis of the director's tasks and role
• Analysis of the intended productive activities of the workshop
• Development of the theoretical basis of the process
• Systematization of the process

Initially, lectures were delivered in English, with either Shona or Ndebele translation. Lectures would last for about one hour, allowing time for questions at the end. Sometimes the question period could last for 30 minutes or more, and depending on the interest the director is able to inspire, the participants can still ask for extended lecture time. The lectures were greatly facilitated by the preparation of more than a hundred overhead projector transparencies, explaining each one of the concepts of the Theory of Organization. At the beginning of our experience in southern Africa, we could see that the participants, especially illiterate women, were taking pains to copy the drawings and the concepts from the transparencies. This was utterly impossible, for they did not have ability to hold the pencil, let alone literacy or drawing skills. The transparencies' presentation time was always too short, and they got frustrated when the next transparency was shown. The authors then developed a second set of teaching aids, with the same content of the transparencies, enlarged to A3 size, conveniently laminated. After the lectures, the posters corresponding to the lecture would hang on the walls of the lecture hall, or even from trees, for the people to study them. It is impressive to see small groups of participants copying from the posters after every lesson, whenever they have the time to do so. The teaching aids helped quite a lot in the directors' formative process, since the basic script of each lecture is already in the transparencies. Therefore, inexperienced lecturers resort to the transparency to remind people of the concepts, until they achieve the ability to elaborate on them on their own, adding real-life examples to the content of the lectures. One of the members of the facilitator's enterprise, acting as the director's assistant on a rotational basis, would initiate the lecture with a quick review of the contents of the previous one, which allowed them to gain lecturing experience, until able to handle a lecture independently. The analysis of the director's role allowed the differentiation of three main functions: lecturer, organizer and organizational instructor. The director performs an 'organizer' task in terms of the facilitator's enterprise, when setting up the conditions for the workshop and directing the team. The director acts as organizational instructor in respect of the participants' enterprise, when allowing them freedom of organization and non intervention in their process, and as a lecturer in respect of both enterprises when delivering the Theory of Organization and other technical advice.

The analysis of the intended activities allows listing of all resources and vocational skills needed, and these, in turn, allow the listing of the facilities required to perform the intended activities. These lists are essential to the procurement and storage process prior to the workshop. The theoretical effort of developing further the social psychology, beyond the limited boundaries of the small group dynamics, allowed the understanding of the organizational processes of large groups of people, and the facilitation of the formation of enterprises and creation of jobs. The systematization of the approach facilitated the dissemination of information and the replication of the workshops. Equipped with these tools, the authors were now in a position to recruit 45 villagers who had showed the best performance as participants in the OWs held so far, and bring them into a one-month theoretical course, where they studied the following disciplines:

- Didactics of the Theory of Organization
- Teaching aids
- Skills of organizing, running and follow-up of an OW
- Large group social psychology
- Self-management techniques
- Theory of Organization
- History of organization of labour
- Political economy

After the theoretical part of the course, successful graduates designed, planned and directed OWs under close supervision. Thereafter, each local director had the opportunity to direct at least one OW by themselves. Lectures were delivered directly in Shona, and in other cases participants asked for English and translation into Shona, so they could pick up from both versions. Participants enjoyed the Theory of Organization, and, even today, they vividly recall its contents. The formative process achieved fifteen local directors of OWs. SADET was able simultaneously to deploy four teams of organizational instructors in four villages at 10 to 40 kilometres from each other, and to run four consecutive workshops attended by an average of 200 participants each. The OW had finally landed and made its home in Zimbabwe.

The Mass Capacitation Operation in Hurungwe District, Mashonaland West, Zimbabwe

The 1992 drought highlighted the need for water resources in most villages pertaining to resettlement schemes and communal lands in Zimbabwe, leading to a large-scale programme, whereby the OW approach was instrumental to the development of water resources through the construction of labour-intensive small earth dams. In this process, the method became a well-known routine of operations that repeated itself about 35 times in three years. Once a community had identified the need to embark on a dam construction programme, the AGRITEX technicians would look at the viability of the intended dams, study the best possible location, and come up with a blueprint. Thereafter, the implementing agency would provide all the required hand tools, food for the first four days, and a development fund that would pay the enterprise of the participants proportionate to the value of labour, properly recorded and calculated at local market rates. During the workshop, participants would start by digging the core trench for the foundation of the dam wall. This could be up to 2 metres wide, 70 metres long, and 2 or 3 metres deep. Later they would locate clay soil, bring it to the site until it filled the core trench, and compact it up to ground level. The actual dam wall would require one or two weeks' tractor work in addition to the labour-intensive effort of the villagers.

Villagers would organize themselves into committees according to different tasks. Committees included the following:

- Measuring and pegging sites
- Tree stumping and removal of roots from the site of the works
- Tool repairs, replacement of handles
- Stone carrying
- Buying and collecting food supplies
- Daily distribution and collection of tools
- Keeping the store-room
- Cooking and distributing lunches

- Supply of drinking water for the workers
- Child care
- Keeping records of individual and committees' labour input
- Keeping records of expenditure
- Attending to specific skills and management courses
- Literacy and numeracy
- Sports and culture

Each one of the tasks on its own is simple enough to be done by people without specialized skills or education, but the whole entrepreneurial set-up is complex enough to impress upon people's minds what management is all about. Within each committee the work is planned for, assigning individual responsibilities to each member. After work, committees learn how to assess their own results, pointing out mistakes and devising ways and means to sort them out. The representatives of the different committees meet to discuss the workplans and critically analyse the work done by the enterprise, combining committees' workplans and assessments into one single document for the whole enterprise. This document goes to a general assembly meeting, where each member has the chance to appraise the proposals. Once approved, the plan is binding for each member of the enterprise, and is therefore enforced by the elected leadership. This is a bottom-up planning cycle, composed of:

- The production of the workplan by each and every committee of the enterprise
- The meeting of the representatives of each committee to sort out resource allocation
- The final approval by the general assembly meeting

In each single workshop, this cycle takes place at least three times, and thereafter the villagers' enterprise is well equipped to continue to work on its own. The OW process takes the participants from a very loose and sometimes chaotic organization to an efficient one. Lectures on the Theory of Organization allow them to reflect on their own mistakes and correct them by themselves. Their level of consciousness rises from a naïve level, where they expect fate to bring something better for them, to an organizational level, where they realize that a better life can come about only if they are properly united and organized around common goals and democratic decision-making. Participants work productively throughout the workshop, and attend vocational and managerial courses as well. As a result, communities can build large infrastructures, which they use and care about, for they will have 'done it themselves'.

The method displays some unique features, the most important of which are:

- Large groups of people, 40 as a minimum, 300 or 400 as an average, and 1,000 or 2,000 at a time when the programme has the necessary resources.
- All villagers participate on an equal footing. This creates an enabling environment for women's participation and empowerment.
- Courses take place on the spot, in the workplace, in the village or in the neighbourhood where people live.
- Courses assist participants in carrying out productive activities identified by the communities beforehand. The programme makes available the resources and the community assumes ownership and control over those resources, as needs arise.
- The workshops develop the capacity of the participants to perform productive and service activities, management techniques, literacy, numeracy development, primary health care for the mother and child and whatever activities respond to immediate needs of the communities.

The programme funded by terre des hommes Germany and the European Union (EU) had a very promising start. During the first nine months, several organizational workshops took place. The mass capacitation operation included a complex logistics, transport, careful financial records and financial management. Later, irregular release of funds slowed down the pace of the process. Funds meant for 36 months trickled through over a period of 57 months. Only twelve communities were able to complete their dams, and 26 others remained incomplete. SADET accumulated a huge debt that determined its fate and eventual closure. While the programme succeeded in accelerating the evolution of the organizational conciousness within the peasantry, it could not control managerial issues pertaining to funding agencies that did not seem up to the challenges posed by a proper developmental process. Agencies, as a whole, are more adept at justifying failures in the field than delivering the goods in a manner that assures success.

Other Experiences

Besides the major thrust described in the previous chapter, NGOs like the Zimbabwe Foundation for Education with Production (FEWP) invited the authors to run several workshops in collective cooperatives in Mashonaland East and Matabeleland South. In general terms, after these workshops the cooperatives were better equipped to deal with their debts to the omnipresent Agricultural Finance Corporation. Shandisayi Pfungwa cooperative, for example, was able to pay back outstanding loans, but it did not want to obtain new credit any more, as the interest rates had made it prohibitive. In the prevailing economic climate, the gains produced by the OW in the organizational conciousness of the cooperators were unable to express themselves fully in economic success. Agricultural cooperatives in Zimbabwe became the only available means for people with low literacy levels to improve their skills. Since the cooperatives had no incentives to offer to retain members that had improved their skills, they usually left to take up gainful employment. While individual cooperatives collapsed, Zimbabwean society gained from improved levels of skills in social strata that, without cooperatives, would have remained barred from education and training.

Ventures in Mozambique

International NGOs like Weltfriedendienst (WFD), Concern World Wide, terre des hommes Germany and Redd Barna did subsequently sponsor OW in Mozambique. In three separate incidents towards the end of the workshops, when the development fund was being calculated and decisions were made on how to use the money, violence broke out, creating difficult situations that were hard to handle. These experiences triggered a process of reflection, which allowed us to realize that our mistakes were the result of an incomplete understanding of the extent to which the OW mirrors the surrounding reality in any given country — in this case, post-civil-war Mozambique, which over sixteen years, had witnessed massive displacement, loss of life and of property, and disruption of the social and economic fabric. Afterwards, emergency aid had flooded in, but the UN and international NGOs were in the habit of doling out unusually high salaries to their own relief workers and their counterparts. People had grown accustomed to receiving handouts. The OW development fund was perceived in a similar manner. A culture had set in of violent demands for what was perceived to be due, in particular by demobilized youths in pursuit of their demobilization benefits. This culture infected the OW processes, especially at the moment when development fund matters came up. This brought the authors seriously to consider abolishing the development fund practice. A deeper reflection made us realize that the Mozambican youngsters who made up the bulk of the OW participants were, in fact, survivors of the civil war. And they owed this survival to their ability to assume the surrounding violence and assert themselves in the only way they knew, out of sheer self-preservation. Use of violence to defend the interests of the group must therefore have come across as a positive attribute, including in the workshops. It should have been possible to turn this negative energy into a positive one. During subsequent workshops we managed to improve the explanations of the why and how of the development fund, appealing to the youngsters' capacity to mobilize their sense of initiative and courage, which could be turned to their own benefit and that of their communities. In this way, the knowledge of the social context, and better reflection on the social composition of the group, allowed subsequent OW directors to foresee the potential problems, to exclude repression as a social response to the demands of the groups, and to establish a cooperative relationship between participants and facilitators.

This Mozambican experience came in very handy when we were called upon to direct OWs in Vitória, Espírito Santo, Brazil, in the course of 1997. Violence is a daily occurrence in the poorest slums of the city, affected by rampant unemployment, crime and drug trafficking. The youth in these neighbourhoods, with a life expectancy of 27 years, are survivors of the prevailing violence of the social environment, too. The insights gained in the process accounted for the fact that in the fourth series of the workshops, held in Mozambique in 1995, and the last workshops held in Brazil in 1997–98, no such violence was encountered.

The behaviour of ex-miners from Lesotho and Mozambique was similarly a rich learning ground for the facilitators. In Village 7B, Nyama Resettlement Scheme, Mashonaland West province, Zimbabwe, a group of eight trade unionists belonging to the National Union of Mineworkers of South Africa performed exactly the contributing role that the Theory of Organization expects from 'workers' (as opposed to 'artisans'). This group, possibly because of their position as trade union leaders in the thick of the apartheid struggle, transferred their experience with the technical division of labour to the participants' enterprise. They constantly encouraged the group to organize, unite and be disciplined. At the end of the workshop, they donated their share of the development fund earned by the participants' enterprise to the capital fund of the recently established village enterprise.

In stark contrast, during a workshop held at the Munguine Cooperative Union, Manhiça, Mozambique in January 1995, a group belonging to the ex-miners' cooperative took over the leadership of the enterprise. While they did contribute towards the establishment of the division of labour, they (ab)used their leadership positions to divert collectively owned resources to their own benefit. They also used their leadership qualities to manipulate the poorest OW participants into working their private plots. At the instigation of the directors and the funding agency, clearly committed to the most vulnerable groups, a democratic discussion took place. This resulted in some of the poorest, illiterate women being voted into leadership positions. It even affected the internal Cooperative Union's power relationships, which had remained unchanged for years and had severely slowed down progress.

Results

Summarizing the results of a twelve-year experience covering 60 OW events, with an average of 200 or more participants each, most of which took place in Zimbabwe, but also in Mozambique, Botswana, South Africa, Namibia, Brazil and Grenada, is not easy. The only systematic impact evaluation performed, so far, took place in November 1998: it covered four cooperatives that had gone through the OW process, even though the focus was more on the aid they had received from Norwegian People's Aid (NPA), rather than on the results achieved by the OW as such. Even so, we think the following can be mentioned.

Social psychology   The 'large group' traits described by Clodomir Santos de Morais proved to be valid across the oceans, notwithstanding the vastly different cultural settings. Moreover, experiences obtained in Mozambique proved to be equally valid in Brazil. As a result of these experiments, social psychology may be redefined as 'a cluster of psychological traits shared by individuals that perform similar types of activities', and 'the science that studies the shared, common or social psychological traits'. At the same time, social psychology may be close to the formulation of a law that establishes causal relationships between the type of activity performed and some of the characteristics of psychological reflection. In other words: change the activity (in a planned manner), and obtain a changed psychological reflection. This relationship has been further defined in a book published by the authors in Spanish and Portuguese, currently being translated into English (*Social Psychology: Responsibility and Need*).

Changes at the individual level   None of the experimental workshops held in southern Africa had a proper follow-up, or a proper impact evaluation. Nevertheless, all data obtained so far, albeit informally and non-systematized, indicate that individuals who have gone through the OW process made considerable gains in their ability to improve their quality of life. The most dramatic example of the difference between what happens at individual versus group level came after the Otse workshop, 1988, Botswana, where a group of unemployed women had formed the Baratani Cooperative making bread and biltong.[8] Twelve years later, Gavin Andersson, one of the cooperative initiators, visited the place and found the buildings deserted; the equipment, however, was still in place: a handwritten sign on the wall warned unwanted visitors: 'Do not steal, for this belongs to the people.' All the women are now in employment.

Changes at the group level: enterprise formation   Compared to mainstream methods, the OW approach provides capacitation and educational opportunities to people otherwise excluded. Compared to the 'enterprise' and 'role playing' games typical of present-day conventional enterprise training workshops, the OW provides participation in a real self-managed democratic enterprise. The element of 'reality', not present in other approches, makes the OW into a unique tool to address the problem of unemployment and social and economic exclusion, so prevalent everywhere.[9]

Agencies While the method succeeds in its commitments to the communities, getting implementing and donor agencies on the bandwagon is still an uphill struggle: agencies invariably lag far behind the leaps and bounds the communities in the field make in developmental and organizational terms. Agencies' failure to put in place follow-up activities that can take communities from the level achieved at the end of the workshops, and usher them into the mainstream economy, has been little short of dramatic.

Notes

1. Gavin Andersson in the then apartheid South Africa had started a woodworkers' cooperative using the artisan form of labour, i.e. with each member making each article from beginning to end. The need to increase production and productivity led this co-operative to introduce the division of labour. When Gavin heard about the role of division of labour in the OW, he had no doubt in his mind about the suitability of the approach to the South African context and became instrumental in the adaptation of the method to the region.

2. Leont'ev, A. N. (1975) *Activity, Consciousness and Personality*, trans. M. Hall, London: Prentice Hall. 'Objectivized activity' – *dyatel'nost* in the original Russian.

3. The term 'pastoralism' has been considered dismissive towards rural communities whose main activity is cattle herding. The intention of the authors is only to describe the general attitude affecting those people who would rather not intervene in matters affecting their social situation in preference to passive acceptance of the natural conditions that govern their habitat.

4. The concept of 'ideological behaviour' has not been defined by de Morais. We understand it as a set of psychological traits shared by individuals who perform the same type of activity and would prefer to call it 'Social Psychology'.

5. *Svetaida* means 'let's learn' in Shona. Meaningful names of development initiatives is a tradition in this part of Africa.

6. Primary structure: the concept is used by de Morais to refer to a small group chosen by the OW director from the larger group of participants, preferably 'workers' who are perspicacious in spotting dangers of group cohesion and discipline breaking up and have the skills to remedy such situations.

7. 'Development fund' is the way we found around the problems of handling money, which is as necessary a capacitating teaching aid as all the others. The development fund allows the participants to be involved in real decision-making about real money.

8. Biltong: from the Afrikaans for buttock (*bil*) and tongue (*tong*): a popular type of dried and salted meat in the region

9. A workshop where people actually work: quite exceptional.

13

Organization Development (OD) and the Moraisean OW in South Africa and Botswana

Gavin Andersson

The discipline of Organization Development (OD) has grown at a startling pace in the decades since its birth in the 1960s, expanding to embrace many different organizational areas and intervention technologies. Management theory has been profoundly affected by its insights. A well-elaborated OD strategy, or access to OD support, has come to be seen as a prerequisite for the continuing health and effectiveness of the organization, its employees and stakeholders. Diverse as the theory that guides OD may be, most of it emerges from and is framed in the language and values of business theory.[1] Over time, this theory has then been applied to the public and to the not-for-profit sectors.

The Theory of Organization first propounded by de Morais emerged within the realm of social development, and specifically in the efforts to build work enterprises by those excluded from the mainstream economy. Just as in the case of business theory, it was therefore interested in increased effectiveness, productivity and efficiency. But unlike business theory, it was also explicitly concerned with issues of equity and human development. The first experimental workshop in the theory of organization (EWTO), later to be called the Organization Workshop (OW), occurred when OD was in its early infancy. Through the formative years of the methodology there was no exchange of learning with those working in the new discipline of OD in the business sector. Moraisean theory thus makes no claim to provide insights for OD practitioners, or to constitute a definitive branch of this discipline. Nevertheless, there is much to be learned from the Theory of Organization, and from the OW method associated with it.

This chapter suggests that a Moraisean OD approach is immanent in the understandings that inform the OW, and that the management system advocated by the theory is particularly suitable for social development organizations (here also called social development enterprises). It looks at some of the organizational changes stimulated by the OW method in experiences across southern Africa, at three levels: within the enterprise established by the participants; within the organization hosting the OW; and within the organizations from which participants are drawn. Thereafter it seeks to pull out the strands of a Moraisean OD approach by referring to experiences in development NGOs in southern Africa.

The Learning Organization

As its name suggests, the OW has as its central focus learning about organization. Three aspects of its design ensure that participants constantly reflect on the organization they have created, with the aim of improving it. First, the freedom of organization, which is unique to the method, forces participants to set forward the patterns, structures and methods that they think are most suitable for effective work. Second, the daily learning event on the Theory of Organization provides valuable insights and information about organizations and their behaviour and so prompts critical reflection on the enterprise, while also introducing tools that enable action on lessons learned. Finally there is a clear incentive to improve organization in that this brings a corresponding improvement in conditions of living and work, and more money for the enterprise as productivity increases. The obverse is also true: if organization is ineffective there are immediate penalties, such as the food running out.

There is a strong body of OD and management theory that recognizes the value of creating *learning organizations*. The priority given to learning in Moraisean thought cannot therefore be said to distinguish it from other approaches to organization development. Nevertheless it should be stressed that a high level of attention is paid to individual, team and organizational learning. Indeed, it could be said that this goes further than is the case with many other methods, since Moraisean practice is rooted in the meta-theory of organization. In other words the method focuses learning attention not only on specific organized actions, and the way in which the enterprise gears up to undertake these actions, but also on the assumptions, beliefs and philosophy of organization that inform these decisions, and even the options for interaction between different kinds of organization. Importantly, this multi-dimensional learning process is not viewed as a task for one or two leaders within the enterprise, but is made part of its everyday life.

Changes in the Enterprise of the Participants

The effect of having the vast majority of enterprise members critically appraising their own organization with the aim of improving it is that organization development proceeds at a rapid pace within the enterprise created by the OW participants. In all workshops in southern Africa over the last ten years there were dramatic shifts in management structure, style and method over a period of four weeks. The Serowe workshop saw three distinct phases of organization, and this pattern was later repeated in workshops at Otse, Zutshwa and Akanani as well as in several other experiences. Part of the strength of the OW method is that there is an acceleration of the organization change process; these three phases could potentially take four years rather than four weeks in everyday life.

The initial management team was elected from the general assembly of the enterprise. It comprised the most learned participants and therefore those most confident in discussion, and thus apparently best qualified to lead the enterprise; indeed the most articulate of these people became the recognized leader of the whole enterprise at its inception. As participants experienced the consequences of weakness of this team and realized that they had power to change it, the first adjustments started. They replaced individual members with candidates who had demonstrated ability or leadership in a particular work process (or who were most articulate in critiquing the management). At this stage management and leadership tended to be seen as the same thing, and management failures were taken as signs of individual weakness of the leaders. The cycles of reliance upon charismatic people, followed by disdain for and anger at them, became shorter and shorter.

Mid-way through the OW, the learning sessions on the Theory of Organization brought realization that failures of management were linked to the very fact of its election from the general assembly. It became understood that effective management required systemic alignment of the various work thrusts (involving planning, resourcing, and reflection on activity) and hence strong links between those tasked with the activities and the coordinating team. This insight precipitated a complete change in the structure and style of management, and the third change began. Within days a system was instituted in which there was devolution of detailed management to each unit but coordination of work across the enterprise. This brought a dramatic improvement in management, the productivity of the enterprise and the pace of individual learning, and these shifts were accompanied by a surge in energy and commitment from all members of the enterprise. New faces appeared in management, people whose abilities were different from those of the orators of the mass meeting. The regular practice of critical reflection encouraged by the Theory then provided stimuli for further adjustments to the organizing patterns, which were steadily implemented as the OW progressed. By the end of four weeks the productivity of the enterprise of over a hundred people was well over the industrial average for the country, and there was also a vibrant crèche, ongoing literacy and numeracy classes, an efficient kitchen with a changing daily menu, and a team engrossed in production of a report summarizing the learning of the four weeks. This was a far cry from the situation during the first week, characterized by long discussions and groups of people waiting to hear what they should do.

Changes in the Hosting NGO

Since the OW is meant to foster learning about organization it is hardly surprising that organizational change occurs in the enterprise formed by the participants. What is perhaps more interesting is that there is immediately also an effect on the organization that arranges the OW, in southern Africa usually an NGO. This can occur at several levels: the leadership and management potential of individual staff members may blossom whereas it was previously hidden; discussion of the behaviour of NGO personnel may provide impetus for a profound culture shift; and the organization may move to improved levels of efficiency and show new confidence in undertaking large-scale projects as it takes on the learning from the OW.

The emergence of previously unrecognized leadership has been a feature of all OWs in southern Africa. At times this is apparent during the OW itself. At Otse a young woman who had not previously occupied any leadership role outside her family circle emerged as the formidable and astute coordinator of an exceptionally complex enterprise. In Zutshwa a potentially debilitating argument, about which individuals should work in the salt-works established in the course of the OW, was resolved by the simple fact that the most capable people proved their worth through the experience.[2] In other experiences there are similar tales about new and exciting leaders emerging.

Sometimes the effects of participation in the OW are apparent only in the months after the experience. A receptionist in an NGO was so changed in her work approach and ability that within months she was nominated to lead a southern African network, a task that she performed with distinction. An unassertive and quiet staff member from another NGO was urged to take up the position of director after a few months, based on the initiative and organizational competence displayed in the period after the OW.

Of course it is not only NGO staff who might grow in this way. Extraordinary people from all walks of life are able to benefit from the experience. And while it is impossible to predict fully the ripple effects of this 'quickening' of leadership, it appears that in every case there has been a substantial strengthening of their organizations and enterprises. Of course, the workshop praxis may also help to reveal weakness in existing leadership; it is after all a real-life situation.

Organizational change in NGOs associated with the OW has been more significant than can be explained merely by describing the effects of participation on a few individuals. Instead the stimulus for change appears to come from the whole organization critically assessing its practice and culture, as it reviews the learning during the OW.

There may be several points that resonate with the NGO. By way of example, it has happened on several occasions that NGO staff are elected to serve on the first management committee of the participants' enterprise. This occurred in Serowe and Otse in Botswana, and at Akanani in the Northern Province of South Africa. This first structure customarily fails rather badly, as is suggested above. But in the workshops mentioned, some individuals in this management grouping were seen to behave completely differently from many of the other committee members from different backgrounds.[3] The strength of Moraisean theory resides in the fact that it is able to interpret this behaviour and show its roots, as well as to suggest ways to deal with it. This means that criticism of the behaviour is not personally threatening, and it is thus easier for individuals to change. This is certainly a strengthening exercise for all of the people concerned; indeed, there is often a great deal of fun as participants discuss behaviour patterns that are unhelpful to the enterprise.

But, continuing with the example of the discussion of 'corrupt intellectualism', there is further consequence if the 'home' NGO is alert to the lessons emerging from the OW. Attention is now focused on the decades-old discussion about NGOs in the 'aid chain', and the positions taken by the intermediaries, the development intelligentsia or elite. This may sound like a return to fundamentalism. Yet the relationship of NGO workers to grassroots organization is central to any struggle for social development, and interactions that raise the problem directly and specify what is a desirable orientation, and what therefore needs to shift, are profoundly helpful. It is not surprising that the OW contributed to a significant culture shift, in favour of grassroots involvement in NGO governance, in two of the organizations that employed the methodology in its early years.[4]

There is a final way in which the OW can affect the organization hosting it. In the first place the exposure to the OW itself may bring a shift in perspective about what is feasible when large numbers of people work together. Second, the 'hosting' NGO is affected by the social mobilization that occurs as a result of the OW; the very scale of the experience means that a range of private, traditional and public agencies may be drawn into the preparations and running of the workshop (and subsequent interaction with the NGO). Third, just as the accelerating learning around organization exposes the inadequacies internal to the participants' enterprise, it also puts under the spotlight inadequate practice in the NGO and offers ways of improving it. The combination of these effects may well induce a great change in NGO operations. In the case of CORDE in Botswana, the organizational activity increased ten-fold in the space of a few months, with commensurate personal development among its staff.

Changes in the Participants' Enterprises of Origin

Change in the enterprises from which participants are drawn is mostly determined by the degree to which individuals are able to influence these bodies upon their return. This means that there is greater likelihood of impact when a group of enterprise members is able to participate in an OW. Experience has shown that there can be rapid changes in the home enterprise in this situation. Having been part of an exceptionally complex enterprise (because of the great numbers of people involved in the OW, and the many different activities that have to be managed), the participants tend to view their home organization through new lenses. What had appeared as very difficult organizational issues appear to be rather simple, while it is correspondingly easier to see how to adjust the enterprise to adopt the patterns and methods suggested by the theory of organization from the OW. Provided there is adequate support at this stage, there can thus be significant improvements as a result of the OW.

Where the home enterprise is debilitated or seriously ill, the OW provides the impetus for diagnosis and treatment. Perhaps the most dramatic known example of this was the effect on an unemployed workers' association whose members attended the Otse workshop.[5] The behaviour of the participants from this organization was seen by others in the OW to be a discredit to the strong union movement that had supported it over the years. Discussion of this behaviour moreover led to agreement that the real problem was the style of leadership of the organization, where a system of 'patronage politics' had become entrenched. The host NGO accordingly wrote a letter to the general secretary of the trade union federation, COSATU, who immediately instigated an investigation into the issues that had provoked the OW participants' concern. Barely two months after the workshop a review process was initiated in the unemployed workers' association, which led to sweeping changes and new leadership.

An Approach to OD?

Up to this point we have briefly looked at the changes brought about during and after the OW. However, this chapter argues that immanent in this method is an approach to OD that can be used in the day-to-day change processes of organizations, and that does not depend on the 'motor' of an OW.

At the outset it should be said that discussion of an approach has not provided a framework for the increasingly familiar OD interventions by an external consultant, so much as it has suggested a method for continual self-strengthening of organizational systems. A Moraisean OD practice would seem to fall broadly into the stream of *process consulting*, led by a team of internal change agents. It is practice that determines this orientation: the NGOs that pioneered the OW in southern Africa were notably stronger after each experience as the theory and method were taken into the life rhythms of these enterprises. In most cases this organizational development was most intense when the NGO concerned was engaged in facilitation of an OW, for then it is inevitable that questions get raised about the NGO operational competence and internal functioning. However, in a few instances a practitioner led an internal change process over a period of time, drawing on Moraisean theory, but outside the context of the OW. A feature of each successful process was that leadership was supportive of the changes, which took a long time to reach their full expression.[6] This need for leadership support also holds, of course, for any other approach.

Defining Characteristics

It is possible to pull out three defining characteristics of a Moraisean methodology. While one or other may be in concordance with other OD approaches, in combination they may suggest a differentiation from other schools of OD. After listing each characteristic, there is a brief discussion about how it may be drawn on in change processes to improve effectiveness of organizations.

Social mobilization In the first place, de Morais' Theory of Organization sets out to inform and support large-scale social processes; it is geared to social mobilization and specifically to capacitation of large numbers of people to take a course of action that will ensure their means of survival and improved quality of life. The encouragement and challenge (even provocation) to think on a social scale means that any enterprise guided by the theory tends to maintain what Mant has called the ternary mindset.[7] In other words the task, product, purpose or ideal for which the organization was established is always at the forefront of attention; little time is given to wrangling over interpersonal power or influence. In itself this is a significant accomplishment. But there is a more subtle consequence of this consistent appreciation of the broader social context. This is that an organization will tend to seek purposeful interaction with a broad array of social actors within the specific context, for mutual benefit and in order that individual efforts will be optimally effective. The 'skin' or boundary of the enterprise is well defined, but so too is its existence as one part of a far greater social system that it is affected by and that it in turn influences.[8]

This orientation towards collaborative work and careful positioning of the organization within its social environment has direct implications for the OD process. If we see each area of work as an 'interaction node' with a range of other stakeholders, then there are obvious implications for patterns of work. It is for instance necessary to devolve the authority to act decisively in 'external policy' to each team member, rather than following the practice adopted in so many organizations where this is the prerogative of a few people 'at the top'. The confidence to act in this way can derive only from thorough understanding of the philosophy and orientation of the organization. This accentuates a need for clarity about the vision and direction of the enterprise by each member, and effective systems for communication and critical reflection across the enterprise.

The link between activity and behaviour A second characteristic of a Moraisean approach is that it integrates issues relating to values, attitude and personal behaviour (in many other approaches separated out into an exploration of organizational 'culture') into every discussion about organizational change. For, of course, the unique contribution of de Morais to social theory was that he showed how experience of organization (especially production organization) contributes to psychological reflection and the cognitive development.[9] It is rather easy to understand that the mental models that are the cognitive product of an experience of organization, or other activity, will powerfully influence subsequent planning and action. Until de Morais' contribution, the extent to which there was a link between certain kinds of individual behaviour and this knowledge production had not been properly appreciated. The conscious attribution of specific 'bad habits' of individuals to a particular background or experience produces a salutary effect when raised within an enterprise habituated to mutual criticism. Since there is an explanation for this behaviour, it is depersonalized and so more easily accepted; this allows the people concerned to look at it frankly and work to improve their own behaviour, just as it empowers others to work constructively with their peers.

The insight that activity or experience itself 'teaches' certain ways of acting and thinking is not only useful to understanding problems *ex post facto*, as described in the preceding paragraph. It also enables the enterprise to anticipate the effect of certain work practices on the individuals concerned, and thus their likely future relationship to the enterprise as a whole.

As a fairly obvious example, the tasks of 'accounting with the need to develop a system of cross checks, and defined hierarchies of responsibility' will lead to a very different orientation and culture than would the experience of facilitating literacy classes. Appreciating this allows the enterprise to pay attention to procedures that maintain the 'whole organization awareness' of each of the actors and provides shifts in activity by individuals to help personal development.

The Freedom of Organization A final distinctive aspect of a Moraisean approach is undoubtedly the freedom of organization. As will have become apparent through other chapters of this book, de Morais understood the freedom of organization in a very direct way: participants in the OW are provided with the opportunity to organize in whatever way they wish, and for whatever end they can define (within the law) as desirable and attainable with the resources at their disposal. This principle extended to a development NGO implies a specific management orientation, flexibility in long-term goals (within a clear understanding of the organization's stance and the contextual demands it strives to meet) and acceptance that there might be frequent changes to structure.

Freedom of organization implies a bias towards what has been called horizontal management or self-management of the enterprise and its constituent parts: a high degree of innovation is allowed, and responsibility given to any department or work team. The core fascination of a Moraisean OD practice is to optimize potential, of individuals and departments/ teams within the enterprise. This innovation and creativity could turn destructive unless a balance is maintained between centralized coordination and decentralized responsibility and innovation, and so clear tools and procedures are introduced to ensure that this can happen. It could be said that the very freedom to organize, and to innovate, is a primary source of motivation for members of the enterprise.

Of course there are also possibilities that a department or team may fail rather badly, or move into a spiral of decreasing learning. The point of the method is not to watch idly to see if these people will 'sink or swim'. In this situation the art of the OD practitioner (here working as part of a management team) lies in weighing up how long it is useful to let people struggle to find the way forward and when it is useful to intervene to assist or to try to provide access to the information or expertise that can assist.

There is no 'level of attainment of the organization' that can be set at the outset, because the degree to which there will be individual and enterprise-wide learning – and the consequences of this learning – cannot be predicted. The enterprise is in essence positioned to learn its way into the future. As it acquires more capability and confidence as a result of practical work undertaken, it is quite possible that there will be a commensurate raising of ambition regarding long-term achievement. This is welcome, and desirable, but if it were unchecked it would tend towards the idealistic and Utopian rather than the practical. The Moraisean approach again introduces balance by the use of very rigorous planning and monitoring tools for immediate projects; the method provides continuity between strategy and the planning detail.[10]

The most obvious consequence of this freedom of organization is that there is an acceptance of the notion that there will be constant change. Rather than focusing on appropriate structures (and tight job descriptions) a Moraisean approach would try, first, to understand the activities and processes that need to be established to reach particular objectives. Then there would be a need to see how these activities can be resourced by the enterprise as a whole, and what the most appropriate division of tasks is to ensure that they are carried out effectively. The process of periodic critical reflection (see note 17) will then provide clarity about necessary adjustments to the organizing pattern or structure (just as it provides learning in the area of activity). In this way the organizational design and change process becomes an arena of work for all enterprise members. This is not to say that there is never going to be a need for external intervention, but rather to emphasize that issues of management and organizational change are part of the everyday discourse within the Moraisean enterprise.

A Note on the Human Relations Movement (HRM)

At first it might appear that de Morais' freedom of organization and attention to participation is in broad alignment with the school of thought pioneered by Kurt Lewin, which at one time was known as the human relations movement (HRM). Nothing could be further from the truth: Lewin's theory in fact deliberately constrains organizational freedom. Leading protagonists of Moraisean thought have railed against the 'small-group social psychology' and all it represents.[11] But there are other critics of this pervasive thinking.

The first element of a critique is the disempowerment brought by the ahistorical and decontextualized approach to any social issue.[12] De Morais' approach is perpendicular to this spirit of enquiry. Instead, as discussed briefly above, he roots all analysis of organization, and of social behaviour, in a detailed examination of history and the prevailing social, economic and cultural-spiritual context. And of course he shows that individual members of a group of three hundred people do not behave in the same way as do members of Lewin's small groups of fifteen or thereabouts.

The second element of a critique has to do with the concept of participation advanced by Lewin and his successors. This is seen to be strongly manipulative. In the words of Peter Drucker: 'Human relations lacks any awareness of the economic dimension of the problem. As a result there is tendency for [it] to degenerate into mere slogans, which become an alibi for having no management policy in respect to the human organization.' Worse still, there is a strong manipulative tendency in the whole concept.[13] As Lefebvre notes,[14] 'without self-management, "participation" has no meaning; it becomes an ideology, and makes manipulation possible'.[15] While the heyday of Lewin has come and gone, there is still a large school of social scientists influenced by this paradigm, which tries to reduce political problems to technical problems.[16] De Morais' approach is in direct contrast to this paradigm. Participation is discussed within the context of full self-management, and with scrupulous attention to the power relationships within society, and the options for organization of the enterprise. There is no attempt to manipulate, but rather an orientation towards constructing a system that optimizes potential.

Giving Priority to Learning

Looking briefly at some of the understandings about (adult) learning that are woven into the OW design, we can start to see the implications for development enterprises. Of course the fact that the workshop is designed to be a practical or activity-based exercise, with a large number of participants, already sets the framework for learning. But the design elements facilitating learning are worth noting so that they can be replicated in everyday life; although it would be a remarkable organization that managed to weave in all these strands consistently:

- The use of reports, the critical balance, and the routines established for enterprise management, establish certain *patterns of information*. Participants gain confidence in 'how to find out about something'.
- The lectures and Theory of Organization help to establish the core concepts or 'big ideas' important for the enterprise, and their relationship. Participants start to learn 'what we need to know': *the organization of knowledge.*
- The allocation of roles across the enterprise to check performance against the plan of another department or team means that participants are helped to build up the overall picture of the enterprise in its full complexity.

- The circulation of reports and critical reflection documents allows appreciation of the scale of the enterprise and the detailed tasks facing different teams.
- The proposals about way forward, and plan elements, at the end of any critical balance, ensures that analytico-synthetical abilities are exercised.
- The critical balance helps build meta-cognition: the ability to monitor one's current level of understanding and decide when it is not adequate.[17]
- Knowledge is made available as it is needed: the situation and context participants are placed in lead them to stretch their cognitive abilities, and information or expertise made available at this point is eagerly grasped since its value is understood.

At the point when the enterprise starts to work really well, facilitators may well work with some of the participants, in optimizing the use of Gant charts, for instance. The difference between accomplishment when working with this support, and that achieved working alone, also increases potential for learning.[18]

Concluding Remarks

Lived experience quickly asserts that a Moraisean approach to OD brings significant shifts to the way that development enterprises organize, and leads to significantly enhanced social mobilization and empowerment. This is not the case in most other experiences of OD facilitation, nor is there a management approach which so consistently speaks to the context, values and imperatives of social development. But it is easier to appreciate the whole systems effect of working in this way than it is to disentangle its constituent parts and present them as elements of a different theory. I am hopeful that this first attempt to do this has at least helped to clarify the orientation and stance of a Moraisean method.

Notes

1. Agencies like CDRA and OLIVE in South Africa, INTRAC in Europe and SEARCH in India (to name merely a few leading examples) have made enormous contributions in contextualizing OD practice to the sphere of social development, and specifically to NGO activity. However, very little of the theory informing it is originally derived from experiences of social development.

2. The Zutshwa OW set up the infrastructure for a salt-works. Each family in the remote village was invited to nominate a participant in the workshop. At the end of the workshop all participants chose the 20 people who had shown themselves best capable of working in the new enterprise. (See *Workteam*, no. 9, 1990.)

3. In the Otse workshop of 1989, participants described the bad habits of some intellectuals, including a few NGO staff, pointing out that they 'give primacy to

theoretical learning over practical experiential learning', resent intellectual challenge and will 'try to maintain intellectual hegemony by personal attack and selecting those facts which bolster [their] position'. This kind of behaviour was dubbed 'corrupt intellectualism' (Andersson, G. et al. [1989] *Organisation Workshops in Botswana*, Gaborone: CORDE).

4. Co-operation for Research, Development and Education (CORDE) in Botswana, and Akanani Rural Development Association in South Africa. It is arguable that another of the NGOs pioneering the method faced internal discord precisely because it tried to ignore the imperative to change its practice.

5. Participants from four countries attended this workshop, and some went on to become well-known leaders in their societies. The workshop provided much learning about leadership and organizational behaviour across different cultures.

6. In one example the organizational change process, led by the CEO, took place over a period of four years. Ivàn and Isabel Labra have also cautioned (personal communication, April 1999) against working in this way unless leaders of organizations are fully aware of the process, and understand its potential and the issues that it may throw up.

7. Mant, A. (1997) *Intelligent Leadership*, St Leonard's: Allen and Unwin, 1997.

8. In other parts of the South, and notably Asia, there has been a similar attention to alignment of multiple organizational initiatives (witness the interest in participatory strategic planning in India and Bangladesh). Richard Bawden's work around the role of critical learning systems in creating couplings for communicative action is a further exciting example of this tendency to move away from 'auto-centric' organizational theory. (See Andersson, 6., 'Unbounded organization', in D. Lewis and T. Wallace, *Beyond the New Policy Agenda* [forthcoming])

9. See Labra, I. and I. Labra (1997) *The Organisational Workshop on Theory of Organisation. Collection of Papers*, Harare: Communication Link Trust, and Carman, R., I. Labra and M. Davis (1999) 'Introduction to the Social Scale Capacitation Method' in *Learning from Brazil*.

10. De Morais did not invent many of the tools and techniques for effective enterprise management. The elegance of the method lies in the way in which they are integrated by the Theory of Organization.

11. The most coherent exposition, in the Moraiscan tradition, of the weakness in this 'small group' and behavioural thinking, and its consequences for social organization, can be found in Ivàn Labra's *Social Psychology* (forthcoming in English) (originally published in Spanish as *Psicologia Social: Responsabilidad y Necessidad*, Santiago de Chile: LOM Editoriales 1992; revised and republished in Portuguese by IATTERMUND, Brasília, 1995).

12. Peter Franks (1993) in *Kurt Lewin and the Foundations of Participative Management*, Johannesburg: HSRC sets forward the objection to Lewin's setting 'boundaries on the gestalt', so it is limited to an abstract ahistorical moment. He quotes Wertheimer and Sarte's objections, and contrasts their approach with the opinion of A. Stephen that 'mankind in a test tube is the hope and aim of social science'.

13. Drucker, P. (1954) *The Practice of Management*, New York: Harper, p. 279.

14. Lefebvre, H. (1976) *The Survival of Capitalism: Reproduction of the Relations of Production*, London: Allison and Busby, p. 120.

15. This intimate link between 'participation' and 'manipulation' is echoed in Carmen's neologism 'participulation', referred to elsewhere in this book.

16. Franks 1993: 21.

17. The critical balance/critical reflection is not a report, although it may refer to a report. The purpose of the CB is three-fold: (1) to assist learning across the entire enterprise; (2) to ensure systemic alignment of the various work thrusts; and (3) to see that attention and resources are made available as needed for the enterprise to succeed in its work.

18. This follows Lev Vygotsky's concept of the zone of proximal development, neglected until comparatively recently in the English-speaking world.

The OW in Europe and Other Industrial Countries

14

The Potential of the OW in the Former Soviet Bloc Countries and in Economies in Crisis

Miguel Sobrado

The Workers' Councils in Poland and the Path Blocked in Russia

Between 1989 and 1991 the old legal economic and social order of the Soviet Bloc finally collapsed from exhaustion. With it ended an era of centrally directed command economics that lasted for 40 years in central Europe and 70 years in the case of the Soviet Union; a new stage was being cleared for structural transformation in which, virtually from scratch, a new institutional framework for a market economy was going to be created. The organizational culture in the Soviet Union, historically based on the central bureaucratic principle, operating through diktat and command, nevertheless inherited new mental models from the new era. In the case of Russia these models, geared to the construction of a capitalism in the Thatcherite mould but directed from above, meant that the pilfering of public wealth became almost child's play. Thus, in the name of the 'free' market, public monopolies were converted, purely and simply, into private monopolies; and at each stage of the distribution process, the Mafia took a generous scoop. The lands of many a collective were redistributed, often against the expressed will of the membership, who preferred to continue producing under the existing collective arrangements.

These authoritarian and centralist mental models, wholly typical of the command economies, were imposed to the interested applause or at least with the silent consent of the international organizations' 'experts in the construction of capitalism'. The crass ignorance, on the part of those organizations, of the sociological processes involved in the construction of a new organizational culture and back-up institutions is plain for everyone to see. The result has been an economic, political and social disaster that has dragged the per capita income of the Russians down to that of a poverty-stricken African state. What was once an opportunity for the development of a major part of the planet has been turned into a growing political crisis that hangs as a looming threat over regional and world stability. That, in a country like Russia, centralist tendencies should have prevailed is comprehensible: it was the Mafia, many of them ex-party cardholders, who grabbed power and who, obviously, benefited; that Western powers should have merely stood by while the economic and military power of their former arch-enemy was being dismembered is also understandable. But that, of all people, 'development experts', because of their sociological blind spot, should have brought this country to the brink of an explosion is not explicable either by their Cartesian upbringing or by a prevailing complacency or a sense of *Schadenfreude*.

But for reasons of a sort of sociological autism, the disintegration and destabilization of an entire region would in normal circumstances, and long ago, have raised the alarm in the circles of international organizations and set off a series of corrective measures. It was not for lack of warning. The great risk that Russia was running had been signalled as far back as 1993, when an ETC (Ecological Training Centre) delegation, composed of myself and Ian Cherrett, visited Russia. In my article 'Entrepreneurial capacitation in conditions of transition in Eastern Europe', which was published by FAO, Rome (Sobrado 1994), we registered our proposal. This consisted in applying the OW approach in Russia, adapted to local conditions, i.e. designed in such a way that the ingrained bureaucratic mentality could be overcome by introducing autonomous management structures. Unfortunately, the potentialities of this approach were not appreciated at their true value, possibly because the inspiration for the proposal originated in the Third World.

In Russia's neighbouring countries, all former members of the Eastern Bloc, the reforms took a different turn. But the most interesting is the case of Poland, this positive 'tiger' of the European economy. One of the fundamentals of the OW is that groups resolve their problems autonomously. Provided people have autonomy, solutions will indeed be found and initiatives taken. It is this very (objective) activity that allows people to recognize the reality of the situation, discard obsolete mentalities and 'learn to learn', from practice. This fundamental OW principle was adopted, broadly, by the new Polish government in 1992, then faced with a floundering economy and rising unemployment, caused by artificial restrictions that had sometimes been inflicted on the former state enterprises at the recommendation of the privatization specialists. The Polish government would, instead, sometimes transfer those enterprises earmarked for privatization to the workers' councils of those factories for decisions concerning their future. The workers' councils took two or three months to decide. They could buy their enterprises with bank credits; look for investors willing to buy the factory and become their employees; they could also enter in partnership with the government, while remaining in the public sector, but on condition that they operate under market conditions and with the understanding that, in case of failure, they would be liquidated.

The majority chose to remain in the public sector, but they insisted at the same time that they be deregulated so that they could operate under genuine market conditions. Some began contracting their own managers with public aid or with the help of international consultants. They reorganized the former state enterprises and began to function. Almost instantly the economy started to pick up and, since then, has maintained an average level of growth at around 5 per cent. Two years after the changes, Poland, the country with the smallest number of privatized enterprises of all its neighbours, boasted a private sector that was already larger than the public sector in terms of contributions to GNP. The growth of the private sector was healthy, with no Mafiosi, and it has been invigorated and stimulated by the rejuvenation of public enterprises. The decentralization of decision-making and the opening of spaces to find autonomous solutions allowed for a great versatility in the paths taken to development, a path blocked off in Russia, where the neo-liberalist radicals held sway.

An in-depth study and analysis of this enormous laboratory of enterpreneurial forms and systems of participation, which blossomed in Poland during the period of transformation and change, still remains to be done. These processes, subjected to systematic analysis, will allow a better design of the type of capacitation processes needed in systemic transformations. The findings would be of great benefit to other regions in the world. From this immense Polish laboratory a number of lessons could be learned that cannot be found in economics handbooks. It could be a source of great inspiration for the multifarious problems with which Russia is afflicted and for which it needs an urgent solution today, if, indeed, it is not already too late before the huge explosion becomes inevitable.

Natural Disasters

Natural disasters such as earthquakes, floods and hurricanes, large enough in size to affect entire countries, bring in their wake the collapse of the institutional structures and provoke a state of social anomy capable of destabilizing a national government or an entire region. Disasters of this kind require equally massive organized responses capable of preventing further damage and initiating reconstruction work in the affected countries or regions. This response can and should basically come from organized civil society. The army, however welcome and useful its intervention at the moment itself, because of its ability to initiate rescue work rapidly, in the long term is not in a position to sustain a long drawn-out effort and, moreover, may give rise to undesirable dependencies among the affected populations.

The fact that the army has assumed leading roles in disaster situations has sometimes served as an excuse for less democratic, authoritarian regimes to legitimize its very existence and has also tended to inhibit the will and the capacity of civil society to organize autonomously. Thus Hurricane Fifi in Honduras in 1974 presented an unforeseen opportunity for the application of mass capacitation approaches to come to the fore and prove its worth. As explained in Chapter 6, a great number of membership associations, which had applied the OW method, had come into being in Honduras in the context of the agrarian reform there.

What was immediately noticeable was that, wherever the local community had gone through the OW experience, people were better able to cope with the disintegrating effects of the hurricane. In none of the affected enterprises of this kind were there any fatalities, whereas elsewhere there were a great number of deaths. This reminds me of an event that occurred in the wake of the David and Frederico hurricanes in 1979, in the Dominican Republic. As recounted by Clodomir himself:

> At that time, I happened to have been directing, together with Hernán Mora, of the National University of Costa Rica, an Organizational Workshop on account of the International Institute for Cooperation in Agriculture (IICA) and the Dominican Agrarian Institute (IAD), with the peasants of the region of Limón del Yuna. This region of a majority of smallholders had been badly affected by the hurricane. We set off using the food aid as launching point for the recovery activities. At first only a couple of hundred people took part, but as the enterprise progressed with its activities, its material work, and the execution of local development plans, the number of candidates increased substantially. The works to be undertaken allowed them to bid for the job of cleaning up the drainage channels, which gave the OW enterprise a great prestige and attracted regional participation. In the end, the enterprise developed into a buoyant cooperative for the purchase and sale of implements and consumption goods for the region's producers. This cooperative was still going strong ten years on and, in all likelihood, still exists.

Hurricane Mitch in Central America: From 'Aid' to Autonomy

Hurricane Mitch, which devastated Central America at the end of 1998, seriously affected or left homeless up to three million people; it virtually levelled the entire banana crop in Honduras and Nicaragua; it seriously affected the coffee harvest and a variety of other cattle and and industrial enterprises, leaving hundreds of thousands unemployed. Neither the army nor the existing institutions in Honduras or Nicaragua were in a position to prevent the disaster, or to provide the necessary back-up in the rescue or recuperation operations. The destruction was of such a magnitude and the means of response of the governments so limited that local communities saw themselves obliged, in many an instance, to organize and take the reconstruction work upon themselves. The latter is an important factor from the point of view of the construction of a civic culture and of a new form of decentralized and participative institutions. The event was of such overwhelming proportions that it transcended the usual channels for reconstruction work. At the same time it opened up a historical opportunity for the construction of a new civic culture and democratic institutions.

With this in mind, the Overarching Council of Central American Universities – CSUCA – took the initiative of setting up an International Civic Committee for the Reconstruction of Central America. This committee has already started work with the channelling of resources and of international aid towards the capacitation, organization and autonomous management of the reconstruction projects by the affected communities themselves. The initiative is important in that it holds the promise of opening up an opportunity for structural transformation in the direction of greater democratic participation in Central America, and towards the channelling of 'aid' towards initiatives that allow people to become organizationally literate, the formation of a civic culture and the building up of social capital, and the promises of a better future for the region.

The civic committee initiative is also important in terms of setting a precedent showing that it is possible to reshape the mould in which the international 'aid' effort traditionally is cast. 'Aid' has the potential here of being transformed into a genuine factor of development that, instead of promoting dependency, stimulates people's organizational literacy and the social synergy towards greater decentralization and participation that tends to emerge in great moments of need and emergency. It shows that it is possible to turn crisis into development opportunities.[1] Debt cancellation for poor countries, certainly, is a positive step, but if this cancellation is accompanied by the positive organization and participation by local civil society itself, it will be possible for public funds to be managed more efficiently and for society as a whole to benefit and progress. If society is not capacitated and if aid is managed in the usual clientelist fashion by the all too familiar political class, the immense local potential for reconstruction will not only not be set in motion, but the possibility is great that in no time whatsoever the country will find itself indebted again while its elite continues to enrich itself in the process by their manipulations of public funds.

That is one of the many reasons why the methodology of mass

capacitation transcends current approaches to organizing of production projects and providing gainful employment for the unemployed. That is also why it is of such enormous importance for state policies dealing with emergencies, development and state reform. The methods of the OW have the potential to become a strategic factor in the design of future state policies and in the construction of a properly organized civil society, in the absence of which the necessary reforms will remain well nigh impossible.

Note

1. The Chinese characters for 'crisis' are those of 'danger' and 'opportunity'.

Reference

Sobrado, M. (1994) '*Capacitación empresarial en condiciones de transición en Europa Oriental*' (Entrepreneurial capacitation in the economies in transition in Eastern Europe) in *Land Reform*, Rome: FAO.

15

Post-Salazar Portugal: The First European SIPGEI[1]

Isabel Labra and Iván Labra[2]

The End of the Salazar Dictatorship and the Independence of the Portuguese Colonies

The demise of the 50-year dictatorship of the Salazar regime only hastened the break-up of the Portuguese colonial empire. During this period thousands of entrepreneurs had lived sheltered lives under the clientelist protection of the state, a sophisticated, institutionalized form of paternalism. They therefore had good reasons to feel indebted to the state, and when the regime collapsed, they came pouring in droves out of Portugal and its colonies, until then euphemistically referred to as Portugal's Overseas Provinces. At the time, metropolitan Portugal held only three-quarters of its total (9 million) population, three million of whom had gone to live abroad, due to the lack of job opportunities at home.

The arrival of more than half a million of *retornados* (returned colonial personnel) made up of Portuguese nationals expelled from the former colonies of Angola, Mozambique, Guinea-Bissau, Cape Verde and São Tomé e Principe, only contributed to a further exacerbation of the inherent structural problems in housing and employment in the motherland. Portugal now was forced to cope, on top, with the structural problem of unemployment.

In this context, hundreds of thousands of paid workers involved in agriculture, industry and service industries were trying to keep afloat thousands of small to medium-sized enterprises, albeit with scant success given the dearth of experience in organizing and managing enterprises of that nature. The workers had quite creatively transformed the enterprises into commonly owned cooperatives with socially divided production. It seemed imperative, therefore, to put in place an organizational skill capacitation programme for those workers, who had become, for all practical purposes, owners and managers at the same time. This would allow them efficiently to confront the unemployment problem and the inherent functional weaknesses of their enterprises.

The situation seemed urgent enough for the government of the then prime minister, Mario Soares, to knock on the door of the ILO for technical assistance, in the form of a Technical Cooperation Programme financed by the United Nations Development Programme (UNDP). The aim was a capacitation programme for the 'Trainer of Trainers' (TOT – formación de formadores) for the social area of the economy, in other words, the cooperative and self-managing enterprise sector.[3]

The Large Scale Capacitation Project: International Aid

The government initiated negotiations for a $500,000 project, and set up the cooperative institute Antonio Sergio, INSCOOP, at the same time. INSCOOP became host to the POR/ILO/UNCP/007 programme. The ILO called upon Clodomir Santos de Morais, who had just directed FAO projects in Honduras and Mexico, to be ILO adviser to the government of Portugal. However, the funds set aside to cover the cost of the course OWs involving six thousand learners were insufficient.

Because of the size of the task at hand, Prime Minister Soares called on the Swedish government, which was able to channel US $250,000 through the Swedish aid agency SIDA to INSCOOP. Furthermore, the Norwegian development agency NORAD provided another $50,000, on condition that the capacitation programme include participants from the Third World. This allowed the project to provide study grants to ten candidates from the Republic of Cape Verde, Guinea Bissau and São Tomé e Principe, as well as to two Guatemalan exiles sent by the Honduran Institute for Rural Development, IHDER. Six exiled Brazilians currently living in Sweden, Switzerland and France were also able to attend.

Portugal had laboured for 50 years under a corporatist regime. Under this form of incipient capitalism, it was sufficient to be in favour with the corporations concerned in order to obtain new investment. To set up a shoe or furniture factory, for example, it was enough to persuade the head-quarters of the corporation concerned that there was sufficient economic space for the business to thrive, for a new branch of that particular industry to be set up in the country. Under these conditions, a country in dire need of experts in development projects had managed for years without them.

It was easy to understand, therefore, that the aspiring (non-corporatist) capitalism of the European Union was only too eager to exploit the 50 economic development specialists (TDEs) the ILO project was going to provide through the 90–day residential course. There was also a big need for the 40 upper-level specialists in investment projects to be formed during a second non-residents' workshop lasting five months, to take place during the second half of 1979.

The directors of INSCOOP and the cooperative leadership of the cooperative unions and federations were not aware of the strong possibility of the new cadres graduated from those courses being diverted from the original purpose that had led to their formation. All of them were united in their opposition to the idea of a special salary being paid.

The salary scale, calculated according to the value and importance of the work done, ranged from investment specialist (TPI), development project specialist (TDC) to project assistant (API). These were to be the backbone of the planned national SIPGEI.

The development experts (TDCs) would train three thousand project assistants, and a further three thousand would be trained by the investment specialists *in situ* at no expense to INSCOOP or to the Portuguese Co-operative Movement and would render their services to the different municipalities.

The Ultimate Destination of the Newly Formed Cadres

Objective factors Some of the 50 TDCs were university students while others were newly graduated. The majority of them had completed higher studies and had not found work, except for a few co-operative leaders and the six Africans on a study grant: four from Cape Verde and two from São Tomé e Principe. The newly formed cadres were full of enthusiasm, not realizing the gigantic problems Portuguese cooperativism was going to have to cope with.

That over four thousand cooperatives and other mutual aid and membership associations existed at that time was no reason for triumphalism. On the contrary, Professor Emeritus Henrique de Barros, the director of INSCOOP, was so worried about the situation that he remarked that 'it would be a grave mistake to take for granted that the cooperative idea had already triumphed in Portugal. It would be more honest to simply admit that it continues to run the grave risk of stagnation, retrogression, not excluding the possibility of total disintegration.' He added, 'Without a sound system for the flow of credit that lays down precise regulations for amounts, timescales, deadlines and strict guarantees, the co-operative movement is doomed to lose steam and may even go into decline.' Protectionist measures, typical of the corporatist state, were done away with in favour of open trade policies, to smooth the path for Portugal to join the then European Economic Community (EEC).

Meanwhile, despite Henrique de Barros' serious warnings, the old and now bypassed cooperative rules and regulations remained in place, and little effort was made to adapt them to the changed circumstances, or to devise a credible and adequate system for the processing of credit. The 50 years of corporatist dictatorship had left Portugal hopelessly overtaken by the other European countries. In the field of education, for example, although 81 per cent of the population received primary schooling, only 8 per cent held secondary certificates. This compares unfavourably with a country like Greece, where the proportions at that time were 55 and 27 per cent respectively.

The cooperative movement could not but reflect this serious handicap. The race towards the adoption of capitalist patterns of operation in the production of goods and services all too soon resulted in a polarization between rich and poor producers. This applied, too, to small and large cooperatives, so much so that a mere 10 per cent of all the cooperatives eventually gobbled up to 90 per cent of the subsidies provided by the European Community. This prompted Ivo Piao to remark that 'for enterprises with a "rating", i.e. the 278 enterprises which represented more than a third of the gross national product, there were no problems of financing'.

Subjective factors Out of the 50 TDC cadres, INSCOOP was able to absorb only five, due to financial problems. Without foreseeing the financial needs of the large-scale capacitation programme it had in front of it, the INSCOOP board of governors spent the greater part of the subsidies on infrastructure and equipment, furniture and vehicles. Rather than delegating to third parties publishing and printing jobs, INSCOOP set up an entire printing plant for the production of cooperative manuals, and undertook also the technical evaluation needed for the thousands of projects identified by the APIs. This task would have been the ideal job for emerging service NGOs formed by the TDCs.

In spite of this, eighteen TDCs from the group of cadres formed in the first cycle of capacitation activities managed to set up their own NGO for the provision of technical support to the project assistants (PAs) and to the cooperatives represented by them. This was despite the fact that most of the cadres were being hired by private enterprises and the bigger co-operatives engaged in the more vigorous sectors of the economy – credit, housing, consumption, agriculture, and milk production.

In line with the INSCOOP capacitation plan, this original TDCs' institution, in reality a workers' cooperative, was expected to be the embryo from which the SPIGEI would spring. Nevertheless, neither the TDC cooperative nor the directorship of INSCOOP had the insight or the foresight to develop a partnership scheme in which, at the very least, part of the evaluation and capacitation tasks were allotted to the new TDC Workers' Cooperative. INSCOOP should have delegated some of its functions to the cadres it had formed, but this did not happen.

The prevailing political instability during this period of Portuguese history saw the premiership of the country pass to successive ministers of varying political hues. This further strongly contributed to the inhibiting climate of mutual distrust between the official bureaucracy of INSCOOP and its first non-state and private 'offshoot', the TDC Workers' Co-operative.

A sharp dividing line therefore developed between the creator and the creature, in stark contrast with what had happened in other countries such as Honduras and Mexico (and would happen later in Nicaragua). These countries used the OW extensively as the method to incorporate the masses in the development process, without such a divorce between the sponsoring institution and the efforts of the newly formed technicians. On the contrary, in these cases they were easily absorbed into the state structures. So, and unsurprisingly, the first TDC Workers' Cooperative in Portugal did not survive for long: it completely disintegrated in only its second year of operation. In the meantime INSCOOP went ahead with the project POR/OIT/PNUD/007, all the while trying to garner financial support from outside the cooperative movement. Shortly afterwards came the transfer of Clodomir Santos de Morais to Nicaragua at the request of the then Sandinista government, who had requested him to set up an identical project under the Capacitation Project for the Organization of Producers and Job Creation under the Agrarian Reform Programe (COPERA)

State Power versus Civil Society: Two Opposing Forces?

Structural reversals notwithstanding, the same phenomenon that was observed in Mexico and Honduras (and afterwards in other Latin American and African countries) could not prevent the unsuccessful attempts of the state to curtail the irrepressible social synergy emanating from the massive organizational capacitation 'job and income generating' workshops. This shows that the broad layers of the population of civil society do not have to wait for development to be done 'for them' by the state. In actual fact the broad layers of the population ('citizens') are quite capable of seeking, on their own, heuristic, self-directed orientations, the necessary energy and material support in organizations set up by themselves.

When it came to offering urgent solutions to fundamental problems besetting civil society, the public powers, whether at state, provincial or local level, consistently displayed a severe case of 'myopia' and 'hemiplegia'. Myopia, because the ideological vision of its officials and bureaucrats prevented them from looking beyond their own immediate small group or party interests. This is symptomatic of all holders of power – a social class that excludes whomever it deems necessary from participating in public budgeting decisions. Hemiplegia, because it behaves as if paralysed on the civil society side of the body, while the active side functions, albeit ineffectively, just enough to guarantee the survival of its jobs and assure its inclusion in next year's budget.

Thus, when it comes to tackling the problem of capacitation of those broad layers of the population, it is the unemployed themselves who are the focal point from which the organizational skills of civil society can be mobilized, and this in the absence and independently from the public powers that be.

The only time the bureaucracy can be persuaded to do something in the interest of the great numbers of the disadvantaged is when they feel it is becoming too apparent that they are not up to the job, and consequently imagine that they will be deemed unnecessary or redundant. On the other hand, when the time arrives for actually implementing mutually agreed programmes, bureaucrats usually seem to be taken by surprise, since they had failed to realize the seriousness of capacitation process at social scale.

By this we mean that there exists an inherent incompatibility between the 'slow' practices prevailing in the public sector bureaucracy and the 'instant' praxis of the new dynamic organizational structures set up by civil society, which are free of the ballast of personal vested interests. They are, instead, thrust forward by extremely urgent social demands that they feel in their own flesh. From this we can deduce that the axiom that 'the state is mindful only of its own interests' is counterbalanced by its immediate corollary, the paradigm that posits the indispensability of the great numbers of the unemployed organizing themselves to solve the great structural and conjunctural problems that affect them.

Further Developments of the INSCOOP Initiative

During the 1980s, the dislocation of the emerging SIPGEI, marked by the premature death of the TDC Workers' Cooperative and that of the UNDP project itself, was the prelude to the disintegration of the vast Portuguese popularly based cooperative movement. Even the national counterpart component built in the UNDP project fell victim to this process. Virtually the only remaining local counterpart is the specialist Arnaldo Leite, principal technical adviser of INSCOOP, who later was also in charge of evaluating the cooperative movement in Brazil.

About a thousand small cooperative and mutual benefit structures, at the end of the 1980s and the beginning of the 1990s, found themselves financially insolvent, principally due to the free market laws regulating all EEC capital injections. The country could not make provisions in time to develop a new cooperative code adapted to the new realities, nor had the Portuguese cooperative movement attained any appreciably high levels of organization. So, the actual practice instilled in remaining cooperatives the need to improvise, to invent, to conceive and accept philosophies and structures allowing them to survive in the pervasive neo-liberal global market, which brought about a high concentration of capital.

This brought the present INSCOOP director, Dr Manuel Canaveira de Campos, to comment that: 'Even though the present environment is characterized by untrammelled competition and a barely controlled market, the truth is that the 240 consumer cooperatives at present in existence in Portugal, to which almost 7 per cent of Portuguese families belong, have succeeded in maintaining and even strengthening their position in the market.'

It so happened that an economic system based on the Darwinian principle of the survival of the fittest was the starting signal for the unleashing of the 'law of the jungle' in the principal branches of Portuguese cooperativism, be it by mutation or by imitation.

The change from cooperative to membership structures was the most commonly adopted means by which the cooperatives increasingly started to fuse with other, more economically sound units, a solution referred to as the 'group strategy for survival'. The Portuguese milk-producing co-operatives setting up their own 'Lactogal Ltd' group is a good example of how cooperatives can confront fierce outside competition by entering strategic alliances that boost their competitive edge. The Lactogal group is in direct competition with multinationals such as Parmalat, Danone and Nestlé, as well as other huge French and Spanish enterprises in the milk sector.

We thus see re-enacted in Portugal solutions similar to those commonly applied in Latin America. In Brazil, for example, the Landless Workers' Movement (MST) completely upgraded its top-heavy cooperative structures. Along the same lines, Central American cooperatives had to confront the united competitive might of American giants such as United Fruit and Standard Fruit by amalgamating a number of cooperatives into mega-structures, such as Hondupalma and Coapalma. These successfully produce palm oil, cocoa butter, margarine and other products for internal consumption and export purposes (see Chapter 6).

Such fusion and absorption processes were adopted by the Portuguese cooperatives involved in the most significant sectors of the economy, such as dairy cattle, agriculture, housing, agro-industry, credit, distribution, industrial and urban services. While it is certain that the European Union brand of neo-liberalism seriously affected the social cement of the Portuguese cooperative movement, it is no less certain that the movement's will to adapt and modernize was mainly due to the existence of a 6,000-strong army of experts at grassroots, middle and higher-ranking levels, who had graduated from the massive capacitation programmes realized by INSCOOP under the POR/OIT/PNUD/007 project. Those experts and their APIs (local project assistants) were trained with a clear view of the dialectical nature of the development process and the socio-economic patterns prevailing in the European Community.

From the capacitation received they were fully aware that cooperatives had to modernize in order to survive amid an increased level in productivity, which is an absolutely determining factor in the organization of large groups of producers of civil society for the generation of jobs and income.

Some Examples of the Influence of the OW in Portugal

Many of the current efforts of cooperative organization show the influence of the mass OW methodology for the training of trainers.[3]

In 1979, one of the participants of the course, José Carlos Albino, initiated what he then called an 'experimental training project' in the framework of FECOOPSERV, the Portuguese Federation of Cooperatives of Associated Workers. This project took place in Mesejana, Municipality of Aljustrel, Beja district, which suffered from heavy depopulation and lagging entrepreneurial initiative, compounded by a 50 per cent unemployment rate. In 1989, José Carlos Albino created the ESDIME service cooperative, and continues to be its president. Explaining the objectives of this project for the INSCOOP journal *Cooperatives and Development* in April 1998, Albino said that the experimental training project for the development of Mesejana (1988–90) was, after tortuous negotiations, eventually financed by the European Commission's Social Fund. In the first phase, the project aimed to set in motion a process of change, by promoting autonomous initiatives among those who had been formed at the project. It would also create a membership cooperative (the present ESDIME) which, beyond the duration of the experimental project, would support the development of professional projects launched by its graduates, as well as giving assistance to the overall development of this Portuguese sub-region.

It was, again in the words of José Albino:

a highly innovative project because it had a stake in capacitation as a prime factor of development. Wholesale tri-dimensional formation to citizenship, enterprise, and professionalism requiring the sustained support and organized involvement of the population. The challenging of people's capabilities and culture, the management of the programme 'in situ' and a sustained struggle against ingrained and backward-looking attitudes.

Subsequent Engagements of the Overseas Participants in the Portuguese OWs

During the first Portuguese OW, three Africans and three Brazilians completed the course, as well as the two Guatemalans. The young ex-combatant of the years of the independence struggle in Guinea-Bissau took up the post of lecturer in cooperative organization at the capacitation centre of the town of Contubo, in the municipality of Bafata, on his return to his home country.

The best Cape Verdian recruit on his return to his home country led, with great success and for several years in succession, the Cape Verdian Housing Cooperative with the rank of secretary of state. The six Africans (four from Cape Verde and two from São Tomé e Principe) who were awarded TPI (investment project specialist) diplomas at the OW, were well received in their respective countries of origin and were appointed to various management posts in local banking institutions, except for one who preferred to go for his own fisheries project, which was approved during the OW.

In fact, this investment specialist graduate, after his return to Cape Verde, sold his house and a piece of land in order to buy a small deep-sea fishing vessel. Three years later he became a fishing entrepreneur who contributed substantially to the increase in employment in the island of Santo Antão. A TPI graduate from São Tomé e Principe could not return immediately to his country because he was recruited by the World Bank to go and work in Washington and in Colombia, from where he was recruited by the FAO to its headquarters in Rome with special duties for Africa and Latin America. Among the Brazilians who completed the Portuguese TDC course workshop, Manuel da Conceição and his wife Denise Leal have revealed their considerable organizational ability. Two years later they created, in the town of Imperatriz, an NGO called CENTRU (Educational and Cultural Centre of the Rural Labourers). They have already built up a Formation of Trainers Network connecting 175 cooperative nuclei and integrating them into a single marketing system for rural products among the landless workers of the state of Maranhão.

Notes

1. SIPGEI: Social Participation System for the Identification of Job and Income Generation Projects.

2. Ivàn Labra visited the project in Portugal in 1979. Clodomir Santos de Morais provided the information for this chapter from his field notebooks.

3. Translator's note: Formation of Trainers, usually known as 'Trainers of Trainers' (TOTs) in development cooperation parlance. As elsewhere in the book, we translate the Portuguese/Spanish/French educational term *'Formação/Formación/la formation/ Vorming'* as 'formation' i.e. not the all-purpose, common English term 'training'. 'Training' is part of the 'formation'/capacitation process, but cannot be reduced to it. (See Preliminary Note.)

16

The Crisis of Work and the Welfare Reform Plans in Western Countries

Raff Carmen

'Grim and Getting Grimmer'

Full employment for all and job security were a deceptively reassuring feature of the immediate post-war years. These couple of decades in mid-century – a mere blip against the backdrop of history – lulled an increasingly prosperous Western society into believing that stability and universal prosperity were conceivable and possible, or, at the very least, were just around the corner. With the illusion of universal employment now a distant memory, but with the New York DJIA at a record 11,000 high by mid-1999, new hopes are raised, if the cheerleaders of the corporate Business press are to be believed, of 'wealth all around'.[1] Little if anything seems to have been learned from limitlessly expanding bubble economies elsewhere (e.g. Japan) or from the consecutive stock market meltdowns in the Far East, Russia and Latin America that this, too, may all be illusion.[2] Even if none of this were a cause for worry, the harsh reality remains that the same global economy that produces such unprecedented highs leaves hundreds of millions permanently excluded while even the 'included' may not be better off, after all, starting with overall quality of life indicators.

The sense of uncertainty, insecurity and powerlessness, at the turn of the century, is all the greater in that the only rule that seems to have become genuinely universal – but over which no one and no institution, not even national goverments or international organizations – seem to have any control, is not universal prosperity but universal economic globalization. Real power is increasingly being wielded by faceless global corporations (Korten 1995). Whatever else may be said about the command economies of the East, their demise in the late 1980s deprived humanity of yet another grand illusion, namely that the 'right to work' and 'universal employment' based on constitutional guarantees underwritten by the state can be a credible, stable and sustainable alternative. Western capitalism, with its unlimited freedom to roam worldwide in a free market environment, eventually proved the stronger, and put paid to that illusion.

How could it be otherwise, if wealth concentration has reached such a peak that, to mention just one example, one solitary individual, Bill Gates, is worth more than the GNP of all the Central American countries combined? That means: the wealth of Guatemala, El Salvador, Costa Rica, Panama, Honduras, Nicaragua and Belize combined. The ILO, Geneva, in 'Grim and getting grimmer – World Employment Report 1998–99' in its *World of Work Journal* (December 1998: 6) reveals that the number of unemployed and under-employed (semi-employed) workers around the world has never been higher, and will go on growing by the million in the twenty-first century. According to the ILO, one billion people are at present in employment, but between 750 and 900 million are under-employed and the rest, simply, unemployed. With the world population soon to peak at 6 billion, these statistics are food for thought. The total number of unemployed workers in the European Union is estimated at 30 million, and rising. In the UK, for example, there is also the extreme imbalance between workers, frequently husband and wife, in employment working copious hours of overtime in order to make up for the low wages, whereas millions go without work and/or have to rely on social welfare handouts.

With the one grand twentieth-century universal employment project, the 'workers' paradise', relegated to the pages of history and global capitalism pushing its competitive logic of total market to its ultimate, globalized extreme, apparently the winner, reaction against the 'There is No Alternative' (TINA) fatalism, most closely associated with the Thatcher–Reaganisms of the 1980s, is steadily giving way to the conviction that reciprocity, solidarity and steady-state economics should be given a genuine chance. Such an 'economy of solidarity' would imply, among other things, a redistribution of wealth, a redefinition of work, a more equal spread of the working time, and a radical questioning of the principles underlying the total market, all the time recognizing that the breathtaking advances in technology, communications and production methods cannot be disinvented nor the clock set back.

Signs that civil society is real abound: the 'social economy' in Western Europe is 'characterized by a plural logic combining voluntary dimensions (importance of social networks, use of voluntary help, etc.), market dimensions (sale of goods and services in the market) and non-market ones (subsidies received from the public purse). Goods and services circulating in these organizations serve as links between persons and facilitate interactions between various actors: workers, users, public officers, etc.' (Verhelst 1997a). 'Social capital', too (distinct from both financial capital and 'human' capital as manifest in the now almost universal economistic 'human resources' parlance), a concept first found in nineteenth-century sociology classics, has been revived and reconceptualized by, among others, R. D. Putnam (1993). Social capital represents people's ability and willingness to create and sustain voluntary associations (membership organizations), based on the idea that a healthy community is essential to economic prosperity. It also represents people's ability to work together to solve their own problems through collective action.

Examples from the South demonstrating that social capital – elsewhere also referred to as 'the relational economy' (in contrast to the 'rational', money-driven economy) or the 'economy of solidarity' (Petrella 1997) is alive and well are legion, notwithstanding daily media reports replete with images of violence, blood, famine, genocide, hijackings and terror. There are numerous examples (e.g. Verhelst's in 'Alternatives beyond Dominant Economic Thinking', 1997b) that show that the social economy is possible, feasible and actually happening even, or rather, particularly so, in the most adverse of circumstances. Organizations of the social economy, it needs pointing out, belong neither to the sphere of the capitalist nor to that of the government/state-managed economy. Neither can they be subsumed in the 'domestic' economy. Modern worker cooperatives in Europe, for example, typically aim at creating their own sources of employment and self-management. An 'economy of solidarity' would imply, among other things, a redistribution of wealth, a redefinition of work, a more equal spread of the working time, and a radically putting into question of the principles governing the 'total market'.

Experiential and Experimental Workshops

The Moraisean OW has been applied, so far, almost exclusively in Third World countries, in economies in crisis, with displaced peasantry, in urban deprivation and inner-city situations such as in Brazil's megatowns and the 'tin towns' of Maputo or, as in the case of Portugal of the late 1970s and early 1980s, in semi-industrialized country contexts, in an economy in transition.[3] Miguel Sobrado shows (Chapters 14 and 20) what the potential benefits can be of applying or integrating the Moraisean vision and methods to membership-based enterprises, and the potential they can have in a country like Poland. He describes what is bound to happen to a once mighty economy such as Russia's if people are 'forbidden', by presidential decree no less, to apply their own nous and their own solutions to their economic and management problems and are driven uniformly down the path of individualism, privatization and micro-enterprise, becoming easy prey to the overbearing Mafia culture, which now is well settled in Mother Russia, allowing a whole rich history and culture of working and managing in common to go to waste, leaving the national economy on the scrapheap.

The Moraisean organizational workshops (earlier known as 'experimental' workshops on theory of organization – EWTO) should not be confused with the so-called 'experiential' workshops popular in the 1970s in workplace training in the West. Organization development (OD) also known as sensitivity training or T-group/small group laboratory training, emerged in the 1960s as a branch of the behavioural sciences and as a reaction against the de-humanizing and alienating aspects (and, therefore, ultimately anti-productivity and anti-profit) of scientific management practices in the workplace as they had developed under Western capitalism. The aim was to improve organizational effectiveness in existing organizations by enhancing the energetic abilities of the individuals involved. The vehicles of OD activities are small teams or groups.

The OD 'Experiential' Learning Workshops

The main theorizers and protagonists of the so-called experiential workshop approach were Elton Mayo and Kurt Lewin. T-group training is an essentially (adult) educational method as it involves learning from experience (hence *experiential* workshops). Mayo and Lewin's 'human relations' perspective is democratically grounded: consensus rather than rules and regulations motivate the participants' commitment to a common purpose. Team spirit, group culture, experience and horizontal forms of organization are highly appreciated and encouraged.

Although a range of similarities definitely exists between the OD and OW approach (explored in more detail by Gavin Andersson in Chapter 13) there are substantial – not to say generic – differences between the OD-style 'experiential' small group training and the Moraisean 'experimental/ organizational' large group capacitation:

- OD training and learning workshop activities are typically conducted with persons already in employment and who are, therefore, more or less economically affluent, well-educated, literate and familiar with the internal workings of a sophisticated, technological society with complex workplace relations inside an enterprise. Since they are employees, the overall management and ultimate power of decision-making about the enterprise, company or institution, though, are usually not theirs.
- Although the normal setting in which OD learning takes place is the workshop, little actual (physical) 'work' occurs: simulation exercises are about as close as the OD workshop will come to actual (productive)

work/labour, with the rest of the time filled with predominantly verbal, interpersonal communications with a maximum emphasis on the free expression of views, opinions and emotions.

- OD methodology is tailored to small groups within the larger setting of company, institution or enterprise ('small group social psychology' for behavioural change that ultimately is to benefit the performance, efficiency and/or profitability of the enterprise).

The 'Experimental' OWs

Participants in the Moraisean workshops, by contrast:

- tend to come from all societal backgrounds, but those for whom the OWs are of primary interest are the semi-employed, the unemployed, those who are displaced by economic or natural disasters, landless or urban squatters, or those whose natural 'artisan' or 'small producer' skills have been put at a severe disadvantage by technological progress and/or the competitive market economy. Whatever the case may be, the primary objective is to (re)-create, for themselves and by themselves, a sustainable foothold in life. The OW starts where the OD workshop leaves off, namely 'where there is no workplace' or wherever, due to lack of 'organizational consciousness', the enterprise or business is in danger of imminent collapse or insolvency, as demonstrated, for example, in the INSCOOP case in Portugal, where the OW (and SIPGEI) came to the rescue of the hundreds of floundering small cooperative and mutual benefit enterprises that were under severe pressure due to pro-EEC free market policies in the early 1980s, or with the Huatusco coffee-growers, who urgently needed 'capacitation' in new mental, social, economic and administrative skills in the Mexico of the mid-1990s.[4]

- de Morais' OW is a workshop in every sense of the word: while a practical learning experience, the OW is also at the same time a *real* enterprise, so much so that sustainable enterprises are actually set up in the course of the OW learning event itself: 'doing enterprises', as Clodomir calls it, after which the OW team moves on. The 'objective activity' of coming to grips with a complex (non-'artisan') large-scale production process generates in the group a different organizational consciousness, which has a deep impact on the organizational psychology of a large group (minimum 40 and up to 1,000 and more) of people, whose individual 'bad habits' had, until then, precluded them from operating in unison and making their organization or enterprise a success.

- The secret of the OW's proven success with such otherwise unlikely candidates, namely the unemployed and the socially or physically uprooted, is the *freedom of organization* that invites the participants – after having gone through a bout of organizational crisis (or 'anomy') – to analyse, and to subdivide in task groups or work committees under the central responsibility of the management committee which they themselves have appointed.

- Last not but least, the OW methodology is rooted in the generically different concept and practice of *capacitation* (objective activity), whereas the OD is part and parcel of the body of mainstream democratic adult learning theories and practices, sometimes grouped under the 'andragogy' heading.

Research into capacitation-type approaches to cognition and learning took off only about fifteen years ago, in total isolation, it must be said, from the achievements in the field in the Third World. In the West (especially USA/UK) 'capacitation' goes under the name of 'situated learning' (for and in the workplace).

We see therefore that the organization of the broad layers of the population, or of 'civil society' does not have to wait to be done 'for them', for example, by the state, in the form of 'workplace provision'. Citizens prove to be quite capable of seeking, in their own, heuristic, self-directed orientations, energy and material support in organizations set up by themselves.

Welfare Reforms and Welfare-to-Work

In industrialized countries, participants in the Moraisean OW will, as already mentioned, typically come from the ranks of the unemployed, the under-employed, semi-employed or young post-sixteen school-leavers. Or from the ranks of the welfare and benefit recipients, the latter a dying breed, now that countries such as Britain advocate the 'Wisconsin model' (USA) of workfare and welfare-to-work, which means that all those capable to work are under a strict, new obligation to take private sector or public service jobs on pain of losing their benefits. In Britain, the New Labour government has poured prodigious amounts of money into 'New Deal' measures. Gordon Brown, then just appointed the new finance minister (Chancellor of the Exchequer), told a hushed public at a press conference soon after the May 1997 (New) Labour election victory that 'the central economic objectives of the new government are high and stable levels of growth and employment', and he announced a 'new golden age' of jobs and prosperity, rivalling the immediate post-war years in the 1940s. A 'New Deal' for the young and long-term unemployed was rolled out.

At the moment of writing (June 1999), the British press announces that the Prince's Trust (Prince Charles' own charity) has won £50 million in taxpayers' money to help young people set up new enterprises with the comment that the 'poor public perception of manual jobs worries the Prince' (*Observer*, 13 June 1999). In its leader comment, the *Observer* editor, however, pointedly goes on to add that 'the Prince, by birth and inclination, is an aristocratic paternalist who is liberal in his concern for the disadvantaged while revelling in small–"c" conservatism over the environment and architecture ... We wish Britain had to rely less on top-down, "noblesse oblige" to advance its social aims' (ibid.).

This top-down 'provision of jobs' approach in the 'training in or for the workplace' fashion by the powers that be, needs to be contrasted with the 'job and income generation' schemes organized by the 'power of culture', i.e. civil society itself as described in this book. All of these schemes are based not on what the authorities do 'for' people, but on the strong conviction that 'people are able' and that civil society can and do things for and by itself.

LETS (local exchange trading systems) – cashless, or 'community money' economies – are an increasingly popular and successful example of what civil society is able to achieve, against all odds, to get the local economy moving, including and especially wherever 'there is no money'. So are the older and more traditional forms of credit union in situations 'where there is little money'. These community initiatives most of the time go hand in hand with measures for the maximum supply of energy and food from local resources: most places, even in over-industrialized Europe, can still develop a combination of wind, hydro and biomass sources to meet their needs, as shown in the examples from a number of industrialized countries including Denmark, Holland, Canada, Mexico and Australia (Carmen 1997). OWs operate in situations 'where there is no work'. It ought to be obvious that 'no money' and 'no workplace' approaches can and should complement each other.

The main reason why civil society in industrialized countries has not embraced the 'OW way' in contrast to the instant success of, for example, LETS, is, no doubt, principally ignorance that such a theory and such a methodology actually exists and has been proved to be successful over and over again. Wider knowledge about the OW is one of the principal rationales of this book. In the meantime, traditional 'training' 'for' (often non-existent) workplaces is the only known strategy, tried and applied in endless variations on the same theme. Drawbacks associated with traditional 'training for the workplace' are that it is prohibitively expensive and, moreover, pointless, if, in the end, there are no stable, rewarding jobs for the unemployed to go to. This has been shown in the United States: since 1996, when President Clinton abolished welfare-as-we-know-it in exchange for 'workfare' and 'welfare-to-work' policies, the results have been far from encouraging.

As the Institute for Women's Policy Research (IWPR) points out:

> in the frenzy to move welfare recipients off the rolls through budget cuts, block grants, time limits, cries to 'end welfare as we know it', and attempts to exclude children and young mothers from coverage, little attention has been paid to 'what works' to help current welfare recipients find work and earn wages that will help them escape poverty. (IWPR 1997)

IWPR's research further suggests that if employment opportunities are not reformed along with welfare, efforts to reduce the rolls are likely to result in increased poverty for many single mothers and their children and increased frustration for tax-payers, who will see yet another reform go awry. In its study sample of 1,181 single mothers who benefited from 'welfare to work' assistance, and who represent about 2.8 million women, or 80 per cent of all adult recipients, it found that 'most welfare mothers are already working, but cannot earn enough or find enough work to lift their families out of poverty. 43% work substantial hours (950 per year on average).' But most tellingly, 'welfare-to-work' jobs are low-wage, unstable, and unlikely to provide health benefits:

- The average job lasted only 46 weeks, less than a year.
- Working mothers held an average of 1.7 jobs during the two–year survey period.
- These mothers also spent an average of sixteen weeks looking for work.
- Mothers' jobs provided health insurance coverage only one-third of the months they worked.
- Their jobs paid an average of $4.29 per hour.
- For those who worked all 24 months of the study period, approximately half earned more at the end of the period than at the beginning, while half earned less.

Their jobs tended to be in the lowest-wage women's occupations: 37 per cent worked as maids, cashiers, nursing aides, child care workers, and waitresses, while 13 per cent of all women worked in those occupations. Their employers tended to be in the low-paying service industries, such as restaurants, bars, nursing homes, private households, hotels and motels, department stores, hospitals, and temporary help services firms. These businesses employed two-fifths of welfare mothers (as compared to 19 per cent of all women) (ibid.). The early indicators, therefore, are that the much vaunted 'New Deal', for all practical purposes, means a 'raw deal' for the individuals concerned, especially if they are women.

De Morais, by contrast, starts from the principle that

> it is the duty of the State to open up spaces for Civil Society to organize

itself and set up enterprises as it can solve most of its problems without intervention. What is urgently needed is the legislation which facilitates such developments. The only way in which those trapped in poverty can escape is by organizing themselves into production/service industries. (de Morais 1997).

In a future 'world without work' (Rifkin and Heilbronner 1996) and without safety-nets, to boot, a lot remains to be learned from the de Moraisean approach with vision and practice: if the problem of unemployment and poverty is, indeed, massive, it needs massive, (not 'micro') solutions.

> Advancing the micro-enterprise model as the universal solution to the un-employment problem, while the new microenterpreneurs have no in-field work experience whatsoever, nor possess the necessary mental models to grapple with the new work environment, is tantamount to missing out on the key element which may crown microenterprise initiatives with success. (Sobrado 1999)

The employment crisis will not be solved, either, merely by dint of 'training' in administrative or merely technical skills. 'Training', as linear transmission of knowledge and skills, does not take in account the different mental models that underlie different modes of work and production. Nor is it possible to continue to rely on the comfortable certainties and associated models that date back to bygone times when 'work was plentiful'. Of course, work needs to be provided, micro-enterprises need to be set up and training needs to take place perhaps more than ever before. Provided, that is, training does not remain a 'one-golf club' strategy, wielded by the powers that be and they alone.

Conclusion

Early indicators are that, even in a booming economy as that of the United States in the latter half of this decade, 'welfare-to-work' reforms will fail if they are driven by the combined forces of the state and of competitive private enterprise alone. What is bound to happen to jobs in a post-industrial economy in deep depression is anyone's guess. Massive problems are not served by piecemeal solutions. Money – 'venture capital' or 'trust funds' – the training of ever more professionals, ever more training courses and more training manuals are important. What is even more important is the knowledge and conviction that people (citizens) themselves can identify promising activities and niche markets and actually do some-thing positive about their situation, 'here and now'.

Notes

1. The Dow Jones Industrial Average had reached 11,299.76 on 23 August 1999; see 'How high is the sky!!' (MD Leasing group on <www.mdleasing.com/djia.htm>)

2. Bubble economy: an economy bound to burst at the top because it has no bottom (i.e. government spending sufficient to balance the removal of money by the tax system). Whenever the US bubble bursts, its effects will be worldwide.

3. This is especially true with the most common form of OW, i.e. the field workshops. However, there are four types of workshop (OW): the centre OW, the course OW, the field OW and the 'enterprise' OW (see Chapter 19).

4. In a recent e-mail message from the University of Chapingo where he is at present visiting professor, Clodomir writes: 'It is important that it be made clear to the reader that the method is not of interest merely in the continents of Latin America and Africa. In the future we are determined to see the method applied wherever unemployment brings violence between individuals, groups, peoples and nations in its wake. Ours is a pacifist task, aimed at dissipating the causes of war. That is why we want to see it applied also in the Balkans, Poland, Slovakia and Russia, all countries with a high degree of unemployment' (Chapingo, 26 June 1999).

References

Campos, M. (1997) 'Dominador de la Miseria' (Conquerer of Poverty) *RUMBO*, Costa Rica, August.

Carmen, R. (1997) 'Local Exchange Trading Systems'? S.A.N.E. (South Africa New Economics Network Site) <http://www.stones.co.za/sane/article6.htm>(18 pages) Hypertext.

IWPR (Institute for Women's Policy Research) (1997) 'Research Report on Welfare Mothers' <iwpr@www.iwpr.org> Hypertext.

Korten, D. (1995) *When Corporations Rule the World*, London: Earthscan.

de Morais, C. S. (1997) 'Los mercados laboriales eficientes', speech at CIEDIA/ICEP Conference, San José, Costa Rica.

Petrella, R. (1997) *The Common Good – In Praise of Solidarity*, Brussels: Vrije Universiteit.

Putnam, R. D. (1993) *Making Democracy Work: Civic Traditions in Modern Italy*, Princeton, NJ: Princeton University Press.

Rifkin, J. and R. L. Heilbronner (1996) *The End of Work*, New York: Putnam Group.

Sobrado, M. (1999) 'Modelos mentales artisanales' (Artisanal Mental Models) *La Nación*, Costa Rica, 7 May.

Verhelst, T. (1997a) 'Economic Organizations and Local Cultures' <http://www.globenet.org/horizon-local/cultures/localeng.html>

— (1997b) 'Alternatives beyond Dominant Economic Thinking' <http://www.globenet.org/horizon-local/cultures/localeng.html>

Part IV
From Local OWs to National Employment-generation Systems

17

The Brazilian PROGEI–SIPGEIs of the 1980s and 1990s[1]

Jacinta Castelo Branco Correia

Background

Clodomir Santos de Morais, on behalf of the ILO, was in charge of the Cooperative Development Project financed by UNDP and SIDA (Swedish Overseas Development Agency, one of the United Nations international organizations) in Portugal from 1977 to 1980. Portugal, in those days, was pulling itself out of the economic chaos that was to a large extent the heritage of thousands of owners of enterprises leaving the country principally because of debt incurred with the banks or with the government, or simply because they were afraid of being held responsible for having trampled underfoot for so long the social rights of their employees during the Salazar dictatorship, which lasted for more than a quarter-century and which was now at long last being swept away in the people's revolution of 1974. Workers and management of the enterprises now abandoned by their owners tried at first to keep them going by trial and error, but their lack of training in how to run commonly owned enterprises soon started to show: hundreds of those enterprises went bankrupt and thousands of their workers were thrown onto the streets, trying to make a living in the so-called informal economy by becoming travelling salesmen, musicians, traditional hawkers and pedlars or working in the traditional family economy.

The field was open therefore for the traditional Portuguese associativist mutual help culture, which reached its apogee under the heroes of Portuguese socialism Antero de Quental and Costa Goodelphin in the nineteenth century, a tradition continued by Antonio Sergio and Henrique de Barros until the present day. From just 600 cooperatives in 1974, their number had soared to 3,800 by 1979. The principal objective of the team working on behalf of the ILO project, which Clodomir Santos de Morais co-directed with the local counterpart, professor of philosophy Ferreira da Costa (who, at that time, was president of the cooperative institute Antonio Sergio, also known in Portugal as INSCOOP) was to instil organizational consciousness and economic rationality and efficiency in the newly set up cooperative enterprises, so that these ventures would be consistent, in a very real sense, with the newly designated 'economic areas for social production' norm. It was indeed INSCOOP that formed the backdrop and support base of the UNDP project.

Two important organizational workshops (OWs, at that time still known as 'experimental' workshops) were initially run with the purpose of building a network that would eventually include 6,000 project assistants (APIs) covering all the cooperatives and most of the municipal councils in Portugal. During the first of those capacitation events 50 middle-level experts (specialists in cooperative development – TDCs) were formed, while the second produced a contingent of upper-level specialists in investment projects (TPIs). It was by means of this capacitation programme that the ground for the economic area of cooperative production in Portugal was prepared in readiness for the free market 'competition economy' under which the French, German and Italian branches of cooperativism operated, thus preparing Portugal, too, for its imminent entry into the European Community. With a population twelve times and a land area 90 times smaller than that of Brazil, the Portuguese, nevertheless entered the 1980s with more cooperatives than the Brazilians.

The UNB, IATTERMUND, Jânio Quadros and the MST

In 1988 the vice-chancellor of the University of Brasília, Cristovam Buarque, who had been one of the principal sources of inspiration behind the elaboration of the 'course'-type workshops for the formation of the TPIs in Lisbon, invited Clodomir Santos de Morais – at that time visiting lecturer at the University of Rostock in the former East Germany to come and set up, in Brazil, the Institute for Technical Support to Third World Countries (IATTERMUND) with the particular intention of confronting one of the gravest problems the country was facing, unemployment. The then mayor of São Paulo, an ex-president of the republic, was the first ever person in authority to lend support to the IATTERMUND discourse, which, among others, projected the view that Brazil was subject to a sort of 'hidden civil war of unemployment' with thousands of people killed (murdered) each day, hundreds of street children summarily executed each year. All this, in the end, was the result of pervasive unemployment, a kind of 'epidemic' sweeping all the big cities and imposing a kind of curfew on everyone, starting each night at nine o'clock, for fear of being punished, be it in the form of physical assault or the pain of death. Every day, from early evening, families and citizens were forced to lock themselves up in their homes and watch soap operas to keep themselves from dying of boredom, while the excluded (euphemistically referred to as 'marginals') and those who capitalized on the situation, always the police, ruled the streets. This made Mayor Jânio Quadros realize to what levels of violence the marginalized had descended in São Paulo City.[2]

However, the credit for having been the first to request IATTERMUND for the OW to be applied in its 30 self-managing cooperatives and to train at the same time its activists in the method has to go to the Brazilian Landless Workers' Movement (MST). Credit for the first publication of de Morais' handbook *Elements of a Theory of Organization* goes to the same MST acting in conjunction with some popular education centres. Soon to follow the lead given by the MST was the Polonoroeste Project, which was a joint Ministry of the Interior, FAO, World Bank and development aid agencies project for the states of Mato Grosso, Rondônia, Ceará, Paraíba and São Paulo. Also involved were the Ministries of Labour and Social Work of the States of Paraíba, Ceará, São Paulo and Espirito Santo, as well as the IBAMA (Institute for Environmental Protection), the INCRA (Institute for Land Settlement and Agrarian Reform) and the UN agencies of the ILO and the FAO.

Mayors Erundina and Maluf

As Jânio Quadros was already thinking of retiring from his job as mayor of the biggest and most industrialized city in Brazil, it fell to Mayoress Maria Luisa Erundina, of the Partido dos Trabalhadores (Workers' Party – PT) to try to prevent the supply line with the government from being cut, and, together with the FAO, the Ministry of Regional Integration and IATTERMUND, to set up the job- and income-generation programme (PROGEI) of the Municipality of São Paulo under the technical directorship of Mstra Jacinta Castelo Branco Correia. The involvement of the FAO in this type of project was due to a large degree to the excellent judgement of the national director of the Programme for Job and Income Generation, Aldenir Paraguassu, who managed to overcome the bureaucratic inertia, compounded by the excessive money devalutions of more than 20 per cent a month that were ravaging Brazil, of the Ministry for Integration. He cleverly managed to transfer the money of the Brazilian government to an international agency, the FAO, which immediately 'dollarized' it so as to prevent it from losing its value, thus allowing it to sustain an uninterrupted support for the fight against unemployment projects. This intelligent resource management opened up the possibility of starting up and running regional and municipal projects of workplace and income generation.

The persistent lack of sufficient financial resources, combined with the paternalistic vision traditionally besetting the counterpart institution of the Municipality of São Paulo, the Municipal Secretariat for Social Welfare, prevented the PROGEI of São Paulo City, which consisted in the creation of a SIPGEI as well as investments system and involved the formation of thousands of project assistants (APIs), who were to make up the main interface between the communities and the financial institutions, from reaching its full potential. Trying to overcome the inefficiencies of the state secretariat, Mayoress Erundina transferred the project to her own secretary for planning, the economist Paul Singer, and asked him to play the role of counterpart of the PROGEI of the Municipality of São Paulo.[3] It was thanks to the influence of Professor Singer that it was possible to have $300,000 devoted to the municipal planning stage, despite the fact that Mayoress Erundina's party, the PT, had already lost the municipal election to candidate Paulo Maluf. Increasing the financial resources available made it possible for two 'course'-type workshops to be organized simultaneously for candidates with secondary schooling diplomas to be trained as economic development specialists (TDEs). Their task consisted of setting up SIPGEIs in their respective destitute neighbourhoods inside the enormous impoverished area of southern São Paulo and, at the same time, dozens of goods and services production enterprises promoted by the APIs. Notable among those enterprises we count the ATDE, which was formed around the approximately eight hundred APIs who were successful in the identification of a considerable number of social ownership and production projects. Their efficiency displayed a considerable impact in Greater São Paulo and some municipalities of the interior.

The PROGEIs of Paraíba, Cuiabá and Alagoas

The Paraíba PROGEI, severe financial constraints notwithstanding, attracted to its gigantic field laboratories, organized by Sebastiao Araujo (one of the IATTERMUND directors), more than four thousand people who participated in 30 different types of courses in semi-professional training, as well as in the capacitation in the running of large-scale enterprises. Not content with developing micro-enterprises in the informal economy, many Paraíbeans pooled their strengths and formed community enterprises, which yielded a considerable number of workplaces. Another PROGEI to result from the IATTERMUND initiative was that of Cuiabà, set up in 1994. The following year, in 1995, the Alagoas PROGEI was inaugurated, under the directorship of Clodomir Santos de Morais. This project covered 90 per cent of all the municipalities of the state of Alagoas, and helped considerably in reducing the grave financial situation that has held down this poor state in Brazil's Nordeste for so long. Forty TDEs were formed here, as well as 1,036 APIs.

The Paraíba PROGEI was the second IATTERMUND project conducted in liaison with FAO and the Ministry for Regional Integration. Due to the lack of financial resources, which had been promised by the Supervisory Committee for the Development of the Nordeste (SUDENE), the associations of APIs for that region met in a matter of four months in Maceió, the state capital, and set up a second-degree structure representing the regional membership associations of APIs and the three TDE enterprises. Joining their forces together, and given the difficult financial predicament in which the state found itself because of its considerable debts and the political corruption of previous state governments, would allow them to survive. From this PROGEI and this second-level association a hitherto unheard-of experience emerged, involving two APIs called 'Marcio and Mercia'. These two set up an enterprise in Palamares, an important town in the interior of Alagoas, and started preparing profiles of projects in which people professed to be interested. These projects were then entitled to apply for funds (up to $5,000) from the Bank of the Nordeste, which had set aside some resources in the Support Fund for the Worker (FAT) earmarked for micro-enterprises. Those two APIs, on their own, during their very first month of operation, managed to identify and obtain the approval for no fewer than 50 projects. The immediate effect of this was that other people became aware of the existence of the fund, and the practice spread to other municipalities in the region. The bank, not really equipped to process such a flood of applications, which kept multiplying almost exponentially, was soon forced to stop project operations. This meant that just two APIs working at full capacity caused the collapse of the financial branch offices of the local municipal agency of Palmeira de los Indios.

The PROGEIs of Paulo Afonso, Vitória and Rondônia

The 'course' OW held in the hydroelectric power-producing region of Paulo Afonso, a few months after the one in Alagoas, was attended by learners from the states of Alagoas, Sergipe and Pernambuco and was funded by SUDENE/CHESF (a hydroelectric company from San Francisco). The PROGEI of the municipality of Vitória, capital city of the state of Espirito Santo, was originally laid on by IATTERMUND in partnership with FAO and with the Municipal Secretariat for Social Action of Vitória as local counterpart. The latter was directed by Professor Vera Nacif. The 42 TDEs formed in Vitória formed the almost 1,000 APIs who became the basis of the start-up of numerous enterprises in the impoverished communities. Those successes in the capacitation programme can to a large extent be traced back to the day Vera Nacif asked for reinforcements from IATTERMUND in the form of specialists able to assist in a number of OWs in the poor suburbs of the capital city of Espirito Santo state.

The rapid increase in the pace of the movement dedicated to the struggle against unemployment by means of the mass capacitation methodology was accompanied, at this level, by an even more rapid increase in the demand for senior OW directors. The municipal PROGEI of São Paulo would subsequently lay on another course OW, under the directorship of its own resource person, Marcelo Martino, responsible for many a SIPGEI in that big Brazilian metropolis. In turn, the secretary of state for labour for the state of São Paulo (and ex-federal minister), Professor Walter Barelli, was instrumental in giving the starting shot to the biggest Brazilian programme so far in the struggle against unemployment, with the launching of the course OW of the Franco da Rocha Region, a workshop directed by José Ambrosis Pinheiro Machado, subsequently co-director, with the president of IATTERMUND, of the course OW preparatory to SIPGEI of the Amazonian state of Tocatins. In the meantime, another senior IATTER-MUND specialist, Paulo Roberto, was busy establishing the PROGEI and SIPGEI of Rondônia, another Amazonian state, which borders on Bolivia.

Given the fact that for each course OW three 'senior' specialists, and for the field OWs at least one senior and two junior experts are required, the great demand for these kind of experts, as the movement against unemployment expanded, virtually exhausted the available Brazilian IATTERMUND cadres. Thus, trying to satisfy the insatiable demand for OW specialists in the state of Espirito Santo, which had pencilled in several mass capacitation events, most of them field-type workshops, thanks to its dynamic Mayor Paulo Hartung and Professor Nacif, IATTERMUND saw itself obliged to call in the help of two Chilean social psychologists, based in Hararc, Zimbabwe for over ten years, who are recognized specialists in the application of the field OW, Ivàn Labra and Isabel Labra. Ivàn Labra, a one-time pupil of Clodomir Santos de Morais in Honduras and, later on, his vice-director during the COPERA project in Nicaragua, together with an expert from the Dutch development agency HIVOS, Ian Cherrett, introduced the method in 1985 to southern Africa (South Africa, Zambia, Botswana, Zimbabwe, Malawi).[4] They had set up an NGO in the style of IATTERMUND, called SADET (Southern Africa Development Trust). The demand for expertise was, however, much greater than expected, which meant that Isabel Labra was recruited by the Mayor's Office of Vitória, while Ivàn was contracted as evaluator by PRONAGER (the Brazilian national project). With the demand at national level proving itself much more acute, Dr Roberto Leno, of the Alagoas PRONAGER board of directors (replaced by Ronaldo Melo), and Vera Nacif herself, were selected to go and work with PRONAGER. The vice-director of IATTERMUND, Dr Sebastiano Araujo, was recruited afterwards by the Brazilian Board of Directors.

In the meantime, the president of IATTERMUND himself, Dr Pedro Cavacanti Filho, was sent out to the Valle del Ribeira to direct the second course OW of the Brazilian PAE programme, the direct initiative of Secretary of Labour Dr Barelli himself. Professor de Morais, president of the board of consultants of IATTERMUND, was entrusted, in 1988, with missions to Haiti, Bolivia, Costa Rica and Mexico to give the initial push in the negotiations for the establishment of a PROGEI in each of these countries, too. This crisis, which was entirely a problem of success, due to the expansion of the movement of struggle against unemployment, did not, however, affect the MST. The reason for this was that during the first Centre OW, which took place on October 1988 in Palmeira de Missões in the state of Rio Grande do Sul, with 106 participants and directed by Clodomir Santos de Morais himself, a number of MST leaders were trained as OW directors, among whom we would particularly like to mention Sergio Fritzen, Adelar Pizeta, Everton Mineiro, Elemar Silva, Deolinda de Ranha and Irma Brunetto. This was a very clear sign of the enormous interest among the membership of the *Sem Terra* (landless) to learn through the mass capacitation method.

With those well-trained cadres the MST was able to come out of its isolation in Rio Grande do Sul state. They went through a rethink of the movement's routine practice of 'invading' unproductive land and then distributing it to its participating militants. The upshot was that from now on they would concentrate, instead, on organizing commonly owned or collectivist enterprises, based on the already excellent organizational consciousness generated in their membership of the states of Santa Catarina, Paraná, São Paulo, Espirito Santo, Bahía, Sergipe and Ceará. Since then, and during the years of the Collor government, in which the *latifundistas* (large landowners) held half of the ministerial portfolios, IATTERMUND tried to convince the MST that it was time to abandon 'ideas about playing soldiers, and concentrate on [forming] civil servants'. What was meant by this metaphor was that, whether now or in the future, there never was going to be any shortage of land invaders as it is in the nature of capitalism indefinitely to continue producing landless peasants; what the MST must concentrate on from now on is forming technical cadres capable of building up enterprises of the ex-landless, in other words, those who are now settled on land and therefore victorious.

That is why the next phase consisted in the organization, in November 1991, of a course OW in Brasília for the formation of a cooperative organization belonging to the MST. The course was directed by the

IATTERMUND president himself, Clodomir Santos de Morais. It so happened that the president of INCRA was the lawyer João Mendoza Amorim, a well-known sympathizer of the peasant struggle and great advocate of agricultural reform in the days of Francisco Julião's Peasant Leagues. He therefore arranged, in order to comply with the MST and IATTERMUND's request, for the use of the installations of INCRA, such as board and lodging for more than a month for the 60 participants who had received financial support from the OCB (Organization of Brazilian Cooperatives) and the ILO. The fact that João Mendoza Amorim was dismissed from his post as INCRA president the very day of the inauguration of this OW was no mere coincidence.

This particular OW produced more than thirty high-level cadres, leaders such as Francisco Dal Chiavon, aka 'Chicão', who was entrusted the following year by MST with the launching and consolidation of the Federation of the Agrarian Reform Cooperatives of Brazil, the CONCRAB, which had its headquarters initially in the town of Curitiba, capital of the state of Paraná. In the same town the MST, but this time without any assistance from IATTERMUND, organized its second OW for the formation of TDCs in 1992. This event was coordinated by Father Paulo Cerioli, a former pupil of Clodomir's at the OW of Tres Pasos, who subsequently, thanks to a scholarship with IATTERMUND, arranged for him by FAO, visited the self-managing mega-enterprise belonging to the sacked agricultural labourers in Honduras, the HONDUPALMA enterprise (see Chapter 6). Paulo Cerioli, after having contributed to the direction of the capacitation centres of Braga and Veranopoles, was, in 1993, with Emanuel Araujo, one of the organizers of the third MST OW for the formation of cooperative development specialists in the capital, Brasília.

Thanks to its newly graduated course directors, the MST was now in a position to set up its own SIPGEI in the rural areas, spearheaded either by its activists (a special version of API) in hundreds of land settlements, or by the provision of formation in capacitation in the three training centres that had rapidly materialized. These centres were situated in the town of Cazador (Santa Catarina), Contestado, Braga and Veranopoles, in Rio Grande do Sul state. The CONCRAB journal *Reforma Agraria: A Struggle which is Everyone's Business* – in which dozens of big regional enterprises and cooperatives involved in producing goods and services are registered – mentions in its edition of 1996 that

> among all the capacitation methods in use, special mention must be made of the Organizational Workshop method which is an experimental exercise, as well as a real one in which a group of settlers organize a self-managed enterprise and organize a series of resources, financial and human. The Field

OWs are promoted inside the new land settlements and the resulting Enterprise, in general, contiunes to function after the Workshop has closed which usually is after 30 days. The Center OWs, on the other hand, are specifically designed to form organizational cadres of membership enterprises. Course OWs, in turn, deal with the capacitation needs of a specific technical area.

The same journal provides the total numbers, for 1996, of the dozens of cooperative enterprises in existence in eleven states in Brazil, some with a membership of more than 500, others with members in excess of 800 while one of them, in the municipality of Cantagolo in the state of Paraná, has 1,328 members. At this rate, the MST, by 1995, already covered the majority of the Brazilian states. Moreover, the landless movement began to exercise an enormous influence on the homeless (*Sem Telhado*) in the inner suburbs, who started up the *Movimento dos Sem Telhado* (Movement of the Homeless). This movement represented those who, after invading the abandoned lands, got engaged in the construction of collective housing, called *mutiraos*. The Mutirantes Movement built thousands of collective housing units in Greater São Paulo, Rio de Janeiro and Porto Alegre. The *DCI (Commercial and Industrial Data) Journal*, in its 'Enterprises and Business' section of March 1992, carries an article under the heading 'Workers who become construction entrepreneurs'. It recounts how more than five hundred bricklayers, engineers, architects, plumbers and other professionals belonging to the Civil Construction Worker Cooperative of Villa Curuza, municipality of São Miguel, earn twice the average salary on the labour market and, at the end of the year, receive, on top, a share in the profits calculated according to the total hours worked. According to the *DCI Journal*, the MST was the driving force behind this cooperative, as a good number of its founder members were militants in the landless movement. This clearly shows that a new social force is in the making, able to counteract and halt the tidal wave of unemployment by the implementation of mass capacitation methods and new forms of ownership and social production, generating thousands of new jobs and new sources of income.

The importance of this movement, which now embraces both rural and urban areas, explains the appearance on the scene of the National Association of Self-employed and Participatory Stakeholders (ANTEAG), which managed to prevent many enterprises with hundreds, or even thousands, of workers from being swept away by the unemployment tide that is the obverse side of the globalization and neo-liberal phenomenon. In an article by Vasconcelo Quadros in the *Jornal do Brasil*, of 2 February 1999, one of the national leaders of the MST, Delvek Matheus, says:

we see here a new face of the MST , built on a social base of 200,000 families, i.e., almost a million small agricultural producers spread over the whole country and controlling the production and commercialization of more than 2,000 settlements through a network of cooperatives. This structure, which contains approximately 100 entities dedicated to the delivery of services and agricultural goods, is linked up under the auspices of CONCRAB. Mediated by this system, for example, 1,200 farmers of the Sarandi region, during the last harvest, produced 230 thousand tons of soya and maize and delivered 15 thousand litres of milk a day, refrigerated in installations set up by the settlers themselves to the transnational 'Parmalat'. In another MST experiment, the Rural Workers' Cooperative, with 3,000 settlers of the municipalities of Nova Laranjeira and Cantagalo, produces 50,000 tons of kidney beans, 60 thousand tons of maize and is investing at the moment in milk production and canned vegetables.

In the same newspaper report by Vasconcelo Quadros, Adalberto Martins, alias 'Pardal' – national MST coordinator for CONCRAB and in charge of the organizational structures of the cooperative system – reports that in the South and South Central region of the country, the settlers have achieved a livelihood for themselves and are fully integrated. Last year (1998) the rural credit cooperative Horizontes Nuevos lent out 5 million reales (approximately $500,000) to small farmers.

There is only one case of insolvency to report, and this was due to the fact that the debtor died before the day repayment was due.

Quadros goes on to say that:

in Pontal do Paranapanema, under the leadership of José Rainha Junior, the system set up by the MST has already changed the physical aspect of the region and transformed for example the town of Teodoro Sampaio into a kind of 'MST Republic'.

Former abandoned landholdings taken over by the land invasions have been converted into settlements that now distribute agricultural produce to nineteen municipalities in the region. Teodoro Sampaio's 'business card' consists of an assembly of silos boasting the MST insignia. In spite of fragility and amateurism, we have succeeded in setting up a 'production system without peer anywhere else in Latin America'. 'No other experience confronts the economic world in quite the same way as ours does,' affirms Pardal in the same article. 'The MST products are preferentially earmarked for low income families. They are cheaper because they are marketed directly, cutting out the middlemen.'

In Guriu de Ceará is an example of yet another model MST enterprise, the Mangue Seco settlement, which was set up as a result of a field OW sponsored by the INCRA and directed by one of the directors of IATTERMUND, Professor Manuel Mozart Machado. This enterprise, although under ten years old, already provides to its membership an average income of five minimum wages combined. Schooling goes up to the 7th grade and the houses all have drinkable running water. They are connected internally and with the world over the telephone. According to the first information newsletter, the *Sipgei Informativo*, the same MST enterprise also has refrigerated storage space for up to five tons of fish; a refrigeration plant capable of producing six tons of ice; two motorized 25-ton boats, which can operate up to 20 days consecutively in high seas, in addition to two heavy lorries and a passenger microbus. Seventy small artisanal fishingboats are linked into its service, storage, refrigeration and transport system. The enterprise also cultivates 200 ha of cocoa palm and has 150 ha of cashews under cultivation. It also has a commonly owned flour production plant, which caters for individual producers of 120 Ha of yuca and cassava flour. The MST is living proof of the existence of a new social force built on the principle of social ownership of the means of production and on forms of self-management capable of counteracting the pernicious tide of unemployment and the resulting crime and violence.

As for Rio de Janeiro, the hidden civil war has turned into open warfare, with thousands upon thousands of murder victims every year. The situation has become so bad that Rio is the first state in Brazil where the army has to intervene. In the second month of army intervention, one major said that he preferred to deal directly with the gangsters than to try to make sense of the compromised policies of the local politicians. Newspapers almost daily relate massacres of the so-called marginalized, who, in fact, are simply people without work, and are therefore excluded from the prevailing economic system. Even in the posh neighbourhoods of the Zona Sul people are killed by stray bullets from the armed clashes between the military and the marginals. That is one of the reasons why Rio, nicknamed the 'Marvellous City' saw itself barred from presenting its candidature for the Football World Cup.

To sum up, it would appear that IATTERMUND has a clear idea of the historical role the MST can play in its fight against unemployment, by means of organizing the vast numbers of the landless and the excluded in urban areas and by its guiding role in the establishment of their own self-managed enterprises. This represents a wholly peaceful way to search for an end to the violence in the countryside and in the towns; it is in this way that the MST is making a huge contribution, notwithstanding the fact that it is precisely they who are the prime victims of the class struggle waged, with government support, by the large landowners. The land invasions coordinated by the MST happen mainly in large abandoned ranches and large agricultural enterprises that owe millions to the public purse in unpaid taxes and unpaid social contributions to their workers, anyway. It is for this reason that IATTERMUND, in conjunction with other institutions, proposed the MST (Movimento dos Trabalhadores Rurais sem Terra) for the 1991 'Right Livelihood Award'.[5] In Brazil, the self-employment programme PAE (Programa do Auto-cmprega), presided over by Professor Walter Barelli, secretary for labour for the state of São Paulo and PRONAGER-AMAZONIA, coordinated by Drs Elien Jaques Eliene Jaques Rodrigues and Romero Ximenes Ponte are the institutions that have made the most intensive use of the mass capacitation OW methodology in the fight against unemployment.[6] There are many other institutions that contribute to the formation of the new social force able to counteract the crime wave in the countryside and the large towns of Brazil.

The Amazonian PRONAGER

The Amazonian PRONAGER made its début in applying the OW method in 1997, with the first course OW in the town of Miracema, near Palmas, the capital of the young Amazonian state of Tocantins, under the auspices of the Supervisory Development Committee for Amazonia and of the state secretary for labour and social action, Dr Homero Barreto. As a result, 54 TDEs and 510 APIs were formed who then went on to identify 597 project profiles. Several field OWs were run there, which resulted in the capacitation of 1,507 persons and gave rise to 35 social production enterprises. In the same year the first SIPGEI was set up in the state. According to the informatin bulletin *PRONAGER Amazonia, Trabalho e Renda* (Amazonia PRONAGER, Work and Income), to these must be added also the field OWs realized in the states of Pará, Amazonas and Amapá, which, following the precedent set by the field OWs of Araguaina in Tocantins, were organized by experts of these states who had experience in the planning and execution of such events, i.e. the habilitating phase of the first national formation course for directors of field workshops.

The next stage in PRONAGER Amazonia will be the realization of course OWs in other states covered by the resources of SUDAN. The information bulletin announces that SUDAN has programmed a repeat performance of the programmes in the states of Amazonia such as Amapá, Roraima, Amazonas, Acre, Rondônia, Goiás and Mato Grosso. In the state of Rondônia, in 1996, a course OW took place that resulted in the local SIPGEI, headquartered in the town of Ji-Paraná and covering about twenty municipalities. The anchor institution of the Amazonia SIPGEI is the Centre for Ecology and Sustainable Development (CEDOCES), administered by the TDEs José Wilson, Lindomar Ventura dos Santos and Nereia Pereira dos Santos. The course OW of Ji-Paraná was sponsored conjointly by the Federal University of Rondônia, IATTERMUND, EMATER-Rn, the local Mayor's Office and the state secretary for planning, Dr Emerson Teixeira. The number of enterprises which have sprung from the mass capacitation method in the state of Rondônia has already acted as an incentive for two 'forums' on self-managing enterprises in Rondônia. The first of these was organized on the campus of the Federal University of Rondônia, in the state capital Porto Velho, while the other took place in 1998 in the town of Ouro Preto. The Rondônia SIPGEI relies on a 'peasant-to-peasant' technical support services network in which ACARAN (Central Articulation of the Mutual Rural Self-help Associations), under the directorship of Carlos Suares de Lima, plays a central catalysing role. They set up the first jobs and income-generating 'labour bank', the BETGER, which was instrumental in overcoming the unemployment problems in the town of Nova Brasilandia. This bank operates on the principle of engaging so-called 'surplus labour' in the planting of young nursery trees, which then are sold on to the local sawmills for reforestation purposes. Another important body to result from the Amazonian OWs is the Amazonian Development Institute, which is based in the town of Guajaramirim, on the border with Bolivia. It occupies itself with the formation of educational cadres at all levels, and is headed by the professorial duo Dorosnil and Carmen Moreira.

'More Than a Job: A Future'

The flag raised in the struggle against unemployment by Walter Barelli and the PAE is viewed with enormous sympathy not only by the long-suffering masses of the unemployed in the state of São Paulo, but also in the Mercosur region (Argentina, Uruguay, Paraguay and Bolivia), and continues to find echos in the press of other Latin American and African countries. Barelli is inspired by the philosophy of Mario Covas, governor of the state of São Paulo, who defines the right to work 'as one of the basic requirements for the exercise of citizenship' and who is convinced that it is 'from the basis of a decent job which guarantees a decent life to a family that the citizen can feel truly an integral part of society, with rights and duties, making their small contribution to the economic and social progress of the state and the country as a whole'.

It is for this reason, emphasizes Mario Covas, who has just been elected governor of São Paulo, that one of the compromises of our electoral campaign was to provide employment to those who want to work and motivate those with the will to produce. The PAE caters for clusters of populations with lower levels of economic development in the rural and urban areas. The PAE programme aims at providing professional qualifications to the unemployed and orienting them towards structuring autonomous, community and cooperative actitivies or engaging in production and service delivery micro-enterprises.

In Chapter 18 Walter Barelli himself explains the philosophy and activities of the PAE.

Notes

1. This chapter is based on the personal recollections of Clodomir Santos de Morais.

2. Jânio Quadros stood against Fernando Henrique Cardoso in the 1985 elections for the state and won.

3. Paul Singer: economist, and professor at the Faculty of Economics and Administration of the Universidade de São Paulo, secretary for municipal planning in São Paulo under Mayoress Maria Luisa Erundina.

4. HIVOS, with its head office in the Netherlands, supports 778 organizations in 32 countries in Africa, Latin America, Asia and Europe.

5. PAE: the Programa de Auto-emprega (Self-employment Project) is a joint venture of IATTERMUND, FAO and the state government (see also Chapter 18).

6. See Right Livelihood Award <http://www.rightlivelihood.se/index.html> : 1991 Awards Recipients (page 3). In March 2000 de Morais was being put forward as an RLA 2000 candidate. He is one of the founders of the MST, which received the RLA in 1993.

18

The PAE and the Self-employment Project in Brazil

Walter Barelli

When the world changes, most of its structures change and are transformed with it. At the turn of the century, a vast process of change is under way in the world of work. Enterprises pass through a slimming process, dumping workers and cadres at all levels. Getting a job does not bring with it any reassurance for anyone that it will last for life. And those who get a good job are few and far between. That is *the* tragedy of the twentieth century. An entirely novel social vocabulary has come into use that classifies a major part of the population as 'the excluded', which is clearly reflected in steeply rising unemployment rates in almost every country in the world. Part of this unemployment is said to be structural, part of the 'normal' cycle of ebb and flow (growth and recession) in the national economy. This is the obverse side of the structural development driven by rapid modernization of technology, which results in the overnight disappearance of a multiplicity of functions in the job market. The state of São Paulo, the most industrialized in the country, has managed to adapt rapidly to the ever-recurring recessions in the world economy. However, the country pays a high price for its modernization drive, so much so that in the metropolitan area of São Paulo alone, 750,000 jobs have disappeared in the industrial sector.

While in charge of employment policy as minister of labour in São Paulo, I went in search of solutions to this enormous problem: the non-existence of jobs for all those who capable and willing to work. In the course of this search I came across an FAO/UNO programme that has proved to be very effective and successful in the countries of Central America and in the towns I was able to visit to investigate the possibilities of applying the method, such as João Pessoa (state of Paraíba) and Cuiabá (Mato Grosso). The meetings I held with the experts who are working with the method and the contacts I had with all those familiar with the different activities of the programme convinced me that I was to be in the presence of something very simple and new which, at the same time, has proved to be efficient in terms of solving the unemployment problem.

The PAE programme starts off with the capacitation of a number of economic development experts (TDEs). It is they who, together with the investment project assistants (APIs) will pinpoint those activities that look promising for setting up businesses capable of generating jobs and income in the community. Once those opportunities are identified, the TDEs and APIs evaluate the potential for implanting related enterprises in the community and the accompaniment of the small entrepreneurs. The TDEs have also the responsibility for the training of the so-called APIs. The main, mass capacitation event used for the capacitation of the TDEs themselves is called the course OW. The entire programme always takes place in the heart of the community, and almost always uses local teams. Only if such teams do not materialize or are insufficient are they supplied by other units belonging to the wider PAE structure.

In a second instance, the programme uses the field OW, which directly engages the local community. The field OW capacitates those who have expressed an interest, always the local unemployed. It allows them to capacitate themselves in the running of their own enterprises. The core principle in action here is that people *are capable* of managing their own businesses, collectively or individually. For this they receive, on top of the course in professional development, information about the Moraisean Theory of Organization. In actual fact, while learning both theory and *practice-while-doing*, they are already in the process of setting up their own enterprises. The proper function of the field OW is helping them to learn how to manage those enterprises. The entire plan for the practical implementation of the PAE programme was built on this theory. The process took off with the signing of the 'Terms for Technical Cooperation' with the UN agency FAO, in July 1996, and with the earmarking of slightly more than $1 million for that specific purpose, soon to be followed by the getting together of the team in charge of organizing the field workshops. A core team was assembled by recruiting persons with TDE potential from the local labour market in São Paulo.[1]

The first course OW was installed in the region of Franco da Rocha, where the poverty rate is very high indeed. During this course OW, 31 TDEs and 493 APIs were formed. The TDSs then went on to set up their own enterprise evaluation enterprise (the IDESE – Institute for Socio-Economic Development) and the IATDE (Membership Institute of the Economic Development Experts). Those two enterprises were very important for the Secretariat for Employment I was then leading because in the later expansion of our activities they delivered the specialists who were needed to direct the numerous OWs that were laid on. In 1997 two more course OWs were run, one in the coastal region of Vale de Ribeira, which comprises 23 towns in the coastal part of the state of São Paulo, and where people also are extremely poor. During this event 45 TDEs and 958 APIs were formed. The other course workshop was laid on in the region of Pontal del Rio Paranapanema, in the extreme western part of the state, and, as in the previous case, in situations where extreme levels of poverty were the rule. This was possible thanks to the intense collaboration of the MST, which provided its members with full land settlement services. In terms of numbers: 34 towns were covered by this initiative, and 96 TDEs and 1,448 APIs were formed.

There were therefore a total of three course OWs during which altogether 172 TDEs and 2,899 APIs were formed. The 172 TDEs were especially important, since, without them, it would not have been possible to set up the different field OWs. Each field OW needs an average of five TDEs who run an average of five OWs. Parallel to this, the PAE developed several enterprise field workshops, in which the TDEs equally played a crucial role, in particular in the case of self-managing enterprises. For example, an OW was offered to the cooperative members of a stocking factory that had been closed down by its owner. The OW came to the rescue here by capacitating all the factory's workers, because what they lacked most painfully were management skills. Today the management of the factory is done professionally by the workers themselves.

In the last two years we have established 20 field OWs providing capacitation to 4,999 persons in professions as varied as: culinary crafts, electricity, domestic skills, brick-laying, tiling skills, confectionery, furniture-making, silkscreen printing, bread-making, tailoring and sewing, cabinet-making, furniture manufacture, hairdressing, manicuring and car mechanics. Of the 170 enterprises generated thanks to the workshops, seven are of the development expert type, 27 are family enterprises, 94 are membership and cooperative enterprises, 16 are autonomous and 26 are micro-enterprises. It is important to point out that the Secretariat for Employment of the PAE was instrumental in bringing the OW to the different municipalities in a total of 80 cities, always in league with the local mayors. This cooperation almost always consists predominantly of the lending of equipment needed for the courses, the provision of meeting places, a house for the specialists to stay in, transport and food supplies for the programme. Not to rely on the cooperation of the local administration would be tantamount to not cooperating with the community itself.

Until now the total sum expended by PAE on the programmes is $3.12 million. One problem that has been observed in the course of running the PAE programme is the difficulty the entrepreneurs, i.e. the owners of the newly created enterprises, experience in running their businesses, because of lack of advice, notwithstanding the training they received during the OW. In order to detect and accompany enterprises in difficulty, the secretary for labour has set up a special team. This team has the special mission of making technical visits and giving guidance of whatever kind the new entrepreneur may need. For example, in the case of an enterprise experiencing problems with securing credit, the specialist will provide the correct information such as where and how to obtain it. Often the difficulties are in the area of marketing, management, quality or the setting of correct prices.

In order to attend to the needs of the micro-entrepreneurs, be they formal or informal, the state government, through its secretary for employment and labour relations, has put in place a 'People's Bank' (Banco do Povo) for the disbursement of small loans valued at between 200 and 5,000 *reales* (in those days the Brazilian *real* was still more or less at parity with the American dollar). What is particular about this bank is that it has no functions other than providing loans. The agents of the People's Bank visit the communities in search of clients, as people in the poor communities are not in the habit of passing the front door of a traditional bank. It is precisely in order to overcome this typical social behaviour that the bank is brought to the people. If that were not done, the main beneficiaries of the People's Bank would certainly be the middle class, and not the poor. This was the reason why the first People's Bank units were set up in those regions where the course OWs had taken place, in Pontal del Paranapanema (town of Presidente Prudente) and Vale do Ribeira (town of Registro). Another delicate question for the entrepreneurs is that of the marketing of their products. To tell the truth, after having made provisions for capacitation and credit, that is a question the Secretariat for Labour is still fighting to find a solution to. We are in the process of motivating the different entrepreneurs to set up a programme around the questions of the flow of goods and products, relying on the know-how of the professionals in fields such as sales, marketing, legislation, quality requirements, and so on.

In some cases the Secretariat for Labour has contributed in helping to set up shops or stalls in public spaces, such as at metro or bus stations or clubs. Without the slightest doubt, this is a matter that needs urgent and serious study because without it, the new enterprises cannot reach their full potential. As yet another means of communication with the TDEs and/or the enterprises, PAE edits periodically a bulletin called *PAE News*. This bulletin is fundamental in keeping the ideals of the programme alive. It has, moreover, generated the writing of numerous letters with commentaries and allowed the provision of information on solutions that peers in the business have devised.

Within a timespan of two and a half years we thus have been able to set up a programme in more than eighty towns of the state of São Paulo. The multiplier effect of this mass capacitation is one of the key virtues of the programme, in which 8,500 persons have so far been involved, be it in the preparation of popular projects or in the enterprises, which continue to expand in number. And so, self-employment has already become a reality for many families. People's enterprises are becoming known increasingly as generators of income in various municipalities. Those who are involved with the PAE programme acquire new perspectives and become propagators of organization and change in the *barrio* or town in which they live. From 'excluded' (negative qualification) they have become promoters of income and jobs. In the fitting terms of Governor Mario Covas, they have become 'ambassadors of new work opportunities'.

Note

1. This first, elementary team consisted of the TDEs Eliseu Lira, Clovis Albano, Nilsa Maria Rodrigues and Marcio Magalhaes, and the executive secretaries Vera Lusia Bagnolesy and Marilene Carvalho. The team was led by Dirceu Huertas.

19

The OW and Civil Society in Brazil

Jacinta Castelo Branco Correia

Introduction

The purpose of this chapter is to analyse the contribution of the OWs to the development of the membership organization movement in Brazil, beginning in the rural areas, and expanding from there, at a later stage, to the urban areas, as well to describe a mould-breaking innovatory experience that, by its ability to generate employment and income, inextricably links the fate of the countryside to that of the town. It is just not possible to do justice to the full potential and impact of this method in Brazil, because of its massive scope. For reasons of lack of space and also because of the logistical problems involved in obtaining all the necessary Brazilian data from our Mexican location at the moment of writing, it is the least of our intentions to want to exhaust the matter here and now. Our aim is more modest: to draw attention to the phenomenon of the OWs in Brazil, and make an analysis of the potential of this mass capacitation approach for the organization of civil society. Or more precisely: the capacitation of both rural and urban communities called 'excluded', to use a term that is becoming increasingly fashionable, and by which we mean the 'rejects' of the capitalist system.

We will start with some comments on the climate for the development of membership associations and cooperatives that prevailed in Brazil at the end of the 1980s, when the first experiments with OWs were introduced after a 25-year hiatus, when, in 1964, Clodomir was imprisoned and subsequently sent into exile by a Brazilian dictatorship that displayed an intense dislike, for reasons best known to themselves, for citizens' organizations in general and mass movements in particular. Into exile with its originator went the theories and practice of the OW. Having set the OW in its historical context in Brazil, we will propose it as a wholly novel approach in the long tradition of associativism and cooperativism. The OW opens up new avenues and ways of thinking about cooperatives as we know them – for example, in the way these are promoted and implemented by the national extension service and by NGOs and governments of all kinds. Consolidating their successes in the rural areas, the OWs then spread out to the built-up areas of Brazil, where they became an important instrument, both in the mega-towns such as São Paulo and in smaller localities, in the fight against unemployment. To stem the urban and rural unemployment tide, a system of job and income generation (SIPGEI) was developed. The PROGEI (job and income-generating project), on the other hand, integrates town and countryside in a common search for the solution, on a massive scale, of the equally massive problem of unemployment.

We will conclude with a balance-sheet of the achievements and difficulties encountered with the implementation of the OW so as to provide a stimulus for those committed to the advance of knowledge about the method and to fostering further research, which, apart from being intellectually exciting, is also urgent in a world climate dominated by the total market which, invariably, militates against the interests of the already least well off, the excluded from the system.

Membership Associations of the Excluded in Late-1980s Brazil

In de Morais' book *Notes on a Theory of Organization*, a classification can be found of the different forms of organization in the rural areas of Central America, which, we think, is still perfectly applicable to the analysis of present civil society initiatives by the excluded while at the same time not exhausting the subject.[1] According to de Morais, rural organizations can be divided into two types: organizations of struggle and organizations for social stability. Militant organizations struggle for the transformation of prevailing structures that, as a natural by-product of capitalism, they understand to be at the root of the problems of poverty, oppression, etc. This struggle is carried out either by force of arms or peacefully, by reclaiming rights through political channels.

The name 'organizations for social stability', on the other hand, is self-explanatory. Brazil, especially in the wake of the so-called 'New Republic' in the 1980s, saw a flowering of organizations of both types. Under the latter we can, for example, list the 21,000 *Comunidades eclesiais de base* (Christian base communities) that emerged in the wake of 'liberation theology' movement in the Catholic Church, the (post-Vatican II) tendency of the Church that had opted for positive action 'on the side' of the oppressed and those excluded. This has been described as 'prayer in practice' and judged to be more effective, in terms of testimonial power, than contemplative prayer, which, if anything, had left the broad layers of the population to their own devices and alienated. Liberation theology, which has achieved so much for the conscientization of the masses, was spearheaded by important thinkers such as Fr Carlo Alberto Betto and Fr Leonardo Boff, and, not least, of course, the great Christian socialist thinker Paulo Freire, whose talents as conscientizer were so much greater than those of literacy worker (*alfabetizador*). His followers during the years of his absence from Brazil – because he too, as is well known, was exiled – notwithstanding the prevailing culture of repression during these years, never stopped their work. Often clandestine, they were very influential in the fostering of a popular culture built on critical consciousness. This critical consciousness, for example, was the moving force behind the MST, which, alongside sister movements, such as the Human Settlement Programme – Moradía – of the state of São Paulo, were the practical outcome of the awareness fostered in the preceding years by the Catholic Church and by political activists of the left.

In the 1990s, the combination of those forces gave birth to the Brazilian Workers' Party (PT), whose militants in the subsequent years founded the Workers' Central Unit (CUT), an important organization of social struggle. Among those organizations (too numerous to mention in this space) we also count the CONAN (National Federation of Human Settlement Associations), with headquarters in Brasília, whose 23,000 associated branches are fighting for a solution to the problems afflicting, in particular, the poorest slums in the towns; there is also the CONTAG (National Confederation of Agricultural Workers), successor of the ULTAB (Brazilian Workers and Peasant Union), which used to be associated with the Brazilian communist movement.

By organizations of social stability we understand the traditional co-operatives and mutuals. The NGOs and rural extension agencies have played an important role in their establishment as well as in that of the small rural producers' organizations (SRPOs) which, for example, go into the pooling of marketing and small machinery use, generally in exchange for votes in the countryside where the mode of small family production still prevails or, alternatively, in the interest of the diffusion of a particular technology promoted by one or other multinational. Rural extension since the mid-1980s has made great strides in taking options 'on the side' of the peasants and against officialdom's dreadful agricultural policies, of which small peasants always are the main victims. This deserves a special mention here. The Organization for Brazilian Cooperatives (OCB) has played an important role in matters relating to agricultural production. Until 1988, however, the law forbade urban cooperatives, a measure that very much restricted the activities of the OCB in the field of social stabilization, especially in the latter years of the dictatorship. But for these legal strictures, a lot could have been achieved, if only their understanding of cooperativism had not been so traditional. We can thus see, in a quick sketch, how the 1980s was a very 'special' decade for Brazil, especially towards the end of the dictatorship, when there was a gradual transition to a civilian government, even though the first democratic elections only took place in the beginning of the 1990s. This gradual change of climate favourable to democracy also gradually brought back those formerly exiled by the military dictatorship. This brought a rekindling of hope for national reconciliation, a new process of healing and the rediscovery of ideals that favour the poorest.

In the years following the 'lost eighties' we see the building up of a 'critical mass' around the need for popular organization and the coming to fruition of the seeds sown, long ago, by those who were exiled for their beliefs and those who remained in Brazil and continued to resist the forces of dictatorship with all their might. Whether dedicated to struggle or to social stabilization, these organizations have in the meantime gone through grave crises, mainly because of their inadequate organization skills. The much talked about 'empowerment' rarely went beyond the popular education' paradigm,[2] which, at best, was able to raise people's critical consciousness, but when it came to equipping the learners with organizational skills invariably fell short of providing useable models. That is the main reason for the lamentable lack of success of the organizations of struggle, consistently failing to achieve group autonomy and, instead, making those groups ever more dependent on what amounts to personal, charismatic leadership. The popular education movement was forever in danger of being pushed into a corner: whenever reactionary forces decided to put a stop to a popular movement or an organization for struggle, it was enough to throw the leader in prison and so demoralize the band of followers. The problems faced by the organizations for social stability were no less and no fewer: they had to contend, in both countryside and urban areas, with the obdurate problem of 'boss-ism' or the personalized artisan leader, leaving the road wide open to clientelism and all kinds of manipulation.[3]

The OW as an Unfolding Form of Associationism and Cooperativism in Brazil

The OW starts from the concepts first mooted by Hegel and Marx, namely that it is 'the conditions of life which are generative of social consciousness (culture)'.[4] This means that, by changing people's conditions of life, their social consciousness will also change. Nothing new up to this point. However, while it is clear *what* needs to be done, knowledge about the '*how to*' – in the case of peasants, for example, with thousands of years of doing things in a certain way, the only option, so far, has been mass emigration to the town. Whenever a peasant or a small producer is in at the deep end of a complex organizational set-up, the 'bad habits' of the artisan culture will inhibit their proper functioning in this context and, because of this, will gradually lead to a crisis or the demise of this organization. As apparently there is no option for the peasant or artisan to change their conditions of life, they are caught up in a vicious circle from which there is no escape. Unless, that is, the principles proposed by Clodomir Santos de Morais are called to the rescue: the OW is a way by which to transform – mediated by an artificial ('experimental'), but at the same time, 'real-life' and intensive process (the workshop) their conditions of life, whether their background is urban or rural.

The OWs are theoretico-practical 'experiments' ('essays', or 'attempts') in which large groups of people are going to learn how to organize by the very act of getting organized. The capacitating learning event lasts between 30 and 40 days and starts from the certain knowledge that only by dint of getting involved in action that is truly capacitating can entrepreneurial literacy be achieved. Using the bicycle metaphor, it is not possible to learn how to ride a bike if there is no bicycle to ride on. In the same way, it is not possible to learn 'another' way of organizing except inside a real enterprise that needs real organizational and real management structures. No amount of 'group dynamics' (with small groups, that is), for example, will be able to achieve this. Only the fact of getting to grips, in actual practice, with the reality of a complex organization will allow the participants to learn how to solve the problems inherent in a complex enterprise. And it is only an inside understanding of 'how' it works that means it will be possible to mount such an enterprise and set it on a successful course. The problems that arise in the course of trying to set up and run such an enterprise become the very pedagogical learning tools in this methodology. Thus, the saying: 'The more problems the better' is pedagogically true in this case. By getting to grips with and solving those problems one by one, the learners evolve a new frame of values: the values prevailing in the complex enterprise. They also learn how those new values and principles are in sharp contrast with the values that prevailed in anything thus far experienced, i.e. their artisan/small producer form of organization, which does not need the assistance or cooperation of anyone. The whole process, from beginning to end, is run by one and the same person (or by the same small group of associates, such as family members).

In the new enterprise, the possibility for which is opened up by the OW learning experience, the 'need' for a strict discipline and a division of labour will become manifest in a very practical way. The OW takes great care that, while the participants are thus engaged in a very practical discovery process, their theoretical understanding is able to keep pace all the time. This is achieved by means of a concurrent lecture series on the theory of organization to which the participants are invited. Practice combined with theory allows the consciousness of reasons for their actions to become ever more explicit. As the process unfolds, the group of participants becomes ever more capacitated inside the very practice of which they all partake. The deeper they get involved in the activities of the workshop, the more they will be capacitated, and the more their organizational consciousness will develop.

The binding and motivating agent of the enterprise is, normally, the lecture series, which is offered in a central location to which all (regardless of age, sex, colour, religion, or whatever) are invited.[5] The community, in this preparatory stage, are at liberty to say what kind of courses they would like to get involved in, where they want them to take place, who they think would like to participate, and at what times of the day they would like them to be run. This is called the 'primary structure' of the event (or the 'organization of the organizers' – Labra). Facilitators and specialists, together with the inventory put at the disposal of the workshop, are all part of this primary structure. As it is not possible to know, beforehand, what tools, machinery or other implements will be required in the course of the workshop, the inventory is supplied as soon as the community has given to the director of the OW the list of courses they want to be taught. The same goes for the type of facilitators and specialists who will be needed for any particular workshop. This is in stark contrast with what usually tends to happen in the relationship between projects ('owners of knowledge' – the 'who-knows') and the community (those 'deprived of knowledge' – the 'don't-knows'). Those relationships are dialogical and democratic.

To sum up: it is inside the organized activities (OW) that the group of participants genuinely acquires the 'capacity to organize' and 'the capacity to manage'. On the basis of this powerful capacitating instrument, it becomes genuinely possible for the community to confront their problems and to actually 'do' something about them, as they know the 'how' and the 'what' to do, be it in organizations of struggle or organizations for social stabilization.

Types of OW

There are four basic types of organization workshop:

1. 'Centre' workshops (centre OW)
2. 'Course' workshops (course OW)
3. 'Field' workshops (FOW)
4. 'Enterprise' workshops (EOW)

Each of these different types corresponds to the particular needs for organizational learning and the formation of cadres. For example:

- A centre workshop capacitates a *cadre* of leaders of membership organizations, of cooperatives or agricultural enterprises.
- A course workshop will be more indicated in the case of *organizers* of systems of mass capacitation for whatever purpose.
- A field workshop is the type that applies in the case of *communities* and their leaders who have put in a request for their community to be capacitated.
- An enterprise workshop is run in the case of an *already existing enterprise*, which has landed in a situation of crisis. In Brazil, three of these four types of OW have been tried out. The most commonly applied type, however, is the field workshop, alongside the course and centre workshops. In these workshops around 60,000 people spread over 100 workshop events, were capacitated in Brazil from 1989 till 1998.[6]

Drawing up a factually correct balance sheet on the exact number of events that took place, and the number of enterprises that actually sprung up as a result of those workshops, is virtually impossible, as this supposes the possibility of quantifying what people have learned and how they subsequently make use of what they learned. We will venture, however, to offer a conservative estimate of the effects of those workshop events, based on the pilot research projects we have run already. From these data we can extrapolate that (to keep on the conservative side) 15 per cent of OW participants subsequently start an enterprise of one sort or the other. We end up with a (conservative) total of 9,000 enterprises – of the family and non-family type – set up in Brazil alone by former OW graduates. This represents an acceptable number of enterprises of different types created as a direct result of the OWs. To this we have to add an approximate 30 per cent of OW participants who subsequently found work or some form of income generation by which they have been able to raise their living standards, as a direct result of participation in the workshops. Translated into numbers, this means that about 8,000 persons overall found employment or income to which they had no access before. When we add to this the family members of those involved in the new enterprises – and not even taking into account the indirect beneficiaries (who have to be multiplied by a factor of 5) we arrive at a total of 27,000 persons who have drawn some economic benefit from those events, at an estimated unit cost of a mere $16 per person.

Up till now we have talked about economic benefits only. The social benefits are equally impressive, as the community, once organized, is able not to solve problems that are strictly the province of the government, but to set up their own projects and run them economically, viably and sustainably. The first OW run in an urban area of Brazil, in the *barrio* of Tancredo in Porto Velho, capital city of the state of Rondônia, in the Amazonian region, is just one example among many: one of the principal problems in this *barrio* was the lack of a sewerage system, which was a public health hazard. The OW project commission, which is still in existence, elaborated, with the voluntary assistance of a number of engineers, an alternative project to the one proposed by the city council (which would have taken decades to complete, let alone to reach the outskirts of this godforsaken *barrio*). The project commission renegotiated the plans with the city council and in consultation with the Canadian Embassy, who were prepared to put up the necessary funds for the project. Subsequently, the project has not only managed to solve the problem, but has also provided a classical example of how it is possible to build, in an alternative way, an urban sewerage system. Moreover, thanks to the money drawn in by the project, the community generated a local source of income.

In the same way, a number of OWs were run in the town of São Paulo. Several cooperatives materialized out of these events, where before there was nothing, or, perhaps, land invasions or traditional self-help types of work, especially in the area of house-building. Only through the OW event did they learn that when you have a house, but no income, the house will eventually have to be sold so that you can eat and stay alive, or pay medical expenses. The city council of São Paulo was firmly set in its paternalistic ways even under the Labour Party government. Instead of helping the *barrios* to organize themselves so that they would be in a position to escape perpetual dependency on food-aid distributed at the *Mutirao* – (a vacant plot of land where the voluntary house-building was taking place), it gave preference to a housing policy that, even after having housed them, left people in the same condition of poverty as before, and dependent on public handouts. The MST had to cope with similar problems. No sooner had it managed to invade and occupy a piece of land, settling a maximum of 30 or 50 families on it, at the cost of enormous struggle and heartache, than it saw those same people back, landless, in the very places from which they originally came, namely the *barrios* in town. What happened was that the new settlers sold their land or passed on the land-rights to others. The whole process having come full circle, the end result was that the lands returned to the big landowners, who were the owners all along.

In 1988 a first OW was held in Rio Grande do Sul where the first cadres of the MST were capacitated. One of the first results of this experience was that the movement's slogan was changed from 'Invade and Resist!' to 'Invade, Resist and Produce!' Another change could be seen in the sheer numbers of people involved in land invasions: a thousand families or more. Those 'with land', who, before, fell completely outside the concerns of the movement – which was, after all, for the 'landless' – now became a real concern, too (be it only to prevent them from joining the masses of the landless) but, moreover, they also became a valuable resource for the budding new settlements. The first cooperative for those 'with land' (*com terra*) was formed in the beginning of the 1990s. From this basis the CONCRAB Terra (Federation of Agrarian Reform Cooperatives) was set up. The great difference between these 'workshop' cooperatives and those with more traditional origin is that the former will not employ salaried labour, i.e. people who are non-members, thus avoiding the otherwise almost inevitable exploitation of paid labour. What they do instead, whenever the cooperative members are not in sufficient numbers or cannot do the work for whatever reason, is set up a sister cooperative, or a 'service' cooperative, which then covers the temporary needs of the mother cooperative. The combination of those cooperatives is known as an enterprise association.

The agglomeration of a number of micro-enterprises into one big enterprise association, or 'second-level enterprises' has meant a saving grace for the otherwise disastrous micro-enterprise approach, which, according to the reports published by SEBRAE (Brazilian Service for Support to Micro-Enterprises) has chalked up a 'mortality rate' of up to 90 per cent (i.e. micro-enterprises folding in the first year after they were set up). That is another important distinguishing factor: the workshops always point in the direction of the formation of large(r) enterprises in the mould of what was directly experienced during the capacitation events. The other major differentiating factor between the OW approach and other events, which may look similar in appearance, is the organizational discipline the participants impose on themselves. It is a case of self-management, or nothing. All decisions are taken in common and are subject to at least 48 hours of scrutiny before they are taken. The decisions of each commission are then proposed to the general assembly, guaranteeing full participation throughout, from beginning to end, from top to bottom.

Conclusion

While, on the one hand, it might appear that we have been viewing things through rose-tinted glasses, and have been intent on demonstrating only the successes, problems with the workshops are nevertheless legion. The same is true when trying to apply the OW method on a massive scale, as is desirable and necessary, taking into account the massive numbers of those excluded. The principal problem derives from funding agencies that fail to understand the absolute need to 'let go', to hand over, lock, stock and barrel, the management of resources and personnel to a collective. Their teachers, facilitators and experts are more part of the problem than of the solution: there is an extreme reluctance to subordinate themselves to the judgement of a group of people who have inferior levels of education, or worse, no education at all ('illiterate'). On the other hand, they tend to (con)fuse their personal experience, based, for example, on traditional *small* group dynamics, with the OW processes, which use principles of *large* group social psychology methods with persons predominantly with lower levels of education. Such an unfortunate mix of two approaches results in mutually antagonistic efforts, which cancel each other out. The whole process gets deflated and in the end no one knows any more what they are doing.

Funding agencies also like to decide for themselves the desirability or not of an OW, often based on a strict cost–benefit analysis. Even though, as we have already pointed out, the cost per person of a workshop is in the region of $16.00 – derisory as far as development projects go – the total sum needed may still seem large, due to the fact that up to five hundred people may participate, necessitating considerable start-up funds. The sums involved in donor agencies' own projects may look small(er), but so is the tiny number of people who eventually benefit. It is indeed very difficult to break old habits and set a new course as this requires questioning fundamental paradigms and replacing them with new ones, which do not end up keeping people dependent. When everything is said and done, it is not possible to come to terms with a problem as large as that of mass poverty as long as the organizations trying to tackle it continue to behave in purely interventionist or assistentialist ways – in other words, such organizations 'need' the people's continued dependence on them for the sake of their own survival, thus, in the end, providing nourishment to that old familiar and sinister enemy: assistencialism.

Notes

1. C. S. de Morais (1986) *Elementos sobre Teoría de Organização*, São Paulo: MST. An English translation prepared by Ian Cherrett is in existence: *Notes on a Theory of Organization*, ETC UIC.

2. On the fundamental distinction between 'education' and 'capacitation', see, for example Correia, J. C. N. (1995) *Communication and Capacitation*, Brasília: IATTER-MUND.

3. De Morais (1986) provides an analysis of the behaviour of the artisan confronted with forms of complex organization. This behaviour is referred to by de Morais as 'a set of bad habits' (habits that are dysfunctional and destructive in a complex organization). For the sake of the successful establishment of the latter, these 'bad habits' need, therefore, to be combated in a large, cooperative organization. This is done by means of friendly reminders and criticisms, and through continued vigilance. Those habits exist,

indeed, at the level of the unconscious and the collective group, understanding what its fundamental organizational tasks are, can stamp them out.

4. On the theoretical foundations of the OW, see de Morais' doctoral thesis, submitted in 1985 in Rostock, Germany, 'The subjective and objective conditions underpinning the transformation of rural life in Central America'.

5. 'Enterprise' is understood here in the sociological sense as defined by de Morais. 'a number of persons who organize themselves for the attainment of a certain goal'.

6. IATTERMUND (Institute for Technical Support to Third World Countries), based in Brasília, is resourced by the officials of the PROGEIs from different states within the Brazilian Federation. Added to them are people belonging to the MST who have a vast experience with the application of this method and in the formation of the settlements, cooperatives and membership enterprises that came in the wake of the land occupations initiated by that movement as well as by the Movement of the Homeless.

20

The OW's Potential: Concluding Observations

Miguel Sobrado

The OW method, as seen in previous chapters, has been applied in three continents, each time in the context of projects with large group participation, resulting in activities that go from simple community actions and survival strategies to the launching of fully-fledged, large-scale agriculture and fisheries industries as, for example, in Honduras. Even though the method often had a rough ride because of adverse institutional environments, the fact that the OW happened at all is due to a fortunate mix of circumstances and concrete results. But what always guaranteed its endurance were, apart from its power of organization, the sympathies and synergies generated between the population and the concrete achievements that invariably ensued. In the locations where the OW was applied there was almost always a frantic race against the clock to consolidate goals and gather the physical and human recources necessary to make the experience self-sustaining from economic, political and social points of view. Given those conditions, there remained precious little time, or, indeed, incentive for the necessary theory-building and further exploration and development of the method.

A path was cut through the undergrowth, though, systematically broadened with successive experiences. This applies to the application of both the theoretical and the methodological apparatus. We will touch in succession on three aspects of further theoretical and methodological development that hold great potential in terms of practical application in programmes and projects. These are:

1. the concept of *social strata* used by de Morais to determine the organizational potential of each group or community in projects with large-scale social participation;
2. the concept of *capacitation–discapacitation*, and
3. the potential of the *PROGEI–SIPGEI* – which take the OW beyond the realm of mass capacitation and into that of social audit and state reform, to name just two.

The Social Composition of the Groups and Large-scale Social Participation Projects

The social strata identified by de Morais, as indicated in previous chapters – artisan, worker, semi-worker and 'lumpen' (social misfit) – do not pretend to replace the concept of social class, but rather serve to highlight the organizational potential of each individual or group within those strata, in terms of their former work and organizational experience. Thus, because in their previous life experience in the planning and production of goods, self-sufficient 'artisans' (small or family producers) are more likely than 'workers' to produce on an individual(istic) basis. The latter, because of the work discipline with which they are imbued, are likely to set up, with far more ease than the former, organizations and enterprises that require forms of social division of labour. Semi-workers, on the other hand, share the skills of either group, depending on the degree of dedication they apply to their double lifestyle as both family-based and salaried workers. And finally, the social misfits ('lumpen') are of course those who will avoid work of any kind.

This differentiation, which, on the surface, may appear to be elementary, nevertheless holds a host of very important practical implications, which make it possible, in the evaluations, to delineate the areas of success and failure, for example in agricultural reform situations. The case of the agricultural production cooperative of Bataán, Costa Rica, in the 1970s will illustrate this. At that time the institute, then still called the Institute for Lands and Colonization, was in search of farmers with a proven track record as 'small entrepreneurs' – and the result was a resounding failure. As they were being selected and put on record under that heading by the institute's administration, without any prior form of training, let alone capacitation in organizational initiatives with social division of labour, their self-sufficient and individualistic ways of operating made sure that any new enterprise went right over the cliff. This contrasts sharply with, for example, the cooperatives Coopesilencio in Costa Rica and of Guanchias and Hondupalma in Honduras (see Chapters 5 and 6). Each of these enterprises started with a land invasion involving the social participation of an important segment of labourers with experience in the industrial banana-production sector – an agricultural enterprise displaying a high degree of social division of labour, and each one of them, 25 years hence, can be deemed an entrepreneurial and social success.[1]

The differences in organizational mental models existing among each of the aforementioned strata are not only important in the evaluation of projects, but also, and more importantly, in the adequate diagnosis preparatory to the setting up of a regional or local development project or of specific group capacitation programmes. It is especially at this level that de Morais' theoretical perspectives hold prospects of major relevance and it has to be realized that his method has, perhaps, been seriously under-estimated and under-used by experts in the field. Instead, the familiar economistic stereotypes blended with crude prejudice have been applied again and again in the type of 'projectile' projects that continue to be launched by both international and national development agencies despite the evidence of the social reality as analysed and articulated by de Morais. Witness the abiding wisdom, during the lifespan of the Costa Rican Institute for Agrarian Development, that self-managing enterprises were 'commie plots' that presumably went diametrically against the individualistic-idiosyncratic character traits of the Costa Rican tenant farmer (small-holder).

On the basis of blinkered views such as these, virtually all commonly owned plots were parcelled out to individual farmers (see also Chapter 5). Today, most of these smallholdings have been absorbed into large-scale commercial farms while, by contrast, the few surviving self-managing enterprises founded by workers and semi-workers that managed to resist, and continued with capacitation events at different stages, are holding their own. Others, such as Hondupalma in Honduras, have grown into big national and regional enterprises. But this obvious lack of vision and of sociological insight is not only a fact of life in, as one might expect, traditional Third World countries: in the course of a consultancy visit to post-Cold War Russia (see Chapter 14), I happened to be visiting a *kolkhoz* (collective) where the conversion of kolkhozians into individual farmers had been initiated by decree. President Yeltsin had, indeed, decreed that the kolkhoz should be disbanded and the land redistributed, but even though most of the kolkhozians abided by the decree for fear of losing their entitlements to the land altogether, they continued to work collectively.

An English agronomist who had been assigned the task of assisting the kolkhozians in the transformation process was wholly disheartened by the lack of interest they displayed in owning their own private plots of land. 'I only managed to persuade a couple of enterprise-minded people to work, not as farmers, but as electricians and plumbers,' he complained. But it was sufficient simply to take note of the real and existing infrastructure of the kolkhoz, the core of which is a commonly owned resource pool, and understand the long historical trajectory travelled by the kolkhozians as salaried labourers, to realize that out of the existing soil and the rich material and social environment a great agro-industrial enterprise could emerge with a minimum of effort. But neither President Yeltsin himself nor the English project manager, a prominent specialist in micro-enterprises in his own right, seemed to be aware of the disgrace and humiliation being inflicted on the collective farmers in Russia, even less, of course, of the sound sociological principles and the verifiable results obtained in the field, in those matters, by the Brazilian sociologist. But the nub of the problem does not so much lie in the area of agricultural projects, nor can it be blamed on Third World syndromes. The total ignorance about those elementary sociological principles that have demonstrated their great operational value in the design and evaluation of projects is also a deplorable fact of life in the so-called developed countries and in the rest of the world.

Here, as elsewhere, assistentialist policies and assistentialist experts peddling their interventionist recipes abound. Much-trumpeted 'empowerment' or 'capacity building' often boils down to little more than technical training courses that keep young unemployed boys off the street, or, at best, get them the occasional salaried job. Alternatively, clusters of training modules and services around the micro-enterprise cure-all are provided. Female heads of household and salaried workers in general with lower levels of education and above a certain age (35 and over), who have lost their competitive edge to the better-trained newcomers, form the bulk of the unemployed who fall outside the grand masterplans drawn up by technocrats bereft of sociological insight. So, for example, the Women Heads of Households organization, one of Chile's star social programmes on which the Costa Rican sister programmes were patterned, has very little to show in terms of concrete results. The in-built limitations of the programme are due partly to the fact that the programme, in its very design, confuses education, understood as 'training', with 'capacitation'. These programmes start from the premise that 'group dynamics' exercises (in no way geared to autonomous organizational capacitation) generate self-esteem as well as organizational discipline so that those women can be reintegrated in the mainstream production processes. As has been shown time and again and as we will explain further in this chapter, such an integration cannot easily be achieved by a disaggregated approach. The lack of sociological insight and the lack of a proper analysis of existing practices restricts the potential of recognizing the organizational potential of salaried workers to create membership enterprises of their own, of a type far more promising than the 'micro-enterprise' strategy enthusiastically endorsed at present at every level.

It is this same lack of vision that makes economists of the type we met at the Punkin kolkhoz in the new Russia indiscriminately dole out uniform recipes to the unemployed that go increasingly under the name 'micro-enterprise'. Never mind that it is a proven fact that up to 80 per cent of those micro-enterprises advertise an 80 per cent-plus mortality rate in their very first year of operation. In actual fact, those who plan social policies and projects not only lack the most basic knowledge concerning these strategically important development approaches (discussed in other chapters of this book), they also automatically interpret the undeniable signs of a healthy growth of the informal sector of the economy as a surefire indicator and an implicit invitation, coming from the grassroots, that 'micro-enterprise' programmes should be stepped up even further. They will point, for example, to the new market niches that are constantly opening up in the market economy in the area of, for example, the new computer technologies and management opportunities in the globalized economy. Unfortunately, they are less keen to admit, in all honesty, that the increase in informal sector micro-enterprises goes hand in hand with a drastic reduction in productivity, which, in turn, would point to the fact that the dramatic increase in micro-enterprises has more to do with the raw survival instincts of those who are displaced by the mainstream economy than with a prodigious sudden flowering of new opportunities or an increase in those who feel a sudden vocation to set up micro-enterprises.

The Concepts of 'Capacitation' and 'Discapacitation'

The conceptual category of 'capacitation' is vital in the design and implementation of development projects, particularly those with specific emphasis on organizational and management capacitation, as the latter is at the heart of the results one would want to see come from most projects. Around capacitation practically all the other disciplines, such as economics, administration, social psychology, (adult) education and sociology, as well as practical skills such as accountancy and financial analysis needed for the achievement of project goals, can be clustered. The importance of 'organizational capacitation' or 'organizational literacy' (understood as a cross-cultural process) is increasing in importance in a rapidly changing world. On the way this concept is understood and applied depends, to a great extent, whether the bulk of development projects, all of which proclaim to want to enhance the participation potential of communities and groups, will result in success or failure. On its application in project design, the preparation of the trainers (*formadores*, in the Spanish original), the logistical support this activity receives, the conditions in which these activities take place, will depend, to a great extent, the expected results.

Even though there is a general consensus that capacitation contains an element of 'enablement towards', there is no uniformity in interpretation as regards the operationalization of this concept, especially in matters of social development projects. When it comes to capacitating subjects in the use of technical-productive instruments or processes, there is, again, a relative consensus as regards the operative processes involved. This consensus is directly related to the very nature of 'the object' with which the subjects interact in the work process. This activity requires training (coaching and instructions) endowing the subject with the necessary skills to manage the object. Thus, in all processes of technical capacitation, such as, for example, the coaching of vehicle drivers, we come across at least two components:

- a module of *instruction*, which inculcates knowledge about road-signs, the highway code, the mechanical components of a car or lorry, etc., and
- a module of *training*, which deals with 'how' the vehicle generally needs to be handled.

In the first module, the subject (learner driver) receives information from another subject (instructor) who holds the necessary knowledge. The second module (training proper) is of an entirely different nature, and the relationships established here are also totally different: no question any more, here, of the learning by heart of concepts and road-signs. The subject is being trained in the handling of 'the object': the traditional relationship between trainee and instructor ceases to apply here and is replaced with that between the subject and the object; this, alone, can instil the necessary capacitation so that the subject is able to handle it. In this relationship, the 'subject' acquires the necessary knowledge about how to handle the 'object'. The subject 'discovers' the qualities, limitations and possibilities of the vehicle only by turning on the ignition and actually driving it, and, in the very process of interacting with the object, acquiring the skills necessary to handle the vehicle.

The instructor sitting next to the learner in the passenger seat is demoted here to playing second fiddle to the object – however necessary the instructor's presence otherwise might be to ensure that the vehicle proceeds in a proper fashion and in all safety. That is because the dominant relationship, in this second module, is not between subject and subject, but between subject and object. It is important here to note that in this module of instruction the need for the autonomy of the subject is absolutely supreme, as this is the only condition under which it is possible for the capacitation process to take place: without this autonomy it is mere training, and capacitation in the handling of the vehicle is impossible. But autonomy does not mean 'lack of direction' or pure 'spontancity', for the simple reason that both training and capacitation require a careful plan worked out in advance by the instructor. However necessary and beyond dispute these distinctions are when purely technical capacitation processes (such as driving a car) are involved, this clarity becomes diffused, or disappears altogether, when it comes to issues of social participation and organization processes where the subjects are at the same time objects of capacitation.

Occasionally, in some cases, the instruction part is oversimplified or disappears altogether. Mostly, however, it is the training part that is docked, suppressed or postponed indefinitely.

The causes of the disappearance of one or another module are varied:

* In instances of suppression or compression of the *instruction* phase, knowledge limitations in knowledge or, simply, a pragmatic corner-cutting exercise on the part of the instructor can be blamed.
* Whenever the *training* phase is suppressed, however, the causes may be more varied and complex, imputable to certain aspects of the way in which training specialists have been trained themselves and due to the prevailing institutional and social context (Sobrado 1994).

Whatever the case may be, the omission or incomplete provision of any part of these modules seriously affects the quality of the process and alters the results obtained. This means that whenever, in the course of social development projects, there is a question of 'capacitation', we are not always talking about the same thing. 'Capacitation' may often mean no more than 'instruction', or 'awareness-raising'. In other cases we may be in the presence of a training process with an obstacle-course thrown, often gratuitously, into the bargain.

Whenever capacitation is confused with instruction, or awareness-raising, understood as a superior level of absorption of instruction, the way or the techniques through which information is provided get pride of place, while training, or the process of learning how to relate with the object, take the back-seat. So as to enhance awareness raising, didactic techniques such as socio-drama, which facilitate the absorption of the course content and which permit, in technical capacitation processes, a better quality of participation, are introduced. The synergies generated in some of those processes fill the facilitators, the politicians and the sponsors of the programmes with enthusiasm ... but no genuine capacitation is taking place at all in these exercises, because no training part was included in the very design of the project. In terms of tangible results, the beneficiaries of these training methods remain incapable of reaching beyond the stage of voicing protests and denunciations of injustice, while the genuine capacity to translate these protests into effective action to overcome the situation remains sorely lacking. What is much more likely to happen is that, as soon as the expectations generated by these group dynamics have dissipated, all that remains is a growing frustration and a sense of powerlessness among the so-called 'beneficiaries' of these types of projects. The following questions therefore then arise:

* How is it that, with such alarming frequency in social participation

projects, such inexplicable alterations in what ought to be a proper capacitation process take place?

- How is it that the experts in charge of the design of those projects – often holders of impressive degrees in education from the best universities in the world – commit with such ease these apparently elementary mistakes?

First and foremost, and obviously, what is glaringly clear to engineers and technicians, because of the very nature of the (mechanical or electronic) objects with which they work, is not so obvious in the case of social development projects. A considerable number of adult educators get absorbed in techno-educational questions around the 'how?' and in a coming together of values that supposedly underpin the process. This results in some cases in a rigid manning of ideological barricades, which makes them lose sight of questions relating to the 'why?', i.e., the purpose and means of education. For example, the so-called 'hands-off' principle applied in certain pedagogical processes, supposedly meant to stimulate creativity and participation, has tended to get confused with reluctance to direct those processes at all, resulting in a crazy 'free-for-all'. Pedagogic principles, taken to their extremes, thus contribute to losing sight of the nature of the object, already contaminated by day-to-day ideological stances.

Second, the theoretical basis of capacitation has never been theoretically explained, except, relatively recently, in de Morais' PhD thesis of 1987. The theoretical framework we propose to offer here is, of course, still far from mature, nor is the OW practice widespread. Even though it has taken root in at least two continents, its practice has remained restricted to relatively small working groups and academic institutions. Theoretical implications such as the importance of the concept of 'the autonomy of the subject' in the capacitation process, as a substitute for the far less accurate concept of 'freedom', still remain to be explored. It is therefore quite useful to be able to offer, in this context, a relational formula that attempts to capture the concept and practice of capacitation, based on de Morais' ideas, allowing us to detect the kinds of problems that may arise in the course of the capacitation process and make it less effective, opening up cracks allowing political clientelism to seep in again; the formula presented here can be found in a more complete form in my publication *Capacitation and Discapacitation in Development Projects* (1994). The formula can be summarized as follows:

$$C = (i + t + ES - ADE) \times K$$

Where: C = capacitation
        i = instruction
        t = training

ES = educational strategy
ADE = assistentialism in the design and execution of capacitation projects
K = outside factors that impinge positively/negatively on the results
(nature, economy, political, cultural)

In keeping with the approach within which this formula was conceived, the outcomes of the capacitation process will depend on the nature of the object which, in turn, defines the sequence and the weight to be attached to the different elements in the relational formula. In the same way as capacitation can be generated, so can discapacitation be understood as a process in which the relationship between subject and object is such that the capacity of the subject to control (conduct) the object properly, for whatever reason, atrophies. Discapacitation results in the subject being handicapped and/or being less able to cope with the surrounding social and economic life.

Capacitation and Discapacitation: Two Faces of the Same Coin

While capacitation is the process that habilitates the subject in 'managing to manage', for example, discapacitation happens when this ability is inhibited or impeded. Discapacitation happens as a result of the very design by which the capacitation process is intended to happen and of the social relations inside which it develops. Discapacitation is not to be confused with incapacity, which is the loss of capacity or the loss of skill caused by disuse or accident. Discapacitation flourishes in a climate rife with relationships of domination. It is these, and never the subject, that decide both the permitted field of action and the permitted level groups are allowed to aspire to. If the prevailing value system has predetermined that groups of people belonging to certain social strata are 'losers' because of their low cultural and social status, they will in no way ever be allowed to take charge of their own capacitation process.

In other words, it is automatically taken for granted that the design is a job for 'winners': it is up to the losers to execute what has been designed for them so that they can get ahead. One of the ways in which dis-capacitation happens is by the wrongheaded design of what is presumed to be a capacitation process but which, instead of habilitating the least advantaged, de facto leads them right down the road to failure – failure for which they, the victims, are blamed because of their 'lack of interest' or their 'lack of gratitude'. Pure ideology takes over, at least subconsciously: that is why training falls by the wayside, along with any other measure, for that matter, that might allow the 'beneficiaries' some modicum of autonomy or the chance to capacitate themselves. Real capacitation is then replaced by 'courses in organizational skills', which, while full of good advice and with plenty of opportunity to 'be' educated, become their only pathway to 'development'.

We have to guard ourselves, though, against imagining that discapacitation is the result of some obscure and perverse conspiracy, a plot dreamed up by 'the dominators' with the sole objective of keeping the dominated in their place and keep them feeling inadequate. All capacitation has discapacitating elements in it. Contemporary education and pedagogics only contribute, by virtue of their lack of conceptual precision, to these handicaps. Similarly, neither are there any processes that are wholly discapacitating. However badly a project may be designed, the participants always learn something. Capacitation and discapacitation are congenitally linked: they form a continuum. Both assistentialism and political clientelism are important factors. The relational formula we are introducing here, especially when applied to development related capacitation processes, allows for a first approximation of the problems that arise in this field, be it at the design stage or at the implementation stage. From that perspective it offers an instrument that may prove to be useful in the methodological design and as a guideline in the analysis of case studies.

Organizational and Management Capacitation as a Civil Society Enabler

In today's world the concept and practice of organizational literacy – which needs to find a proper place in development projects and programmes of continued education in the public sector – shows the kinds of challenges faced and the possibilities open to groups, societies and nations. Europe, left devastated after the Second World War, managed to recuperate in record time, partly because of its high level of organizational literacy. The Shah of Iran, by contrast, with high incomes from petrol at his disposal, went on a spending-spree in the West, acquiring a number of ready-made factories or 'key in hand' factories. Such an approach does not pose any problems in highly developed countries because of the high quality of human capital and the organizational skills prevalent there. This, however, was not the situation in Iran, and many of the factories purchased by the Shah stood idle for a long time. It was not until administrators from the countries of origin were shipped in, and only after they had properly trained their counterparts in Iran, that at last they could start up the factories.

The need for organizational literacy in situations with a strong division of labour is all the more important because it forms the basis of a society's social capital and sets the course of the progress of nations. The above Iranian example raises profound questions around the type of consensus that exists in the world concerning the need for strong organizational apprenticeship, a need that, however obvious, does not even form part of the educational programmes of those countries that claim to be spear-heading the development of the next century. Learning how to organize, especially how to organize autonomously as a means of becoming enabled to face up to the challenges of life, means coming into possession of the main strategic instrument for participation. Habilitation in organization also performs a key function in all development and change: it breaks the vicious cycle of social inertia caused by relations of domination.

Becoming organizationally literate also plays a key function in the processes of development and change: it breaks social inertia caused by relations of domination. It is indeed the passivity deeply ingrained in age-old mental attitudes that puts a damper on all forms of change. Organ-izational know-how opens up possibilities for individuals and groups to broaden their horizons, raise their aspirations and boost their self-confidence and self-esteem. Thanks to this process, the patterns of dependency accumulated historically due to clientelist power relationships are first eroded and then broken down. Social determinisms, too, as well as mental attitudes, limit aspirations and the ability to spot opportunities. In this way, organizational capacitation not only becomes a means for the 'literacy of life', it also loosens up mental bonds and builds up human beings who are able to be increasingly free. Becoming equipped to act in an organized way and breaking down inveterate mental models that perpetuate relationships of dependency go hand in hand. This fundamental point has, unfortunately, not been understood by development agencies. Relations of dependence and domination are perceived to be inevitable, as the most natural of things, as an independent variable upon which projects have no grip and cannot act.

Organizational capacitation is not perceived to be the fundamental obstacle it is, which needs to be pursued vigorously, so that people's capacities can be released. To complicate things even further, the much talked about organizational 'capacity building' and 'empowerment' confuse instruction with genuine capacitation and these fundamental misconcep-tions are, of course, reproduced in the programmes themselves.

The PROGEI and SIPGEI as Mechanisms of Social Auditing and of State Reform

Employment and income-generation projects (PROGEI) and systems (SIPGEI) in actual fact are the keystone and focal point whenever a mass capacitation process is launched. These large-scale projects intend to put in motion production-related and social participation community initiatives.

This is done by way of putting in place, first of all, a team composed of a number of professionals called 'frontline economists' or 'economic development experts' (TDEs) and a great number of 'investment project assistants' (APIs) who belong to the communities from which they are drawn. From there on, and using the field OW as the principal tool, a number of APIs are identified, and, with their positive input, a number of community and productive projects are set in motion. These projects rely, for the duration of the initial start-up, on public institutions or on second-degree producers, always remembering, though, that the ultimate objective is the establishment of autonomous modes of operation.

To a large extent, the aim of the PROGEI is to manage the SIPGEIs. We are in the presence here of a new, independent institutional structure, operationalized in close association with budding self-managing entre-preneurs and offering them the technical and professional services they need for their further development. Even if there is no example, as yet, of such a fully autonomous system, at least not on a universal, country-wide scale, the PROGEIs that have been started in Brazil (see Chapter 19) have real achievements to show and are very significant and promising. Quite a number of technical and political difficulties remain to be overcome, but they clearly show what can be achieved in practice, as well as suggesting the possible role and place of the SIPGEIs as active agents in the reorganization of the institutional delivery of services. And this always in view of responding more effectively to the needs of those who need them most, i.e. the unemployed and the excluded.

Many a positive step has been made in Brazil in the direction of the formation of 'frontline economists' (the TDEs) as agents of organizational literacy and development, in the formation of a new type of professional who is capable of the activation, mobilization and putting into effect of projects on behalf of the unemployed; capable also of integrating in actual practice – in person, or with the help of other specialists – the technical knowledge required by the budding enterprises and organizations. There is still a lack of precision about what the proper niches are that need identifying – due to the enduring clientelist tendencies of the state in development matters – for the development, consolidation and take-off of this type of project, but a number of important suggestions have already come out of those initial experiences.

In this context it is worth mentioning the most recent initiative under-taken by the National Employment and Income-Generation Project in Deprived Areas organized by the Ministry for Planning and Budgeting – the MPO – in Brazil. The objective here is to push, mediated by the PRONAGER programme, for the establishment of SIPGEIs in the entire country, inside a period of two years. The conceptual framework within which they operate is that of institutions of civil society with state participation. These SIPGEIs will have, as one of their principal objectives, 'to articulate various public policies for poverty alleviation, workplace creation, income generation and local development in close coordination with the government and non-governmental institutions (NGOs) so as to realize the maximum potential of available resources'. This is an extremely interesting and daring proposal and it will take a high degree of political will for it to be brought to a successful conclusion within so narrow a timescale. Whatever the case may be, the proposal is an important landmark on the road to state reform in that it integrates the solution to the two-pronged problem of poverty and unemployment with the necessary structural and institutional reforms.

It is a generally recognized fact that state reform, conceived of in structural and institutional terms – and not restricted only to the opportunistic wild growth of wholesale privatizations – has to overcome numerous obstacles put in its way by vested interests as well as historic inertias. It is therefore not surprising that the new institutions, or the reform of the existing ones, usually happens under a great deal of pressure. The now well-rehearsed 'reforms from above', by contrast, usually do not amount to much, not least because they are mediated by the same old tired executive for their assistentialist clientele, neither of whom are really interested in changing their status.

One could look at the PROGEI–SIPGEIs as support organisms in the process of a much-needed decentralization of power and also as organizations that are capable of stimulating, reorienting and reorganizing institutions. In other words, the PROGEI–SIPGEIs are active instruments in the process of the otherwise much talked about decentralization and structural adjustment, geared, in this case, to the actual real needs of the population. They would also be a stimulus towards a new institutional structure, progressively less dependent on the government and ever more directly under the direct management of civil society. Seen from this perspective the PROGEI–SIPGEIs acquire a strategic role in the context of overall development. The fact that they emerge 'from below' with the possibility of genuine support 'from above' endows the SIPGEIs with a particular vigour in the project of institutional reorganization. They have the potential of becoming a real avenue in the processes of change and strategic state reform, towards the establishment of a regime based on human rights as well as the construction of a participatory democracy.

To summarize, then: the theoretical-methodological concept, evolved by de Morais and spearheaded in Brazil by IATTERMUND, has a definite renovating potential; it also offers a model, based on actual experience in real-life situations, of how to define and hone social policy, rendering it both more operational and efficient. In that sense the de Moraisean theory and method offer an operational perspective far superior to what is commonly the rule in the social sector institutions in the majority of countries across the world. But this strength only increases in so far as they succeed in consolidating their organizations into transforming themselves into SIPGEIs, which then shape the decentralization processes and institutional services in tune with the needs of civil society, especially those members of society who find themselves excluded.

As can be gathered from the above, de Morais' theory and practice did not set out as an academic construct, but is first and foremost the product of an actual field practice with a track record of over a quarter of a century. Its further development, especially in terms of theoretical elaboration, deserves the full attention of the academic community, of development agencies and of governments keen on ending the festering unemployment problem, and in need of a reform of the state in the direction of a more participatory democracy. We are dealing here, therefore, not with a finished product, but with a building-site. But, at the same time, there are real and substantial achievements on record. In other words, it is a concept full of promising possibilities provided the experience so far is sufficiently systematized and new projects continue being launched. As the Mexican experience with small coffee-producers in the Huatusco region (Chapter 7) shows, the hybridization of the original method with methods of strategic planning – such as a specialized module in management – as soon as a basic level of organization has been achieved, can increase considerably its scope and potential.

In this sense, and overcoming the historical allergies we have mentioned, it is necessary to sow in the open furrow ploughed by the live methodology of massive capacitation the best of what has been developed by other techniques and approaches. Together they can render a more efficient service in the development of the organizational capacities in processes owned and controlled by the excluded.

Note

1. See Barrantes, V. (1998) *La construcción de un sueño – Coopesilencio 25 annos despues*, EUNA, 1998 (The Building of a Dream – 25 Years of Coopesilencio), Heredia, Costa Rica: EUNA.

Reference

Sobrado, Miguel (1994) 'Capacitación y discapacitación en los proyectos de desarrollo', *Cuaderno de Ciencias Sociales*, no. 68, San José, Costa Rica.

Selective Bibliography of Works by and on Clodomir Santos de Morais

Note: preference has been given to the rarer English-language texts.

Andersson, G. (1986) 'Another battle begun. Images of collective cooperatives in Zimbabwe', *Education with Production*, vol. 5, no. 1, December.

— (1987) 'Cooperative management – self-management: cooperative research, development and education', *Workteam*, no. 3, Gaborone, Botswana.

— et al. (1989) *Organisation Workshops in Botswana*, Gaborone, Botswana: CORDE.

— (forthcoming) 'Unbounded organisation', in D. Lewis and T. Wallace, *Beyond the New Policy Agenda*.

Antoine, G. (1980) *Enmi Koperasion* (Cooperative Enemy), Port-au-Prince, Haiti: FEDE-COOP.

Barelli, W. (1998) *Programa de Autoemprego (PAE): mais que um Emprego: o Futuro* (More than a Job: a Future), São Paulo: Ministry of Labour.

Barrantes, V. (1999) *La Construcción de un Sueño: Coopesilencio 25 Años Despues* (The Construction of a Dream: Coopesilencio after 25 years), Heredia, Costa Rica: Euna.

Campos, M. (1997) 'Domador de la miseria – Clodomir Santos de Morais lleva su voz y soluciones contra la pobreza' (Conqueror of poverty – Clodomire Santos de Morais raises his voice and offers his solutions to poverty), *Rumbo*, no. 658, 11–18 August, Costa Rica.

Carmen, R. (1995) 'Workshop for enterprise management vs "British" enterprise education', *Convergence*, vol. xxviii, no. 1, Toronto.

— (1996) *Autonomous Development: Humanizing the Landscape*, London: Zed Books.

— (1998a) 'Production works!', *Development*, vol. 1, no. 41, Rome.

— (1998b) 'Global Conferencing on <Facilitate.com> <http://www.man.ac.uk/education/intconfl.html> conference report URL Hypertext.

— (forthcoming) 'Where there is no workplace', in N. Boreham (ed.), *Situated Learning and the Workplace*, London: Routledge.

Carmen, R., I. Labra, I. Labra and M. Davis (1999) *Learning from Brazil*, Manchester: Manchester Monographs.

Cherrett, I. (1986) *Collectivism Leads to Self-sufficiency*, Borrowdale, Zimbabwe: Glenn Forest Training Centre.

— (1989) *Report of the Mauya Experimental Workshop on Theory of Organization – EWTO*, Mauya, Zimbabwe.

— (1992a) *The Theory of Organization, a Tool for Mass Training for Development*, Newcastle and Manchester: ETC UK.

— (1992b) 'Algunas reflexiones sobre los resultados e implicaciones del laboratorio experimental' (Some reflections on the results and implications of the OW), in FAO/INA Conference Proceedings, RLAC/92/35 DERU-44, Tela, Honduras.

— (1993) 'The crisis of sustainability and EWTO', presented at Conference on the OW Principles and Practice, 25 February, Centre for Adult and Higher Education (CAHE), Manchester University.

Cherrett, I. and M. Sobrado (1992) *Eastern Europe: Enterpreneurial Training in Conditions of Social Crisis*, Newcastle: ETC UK.

Comunitario, (1993) Special Issue on Cooperativism, São Paulo, September.

Correia, J. C. B. (1994) *Comunicação e Capacitação* (Communication and Capacitation), Brasília: IATTERMUND.

— (1998) 'De Paulo Freire a Clodomir Santos de Morais: de conciencia critica a la conciencia organizativa', presented at Iberoamerican Congress on University Extension, UNA University, Heredia, Costa Rica.

Erazo Midence, B. and C. A. Tovar (1975) *Diccionario de la Reforma Agraria* (Small Dictionary of Agrarian Reform), Tegucigalpa.

— (1985) *La Dinamica Social de los Laboratorios Experimentales*, IICA/UNACR.

FAO (1992) 'Consilidación de empresas campesinas de reforma agraria y metologias para la organización de comunidades rurales', presented at meeting on workshops, FAO/INA Conference Proceedings, RLAC/92/35 DERU-44, Tela, Honduras.

FAO (Brazil) (1987) *Apostila de Planjamento e Projectos – Curso de Formação de Auxiliar de Projectos e Investimentos – APIs* (Courses for APIs – Investment Project Assistants), São Paulo.

— (1997) *PAE (Programa do Auto-Emprego)* (Self-employment Programme), São Paulo.

Freire, P. (1985) *The Politics of Education*, London: Macmillan.

— (1987) *Aprendendo com a Própria Historia*, Rio de Janeiro: Paz e Terra Ediciones, pp. 135–7.

— (1996) 'Carta de Paulo Freire a Clodomir Morais – lembrando os ensinamentos da prisão' (Letter from Paulo Freire to Clodomir – sowing the seeds learned in prison), in *A Voz da Espos*, A. M. A. Freire, <http://www.ppbr.com./ipf/bio/esposa.html>

— (1997) 'Tribute to Clodomir', video cassette, University of Rondônia, Brazil (event related in Chapter 4).

HIVOS (Humanistisch Institut voor Ontwikkelingssamenwerking) (1984) *The Experimental Workshops in Anglophone Countries of the Caribbean*, Tegucigalpa, Honduras.

IATTERMUND Archives, Brasília.

INAGRO (1982) *Audiovisual Tools for the OW*, Caracas, Venezuela: IICA.

Juarez, B. (1977) *Memoria del Primer Laboratorio Experimental de la Selva Lacandona* (Record of the first experimental workshop in the Lacondona forest), Mexico: CECODES.

Hanley, J. C. (Fr. Guadelupe) (1985) *Asi es la Iglesia*, Managua, Nicaragua: CENIH.

Labra, I. (1984) *La Division del Trabajo Como Prerequesito de la Formación Profesional* (Division of Labour as Prerequisite to Professional Training), Managua, Nicaragua: INFORP.

— (1998a) *Glenn Forest Training Centre: Cooperative Management*, Harare, Zimbabwe: SADET, June.

— (1998b) *Introducing Southern Africa Development Trust*, Harare: SADET.

— (1992a) 'Talleres de experiencias con laboratorios de organización y talleres de gestión empreserial' (Experimental Workshops and Entrepreneurial Management Workshops), FAO/INA Conference Proceedings, RLAC/92/35 DERU-44 Tela, Honduras.

— (1992b) *Psicologia Social: Responsabilidad y Necessidad* (Social Psychology with Large Groups: Responsibility and Need) (English trans. forthcoming), Santiago de Chile: LOM Editoriales.

— (1996) 'Communication link trust. Impact evaluation of the organizational workshop approach – draft', Harare: SADET.

Labra, I. and I. Labra (1992a) 'Contribuciones de la psicologia educativa al desarollo del laboratorio experimental', FAO/INA Conference Proceedings, RLAC/92/35 DERU-44, Tela, Honduras.

— (1992b) 'El pastoralismo, un tipo de comportamento ideologico encontrado en Africa' (Pastoralism: an ideological behaviour found in Africa), FAO/INA Conference Proceedings, RLAC/92/35 DERU-44, Tela, Honduras.

— (1999) 'Introduction to the Social Scale Capacitation Method', in R. Carmen, I. Labra, I. Labra and M. Davis, *Learning from Brazil*, Manchester Monographs, no. 38.

Lewis, J. (1998) 'Massive phenomenon – massive solutions needed', *New Economics*, London, Summer.

Monteiro, S. T. (1992) 'O método de capacitação para a formação de empresas associativas', *Revista Perspectiva*, Erechim, Brazil.

— (1993) *A Capacitação para Formação de Empresas Associativas* (Capacitation for the Formation of Membership Enterprises), São Paolo, Brazil: IATTERMUND.

Mora Alfaro, J. A. (1978) *Autogestión y Capacitación Campesina* (Peasant Modes of Self-management and Capacitation), San José, Costa Rica: IICA.

— (1980) *Apuntes Sobre la Evaluacion y Seguimiento de la Capacitacion en la Organización Campesina* (Notes on the Evaluation and Follow-up of Capacitation with Peasants), San José, Costa Rica: ANACR.

Moraes, A. A. da Costa (n.d.) 'Gerar o proprio emprego é opção do futuro' (Manage your own enterprise as an option for the future), *Alternative*, journal of the Vitoria PROGEI, vol. 1, no. 8, Brazil.

de Morais, C. S. (1969) *Algunas Consideraciones en Torno a las Organizaciones Campesinas en Latinoamerica* (Some Reflections on the Peasant Organizations in Latin America), Geneva: ILO.

— (1970) 'Peasant leagues in Brazil', in R. Stavenhagen, *Agrarian Problems and Peasant Movements in Latin America*, New York: Doubleday.

— (1973) *Dictionario de Reforma Agraria Latino America* (Dictionary of Agrarian Reform), San José, Costa Rica: EDUCA.

— (1975a) *La Marcha Hacia la Ciudad* (The Flight to the City), Tegucigalpa, Honduras.

— (1975b) *The Honduran Development Model*, Tegucigalpa, Honduras: PROCCARA.

— (1976a) *Movilidad de la Mano de Obra en Centro America* (Workforce Mobility in Central America), Tegucigalpa, Honduras.

— (1976b) 'Capacidad de la tierra para retener el hombre en el campo' (The capacity of the land to continue to support human habitation), presented at the UNO Global Forum Conference for Habitat, Vancouver, Canada.

— (1979) 'La capacitación masiva para el desarrollo rural' (Large-scale capacitation for rural development), *Cinterfor*, no. 64.

— (1986) *Notes on a Theory of Organization* (trans. I. Cherrett), Newcastle: ETC UK.

— (1987a) *Elementos da Teoria da Organização no Campo* (Elements of a Theory of Organization), São Paulo: Movimento dos Trabalhadores Rurais Sem Terra.

— (1987b) 'Condiciones objetivas y factores subjetivos de la incorporación de las masas rurales en el proceso de desarollo progresista de la agricultura en Centroamerica' (Objective conditions and subjective factors in the incorporation of the rural masses in the progessive development project in Central America), doctoral thesis, W. Pieck University, Rostock, Germany.

— (1989) *A Capacitação Massiva: Uma Proposta para o Desenvolvimento Rural* (Mass Capacitation: A Proposal for Rural Development), Porto Velho, Brazil: EMATER.

— (1992) 'The imperative for social engineering in the agrarian development processes', seminar, Humboldt University, Berlin and Capingo University, Mexico.

— (1994) *A que é a Organização?* (What is an Organization?) (the Theory of Organization explained in cartoons), Alagoas State, Brazil: Trabalhadores sem Terra.

— (1995) *Cual é o Mérito do Método Paulo Freire* (What is the Merit of Paulo Freire's Method?) Rondônia, Brazil.

— (1997a) *Historia das Ligas Camonesas do Brasil* (History of the Peasant Leagues in Brazil), Brasília: IATTERMUND.

— (1997b) *El Reencontrado e lo Perdido de las Reformas Agrarias* (Agrarian Reforms Lost and Found), Brasília: IATTERMUND.

— (1997c) 'Los mercados laborales eficientes: un desafío para América Latina' (Efficient labour markets: a challenge for Latin America), keynote address at the K. Adenauer Foundation International Seminar, San José, Costa Rica, 30 July.

— (1997d) *Teoria de la Organización Autogesionaria* (Theory of the Self-managing Organization), Brasília: IATTERMUND.

— (1997e) *Uma Nova Visão da Extensão Rural pelo Geração do Emprego e Renda* (A New Vision for Rural Extension of Job and Income Generation), Porto Velho, Brazil: EMATER.

de Morais, C. S. et al. (1976) *PROCCARA 46 Months*, Tegucigalpa, Honduras: INA.

Morales Marin, R. et al. (1986) *El Laboratorio de Organización, Una Metodologia para la Capacitación en Organización* (The Organization Workshop, a Methodology for Capacitation and Organization), Cartagena, Colombia: SENA (Servicio Nacional de Aprendizaje).

O'Neill, M. (1997) 'From projects towards process: a case study of a CONCERN-initiated programme in Mozambique', MEd thesis, CAHE, Faculty of Education, Manchester University.

Pinheiro Machado, J. A. and C. S. de Morais (1996) *Avaliação dos Laboratorios Organizaciais do Estado da Paraíba* (Evaluation of the OW in the State of Paraíba), Brasília: IATTERMUND.

PROCCARA (1976) *Empresa Asociativa Campesina 'Isleta'* (Report on the Membership Enterprise 'Isleta'), Tegucigalpa, Honduras: INA.

Puga, G. (1975) 'Honduras: forms of agrarian self-management', presented at Second Conference on Self-Management, Cornell University, Ithaca, NY.

Reveau, R. (1980) *Défendre l'Unité et la discipline dans la cooperative* (Defending Unity and Discipline in the Cooperative), Port-au-Prince, Haiti: Editions Marcel Herz.

Rojas, J. J. (1988) *Auge y Decadencia del Corporativismo Agrario en México* (Rise and Fall of Agrarian Cooperativism in Mexico), Chapingo University.

SADET (n.d.) *Organizational Workshops: What are They?*, Harare, Zimbabwe: SADET.

Sariego, J. and A. Gonzalez (1997) *Seminario Taller de Capacitación en Organización: El Caso de la Cooperative 'El Tigre' (El Salvador)* (The Case of the Cooperative 'El Tigre' in El Salvador), San José, Costa Rica: IICA.

Seidman, J. (1986–87) 'De Morais' Organizational Theory', cartoon series in *Workteam*, Gaborone, Botswana: Design Layout Graphics.

SENA (1986) *Experimental Organizational Workshop. A Methodology for Capacitation and Organization*, Caracas, Venezuela: SENA.

Silveira, C. M., R. Mello and R. Gomes (1997) *Work and Income: Three Capacitation Models* (one chapter devoted to de Morais' OW), Rio de Janeiro: FASE/GTZ.

Sobrado, M. C. (1981) *Apogeo y Decadencia de los Artesanos* (Rise and Fall of the Artisan Way), Heredia, Costa Rica: PRACA/UNA.

— (1990) *Teoría de la Organización para Talleres de Generación de Empleo* (Theory of Work-Generating Workshops), Panama: UNDP–ILO.

— (1994a) 'Capacitación y discapacitación en los proyectos de desarrollo', *Cuaderno de Ciencias Sociales*, no. 68, San José, Costa Rica.

— (1994b) 'Capacitación empresarial en condictiones de transición en Europa Oriental', *Land Reform*, Rome: FAO.

— (1994c) 'Interferences of relations of domination in the capacitation process' research paper, Heredia, Costa Rica.

— (1996) *La Autonomía de la Organización es la Enzima del Desarollo: El Clientelismo, la Discapacitación* (The Autonomy of the Organization is the Yeast of Development), Chapingo University, Mexico.

— (1997) *Germinadora Masiva de Empresas y Empleo* (A Massive Enterprise and Workplace-generating Model), Universidad Nacional, Heredia, Costa Rica.

— (1999) 'Coopesilencio: un cuarto de siglo', in V. Barrantes, *La Construcción de un Sueño*.

Sobrado, M. C. and C. S. de Morais (1981) *Guia Tematica para Participar en el Simposio de Analisis Sobre los Laboratorios Experimentales* (Thematic Guide for the Participants in the Symposium on the Analysis of the Organization Workshops), Costa Rica: IICA.

Sunday Mail (Zimbabwe) (1983) 'Burglar bars, security walls tell the story', article on Clodomir Santos de Morais.

van Dam, C. (1982) *Het Experimenteel Laboratorium: de Methodologie van Santos de Morais*, The Hague: CESO.

Wilson, J. (n.d.) 'Diary of a resource person from PELUM, Zimbabwe at the organizational workshop held at Munguine, Mozambique' (unpublished).

Index